TRACY M. SUMNER

The COMPLETE GUIDE to the BIBLE for Kids

PLUS **BONUS GUIDE** TO **GOD'S CREATION!**

BARBOUR kidz
A Division of Barbour Publishing

ISBN 979-8-89151-184-2

Previously released as separate books: *Kids' Bible Handbook* and *Discover Creation.*

Cover, interior design and layout by Greg Jackson, Thinkpen Design

Published by Barbour Publishing, Inc., 1810 Barbour Drive, Uhrichsville, Ohio 44683, www.barbourbooks.com

Our mission is to inspire the world with the life-changing message of the Bible.

ecpa Member of the Evangelical Christian Publishers Association

Printed in China.
002615 0825 XY

So you think you know the Bible? Great. . .but you'll learn even more here.

The Bible, scripture, the Book of books: From Genesis to Revelation, it is God's word to humanity, telling us everything we need to know for life!

The Complete Guide to the Bible for Kids is for 8-to-12-year-olds like you, written to help you understand the most important Book in human history. Find out

- How we got this ancient, incredible Book
- Why God chose to "speak" through words on a page
- What the 66 books of the Bible contain and mean
- Who the most important characters are, and what they have to say to you today
- How you can read and enjoy the Bible yourself

Plus you'll find a whole section on the "book of nature" that puts God's creativity and power on full display. This bonus guide to Creation starts on page 161.

Read on to learn more about God and His Word, plus the world He created. . .and where *you* fit into it all. This could be a life-changing journey!

What's in This Book

Before You Get Started

Chances are, you've got at least one copy somewhere in your home. Maybe more than one copy. And maybe more than one version.

What are we talking about?

The bestselling book of all time.

The Bible!

It only makes sense that the Bible, also called "God's Word" or "the Word of God," is the world's all-time bestseller. After all, it's been around for almost 2,000 years (actually, the books of the Old Testament have been around for a lot longer than that) and has been translated into hundreds of languages.

The Bible is easy to find in most parts of the world. In America, we have dozens of translations and styles available in just about any bookstore. There are study Bibles, children's Bibles, pocket-size Bibles, hardcover and softcover Bibles, and Bibles that include easy-to-follow reading plans for people who want to read through the entire Bible in a year.

Did you know that the word *Bible* actually means "book"? In reality, the Bible isn't just one book. It's a collection of 66 books (39 in the Old Testament and 27 in the New Testament) written by about 40 different writers over a period of several centuries. The oldest books of the Bible (including Job and the first five books of the Old Testament) were written 3,000 to 3,100 years ago; and the youngest book (Revelation, written by the apostle John) was written around 2,000 years ago.

We'll get into more detail about the Bible's writers and when they did their writing later on, but first let's focus on what the Bible means to us.

If someone were to ask you what the Bible is (other than a book that's been around for a really long time), how would you answer? Would you say that the Bible is a collection of stories about God's people going back thousands of years? Would you say it's God's book of promises for people who put their faith in Him? Would you say it's a book of God's commands for people who want to please Him in the way they live, talk, and think?

Well, none of those answers would be wrong. In fact, they're all 100 percent correct. But there's a lot more to the Bible than that. You see, the Bible is more than a collection of stories about a bunch of people who died a long time ago, and it's more than a book of God's promises and commands. The Bible is the account of how God has communicated with the most prized part of His creation—His people!—from the beginning of time until the beginning of the Christian church. And it's also about how God communicates with you and me today.

With so many Bibles in the world, it's easy sometimes to start taking God's Word for granted. That's partly why I've written *this* book. I want to help you come to a greater appreciation for the Bible, and I want to give you some of the basics that will help you understand where it came from, how it became the book it is today, and how you can better read the Bible and understand what it is all about.

This book will give you a brief look at all 66 books of the Bible, including information about the people who wrote the books, the men and women they were written to, what the books mean, and how the message of the Bible applies to your life today.

Each of the 11 chapters in this book includes a story about how the Bible came to be, as well as some fun and interesting features about the Bible and what you'll find in it.

Here are some of the fun features you'll find in this book:

Power Words: Important verses you can memorize from different books of the Bible.

Who, What, Where? Important people, things, and places mentioned in the Bible, as well as the people and events God used to give us the Bible.

Fun Bible Trivia: Some not-so-well-known facts about people and events you can find in the Bible.

What's in It for Me? How you can apply what you read in the Bible to your own life.

Did You Know. . . ? Fun facts about the Bible itself and how it came to be the book it is today.

This book won't teach you everything there is to know about the Bible. To do that, it would have to be many times longer than it is. What it will do, though, is give you a good place to start as you read, study, and learn what the Bible has to say and what it means to you.

When you're finished reading this book, you'll have a pretty good idea of how wonderful and amazing the Bible really is. And you'll probably think to yourself, *Wow! The Bible is a really cool book!*

CHAPTER 1

How Did We Get This Book Anyway?

The Work God Did—and the People He Used—to Give Us the Bible

Take a look at your own copy of the Bible. If you don't have it nearby, take a minute to go get it. Then just look at it for a moment. You've probably read at least some of the Bible, and you might even have a pretty good idea about what it says. But have you ever stopped to think about what it took to give you an opportunity to have your very own copy?

A lot of Christians, even some who know the Bible very well, don't really understand how we got the 66 books that make up the Bible. That's what this chapter is all about. It gives you a quick look at how God used different people from all sorts of backgrounds to record His words, to gather them all together to make up one book, and to help make the Bible available in the language that you speak, write, and read.

So read on! You're about to discover the amazing story of how God's Word became the book we know as the Bible.

Writing Down God's Words

The first thing you should know about the Bible—if you don't already—is that God didn't just give someone a completed manuscript and send him off to a printing press. Actually, the story of how we got the Bible is a lot more interesting than that.

You probably know—even if you haven't given it a lot of thought—that someone had to write down the words that are in your Bible. Actually, the books of the Bible were written by about 40 men (and possibly a few women). These writers came from a lot of different backgrounds and professions. For example, Moses was a shepherd, Amos was a fig farmer, Matthew was a tax collector, and Peter and John were fishermen.

Did You Know?

The apostle Paul writes, "All Scripture is inspired by God" (2 Timothy 3:16). The idea behind the word *inspiration* is that God "breathed out" or "spoke" the words that are in the Bible. In other words, the words you read in the Bible are the words of God Himself!

Yet all these people, from different backgrounds, writing over a span of about 1,500 years, together produced a unified book that never disagrees with itself, never moves from its main message, and always presents God's perfect plan for the salvation of humanity.

How did such a group of writers—most of whom never met one another—pull that off? The answer to that question is in the word *inspiration*. One of the Bible's main writers, the apostle Paul, writes, "All Scripture is *given* by *inspiration of* God" (2 Timothy 3:16 NKJV, italics added). What Paul means is that God, through His Holy Spirit, spoke through the Bible's writers and gave them His very own words to record. In other words, the people who wrote the books of the Bible were tools that God miraculously used to give us His written Word.

This means that even though the Bible was written by dozens of people from different backgrounds and points of view, it has one ultimate author: God Himself. That's why you can count on the Bible as your final source for everything you need to know about how to live a life that pleases God.

Power Words

No prophecy in Scripture ever came from the prophet's own understanding, or from human initiative. No, those prophets were moved by the Holy Spirit, and they spoke from God.

2 PETER 1:20–21

Why *These* Books?

All 39 of the books in the Old Testament had been written by about 400 BC (*before* the birth of Christ), and all 27 of the New Testament books were finished by the end of the first century AD (*after* the birth of Christ).

But these weren't the only books written that contained teachings and history that are very much like what we have in the Bible today. For example, during the first few centuries after Jesus' life here on earth, dozens of letters and other "gospels" were circulated in the Christian church.

So how do we know that all the books in the Bible are the ones God wanted? The answer lies in the great care He put into making sure all the words He inspired the biblical writers to record were kept in the book He has prepared and given us.

By the time of Jesus' birth, the collection of books included in the Hebrew Bible (the Old Testament) was pretty much decided. The Jewish people recognized that Moses,

Did You Know. . . ?

Moses and Jesus both spent part of their lives in Egypt!

the prophets, and other writers were God's messengers, so they accepted their work as the inspired Word of God. This collection is sometimes called the "canon of Scripture," and the act of declaring individual books as part of the Bible is called "canonization."

Power Words

Your word is a lamp to guide my feet and a light for my path.

PSALM 119:105

By the mid-third century AD, almost all Christian leaders agreed that the books we now have in the Old Testament belong in the canon of Scripture. But there was some disagreement about certain books that are not in the Bible but are part of what is called the Apocrypha (see the Did You Know. . .? sidebar on this page).

The process of accepting the New Testament books as part of the Bible began in the first century AD and continued on into the fourth century. By the beginning of the fourth century, Christians had already accepted most of the books now in the New Testament as God's Word. But a few books still needed final approval before they would be accepted as part of the canon.

Around AD 363, about 30 Christian leaders from what was then called Asia Minor (now part of the nation of Turkey) held a meeting called the Council of Laodicea. One of the things they talked about was the final acceptance of the canon of Scripture. This council decided that only the Old Testament, including the Apocrypha, and the 27 books in the New Testament could be read in the churches. Two other meetings—the Council of Hippo in AD 393 and the Council of Carthage in AD 397—also agreed that those same 27 books would be part of the New Testament.

Same Message, Different Languages

Okay, now you have a basic idea of how we got the books we have in the Bible today. But there is more to the story. Not only did God use some very brave people to record His words; He also used some very dedicated men to keep the original words in the Bible from being changed. That's why we can count on the fact that the message of the Bible is the same today as it was when it was first recorded thousands of years ago.

One thing that *has* changed is the languages people use. Very few people in the world today speak Hebrew or Greek, the languages used when the Bible was written. That means God's Word has had to be translated into languages that people could understand. God again used gifted and devoted

Did You Know. . .?

Several books that are included in some Catholic versions of the Bible aren't found in other versions. The reason? These books are part of what is called the Apocrypha—which means "obscure," "hidden," or "secret." The books that make up the Apocrypha contain a lot of wisdom and historical teaching, but during the 1500s, during a time called the Protestant Reformation, they were taken out of the Bible for various reasons.

men to do His work, making it possible for people to read and understand the Bible in their own languages.

The translation of the Bible into other languages actually began even before Jesus was born. Starting around 285 BC, a group of 72 men began translating the Old Testament books from their original language of Hebrew into Greek—the common language that most people spoke back then. This translation was called the Septuagint.

The word *Septuagint* is Greek for 70, which approximates the number of translators who worked on the project. According to one story about this translation of the Hebrew Old Testament into Greek, it took the 72 translators 72 days to finish the project. But it actually took a lot longer than that!

The project was started because Ptolemy, the Egyptian king, wanted to include the literature of all the world's ancient religions in his library at Alexandria. Ptolemy contacted a man named Eleazar, the Jewish chief priest at the time, and asked him to assign Hebrew scholars from Jerusalem to work on the translation. Six men were chosen from each of the 12 tribes of Israel, which accounts for the 72 translators. At first, they translated only the five books of the Old Testament, the Law of Moses; but after a while, they translated the other books and added them to the collection.

By the time Jesus was born, the Septuagint was read by most Greek-speaking Jews. It was also read in church gatherings during the first century AD—because the New Testament had not yet been completed, the first Christians didn't have it to read like we do now.

The Bible in the "Common Language"

Most of the New Testament was originally written in Greek. But as the years passed, Latin replaced Greek as the language that most people spoke in the Roman Empire—which meant that someone would have to translate the New Testament into Latin.

That someone was Jerome, a church leader who lived from about AD 347 to 420.

Around AD 382, Pope Damasus I asked Jerome to translate both the Old Testament and the New Testament into Latin. Jerome used the Greek copies of scripture as his starting point. He began by translating the Gospels—Matthew, Mark, Luke, and John—and the Old Testament. Jerome finished his work around AD 400, and it came to be known as the Vulgate.

The Vulgate was used in the Christian—mostly Catholic—church from the 4th century to the 15th century. Even though the primary language of the people continued to change, there were no new official translations done during this time. That's mostly because the Catholic Church, which was very powerful at the time, wouldn't allow anyone to translate the Bible into the people's spoken and written languages. So only the pope and the priests, who learned to read and write in Latin, could read and understand the Bible.

That began to change when brave men such as John Wycliffe and William Tyndale risked everything—including their lives—to make sure that people could read the Bible for themselves.

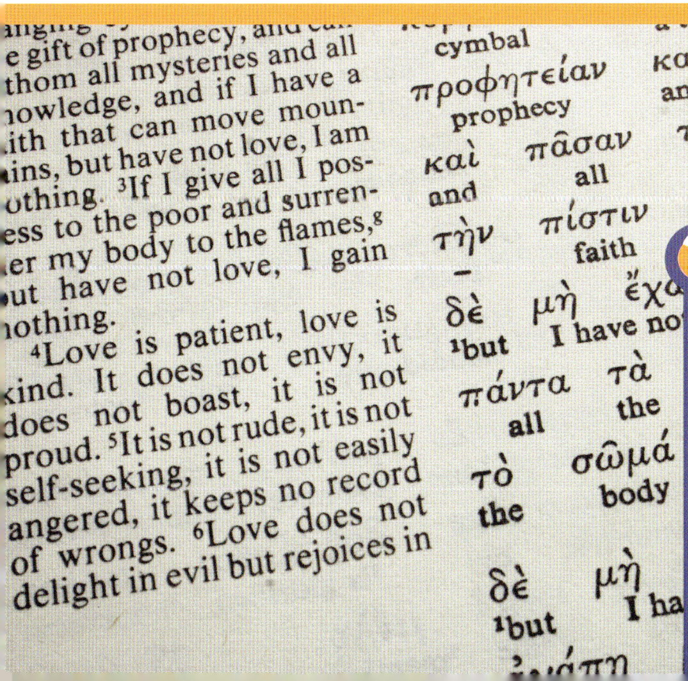

Did You Know. . . ?

Even though there wasn't much Bible translation going on between the 4th and 15th centuries, some translations of the New Testament into the language of the Anglo-Saxons—an early form of English—began showing up late in the tenth century (the AD 900s).

A Big Step toward an English-Language Bible

John Wycliffe was a Catholic priest who lived in England in the 1300s. Even though he was a Catholic, he believed—and said—some things that got him in trouble with the church. One of the things he believed was that every Christian should have the right to read the Bible without the interference of the church.

Wycliffe knew that the Roman Catholic Church wouldn't allow anyone to translate the Bible into the languages that the "common" people spoke and read. But he was willing to risk trouble with the authorities, so he moved ahead with his plans to translate the Bible into English.

Wycliffe—and probably several of his closest friends—began their work by translating Jerome's Latin Vulgate into English. It is believed that Wycliffe translated the four Gospels himself and that he may have translated the entire New Testament. The work of translating the whole Bible into English wasn't finished until several years after Wycliffe died of a stroke in 1384.

Wycliffe's work was just the beginning when it came to translating the Bible into English. Another Englishman, William Tyndale, picked up where Wycliffe left off.

This is Merton College at Oxford University, where William Tyndale attended college.

William Tyndale Gives His All

William Tyndale was an amazing man who attended college at Oxford University, one of England's best schools. By the time he graduated, he had mastered seven languages, including Greek and Hebrew. Because he knew those languages so well, he was able to read the Bible for himself—in its original languages.

Tyndale knew what he wanted to do more than anything else, and that was to translate the Bible into English so that even the most uneducated Englishman could read it for himself. But he also knew that the Catholic Church was against the idea and that working on translating the Bible into English could cost him everything—including his life.

At first, he asked the church authorities for permission to translate the Bible into English. But because the leaders of the church believed that only the pope and priests were educated enough to truly understand the Bible, the answer was a big no!

Still, Tyndale wouldn't stop talking about how he disagreed with the church about many subjects, including translating the Bible into English. He began his translation work while he was still in England; but when the authorities found out what he was doing, he had to leave England. He traveled to Germany, where he could continue his work.

Did You Know. . . ?

It took a lot of courage for William Tyndale to work on translating the Bible into English. As an example of how brave he really was, consider this story: One day, Tyndale shouted at an English bishop who told him that the common people didn't need to read the Bible but only needed to listen to the words of the pope. "I defy the pope and all his laws!" Tyndale said. "And, if God spares me, I will one day make the boy that drives the plow in England to know more of the scriptures than the pope does!"

Who, What, Where?

Even though he never worked on translating the Bible, a German inventor named Johannes Gutenberg played a huge part in making the Bible available to all people. Gutenberg developed the movable-type printing press, which made it possible to mass-produce printed materials—including the Bible. In fact, the world's first printed book was the *Gutenberg Bible*, a 1,286-page printed version of the Latin Vulgate that came off the presses in the 1450s.

Did You Know. . . ?

By the time William Tyndale arrived in Germany, a man named Martin Luther had already begun translating the Bible into the German language. In 1523, Luther published the first five books of the Bible in German. By the 1530s, he had published the entire Bible in German.

Translating the Bible into English was no easy job, and it took Tyndale more than a year just to complete the New Testament. After he finished, he and some of his friends arranged for the English Bibles to be smuggled into England. The people loved the "new" Bibles, but the authorities weren't impressed. They made plans to stop Tyndale for good.

Tyndale knew he could not return home to England. He loved his native land and missed his friends and family there, but he knew that going home would mean almost certain death. Instead, he left Germany and traveled to Antwerp, Belgium, where, in 1530, his translation of the first five books of the Old Testament was printed. He also planned to translate the remainder of the Old Testament.

Tyndale didn't live long enough to realize his dream of an English translation of the entire Bible. In May 1535, he was arrested in Antwerp and thrown into a prison cell. The following year, he was executed.

Finishing What William Tyndale Started

After William Tyndale's death, one of his friends, a man named Miles Coverdale, completed the translation of the Old Testament. In 1535, Coverdale printed the first complete Bible in the English language. It was called the Coverdale Bible. Two years after that, John Rogers, another friend of Tyndale's, printed the second complete English Bible. He translated his Bible directly from Hebrew and Greek manuscripts. It was called Matthew's Bible.

In 1539, Coverdale published what is now known as the Great Bible (it is called that because it was really big—about 14 inches thick). Even though the "common" people still weren't allowed to own copies of the Bible or to read the Bible on their own, the Great Bible brought English Christians a step closer.

The King James Bible—the World's Number 1 Bestseller

In 1604, King James I of England appointed 54 of the world's best Bible scholars and language experts of the time to translate the Bible into English. Each of these men knew the Hebrew, Greek, and Aramaic languages well. It wasn't easy work, and it took several years to finish. Their final product came to be known as the King James Bible (also known as the Authorized Version), and it was completed and printed in 1611.

At first, the people of England—and other English-speaking places—didn't like the King James Bible as much as other translations. They preferred the Geneva Bible, an English translation that had been around for several decades. But in time, the King James Bible became more and more popular. Eventually, it became the world's all-time bestselling book. By the end of the 18th century, the King James Bible had become the only Bible used in English-speaking Protestant (non-Catholic) churches.

Look How Far We've Come!

You're fortunate enough to live in a time when you can walk into any bookstore and buy your own copy of the Bible. Not only that, but you can buy one of literally dozens of translations. All you have to do is find one that is easy for you to read and understand, plunk down your money, and take home your very own Bible.

Translation of the Bible didn't stop with the King James Bible. Since the King James Bible was first printed and distributed in 1611, Bible translators have worked tirelessly through the years to adapt the language of the Bible—while keeping the content the same.

Power Words

"People are like grass; their beauty is like a flower in the field. The grass withers and the flower fades. But the word of the Lord remains forever."

1 PETER 1:24-25

Here are some of the versions translators have produced since the King James Bible first came on the scene:

- 1885—The English Revised Version, the first major revision of the King James Bible
- 1900-01—The American publishing company Thomas Nelson & Sons publishes the American Standard Version
- 1952—The Revised Standard Version
- 1965—The Amplified Bible
- 1971—The New American Standard Bible and *The Living Bible* (a paraphrase)
- 1976—*The Good News Bible*
- 1978—The New International Version
- 1982—The complete New King James Version
- 1989—The New Revised Standard Version
- 1995—The Contemporary English Version
- 1996—The New Living Translation
- 2001—The English Standard Version
- 2002—*The Message* (a paraphrase)
- 2004—The Holman Christian Standard Bible

With all these versions of the Bible—and many others—around, it's hard to believe there was a time when ordinary people weren't even allowed to *read* the Bible themselves, let alone own one. But it's true.

We can be grateful that God used so many people to put His thoughts and deeds down on paper, and then to make the Bible available to anyone who wants one.

As you're starting to see, the Bible really is an amazing book. . .and the God who gave it to you really is an awesome God!

CHAPTER 2

In the Beginning. . . and Beyond

How It All Started (Genesis through Deuteronomy)

The Bible begins with five books that, as a group, are called the Pentateuch. The word *Pentateuch* is a Greek word that means "five rolls" or "five cases." Jewish people call the first five books of the Bible the *Torah*.

The first five books of the Old Testament are a set of books about beginnings—the beginnings of the universe and the world around us, the beginning of the human race, the beginning of God's plan for the salvation of humankind, the beginning of the Hebrew people and the nation of Israel, and the beginning of God's rules, laws, and guidelines for living.

By the time you finish reading those five books—Genesis through Deuteronomy—you will have read everything the Bible says about human history, starting with Adam and Eve and ending with the death of Moses.

Does that sound like fun reading?

Let's get started!

Genesis

What It's About: The word *genesis* means "beginnings," and that's what the book of Genesis is all about. This book is about the *beginning* of the universe and the world around us, the *beginning* of life, the *beginning* of the human race, the *beginning* of sin, and the *beginning* of a special race of people through whom God chose and prepared to bring salvation to the world.

Important Characters/People: Adam and Eve, Noah, Abraham, Sarah, Lot, Isaac, Rebekah, Jacob, Esau, Joseph, Potiphar, Pharaoh

Adam and Eve

Noah

Abraham and Sarah

Jacob and Esau

Joseph

The Writer: None of the first five books of the Bible names its writer, but many centuries of tradition say that Moses wrote all of them. Moses lived around the 1400s BC.

What You'll Find in the Book of Genesis

Knowing what the word *genesis* means, doesn't it make sense that the book of Genesis begins with the words "In the beginning"? This was the moment when God began the miraculous six-day process of creating everything you see around you—the universe, our solar system, our planet, and every living thing that inhabits the earth.

The first two chapters of Genesis give us a bare-bones outline of what God created and when He created it. You won't find a lot of detail about the process of creation in Genesis—or anywhere else in the Bible, for that matter. How God did it remains a mystery. But as someone once wisely said, "I don't know *how* God did it; I just believe Him when He says, 'In the beginning, God created. . .'"

Genesis 1 divides the process into six days of creation. On the first day, God laid the groundwork for all life on earth when He created light. Without light—light from the sun, that is—nothing could live, grow, or reproduce here on earth. Here is a basic list of what God created on each creation day:

Day 1: The earth itself and light (1:2–5)
Day 2: The sky and the oceans (1:6–8)
Day 3: Dry land and plants (1:9–13)
Day 4: The sun, moon, and stars (1:14–19)
Day 5: Birds and fish (1:20–23)
Day 6: Other animals. . .and people! (1:24–31)

When God finished the job of creation, He looked at everything He had done and "saw that it was very good" (Genesis 1:31). God had just made *paradise*, and He told Adam and Eve, the world's first two humans, to reproduce and to care for His creation.

Everything was perfect, *until*. . . !

It Was All Downhill from Here

The third chapter of Genesis tells us that the serpent—actually the devil in the guise of a snake—deceived Adam and Eve and got them to do the one thing God had told them not to do: eat from the tree of the knowledge of good and evil. And when they did that, they brought on another beginning from the book of Genesis: the beginning of sin.

From that moment on, it was all downhill for the human race. Adam and Eve were kicked out of the garden of Eden. Genesis 4 reports how jealousy, anger, and even murder became a part of human life. And as the years went on, things only got worse. In fact, things got so bad that God decided to scrap the whole thing and start over.

Did You Know. . . ?

The Old Testament is filled with what are called "messianic prophecies"—predictions of the coming Messiah, Jesus Christ. The first prophecy is found in Genesis 3:15, where God says to the serpent (Satan), "I will cause hostility between you and the woman, and between your offspring and her offspring. He will strike your head, and you will strike his heel." This meant that the Messiah would be born from a woman and that He would one day destroy the devil.

Water, Water Everywhere—the Flood

You've probably read or heard the story of Noah (Genesis 6–9). Several hundred years after God kicked Adam and Eve out of Eden, humans had become so sinful and violent that God decided to send a huge flood to destroy the whole human race—except for Noah and his family.

God told Noah to build a huge boat called an ark. The plan was for Noah, his family, and some of each kind of animal to get in the ark before the rains came and stay there until dry land appeared again. Five months after the flood started, the ark came to rest on a mountain called Ararat. A few months later, more land started to appear. Several more months later, Noah and his family—along with all those animals—left the ark and began repopulating the earth all over again.

Abraham and Some Other Biblical "Fathers"

The book of Genesis shifts gears in chapter 12. While the first 11 chapters tell us the story of the beginnings of the universe and of human history, chapter 12 is the start of what is called *patriarchal history*.

The word *patriarch* is kind of a fancy name for "father." The four patriarchs of the book of Genesis are Abraham (Genesis 12–25:8), Isaac (21:1–35), Jacob (Genesis 25:21–50:14), and Joseph (Genesis 30:22–50:26). When you call these men patriarchs, what you're really saying is that they are fathers of the nation of Israel.

There are a lot of important characters in the book of Genesis, but probably the most important is Abraham, the man God chose to be the father of the Hebrew nation. You can read all about Abraham (or Abram, as he was called earlier in his life before God gave him a new name) in Genesis 12–24.

Even though Abraham wasn't a perfect man—he made more than his share of mistakes—he was still a man who believed that God kept His promises. That made a difference in nearly everything Abraham did!

When you first start reading about the patriarch Abraham, you may wonder if someone misspelled his name in the first few chapters that tell his amazing life story. But the name *Abram* is not a typo. Abram and Abraham are the same guy. After God called Abram and told him to move to Canaan, He promised Abram he'd be the father of a great nation and a blessing to the entire world.

Abraham (we'll use this name from now on to avoid further confusion) is first mentioned in Genesis 11; but it's in chapter 12 where his life gets really interesting. Abraham was 75 years old when God told him to leave Ur and travel to Canaan. But he never questioned God—he just did what he was told.

It probably helped that God made him an amazing promise: "I will make you a great nation; I will bless you and make your name great; and you shall be a blessing. I will bless those who bless you, and I will curse him who curses you; and in you all the families of the earth shall be blessed" (Genesis 12:2–3 NKJV).

Who, What, Where?

Ur was a place—probably a large city—located in what is now Iraq, about 600 miles east of Canaan, which is the land in and around Israel today. Ur was the birthplace of Abraham and Haran, his brother. Abraham and his family lived in Ur before God commanded him to travel to Canaan.

The Promise of a Son. . .and Millions of Family Members

Power Words

And Abram believed the LORD, and the LORD counted him as righteous because of his faith.

GENESIS 15:6

What's In It for Me?

The story of Isaac's birth is a good reminder of two things: God always keeps His promises, even when it doesn't seem humanly possible; and we need to wait patiently—sometimes for years—for God to keep His promises. You can never go wrong when you simply trust God to do what He says He will do.

Later, as you can read in Genesis 17, God repeated His promise to Abraham, only this time He was a little more specific. God promised Abraham that He would begin a new race of people through him and his wife, Sarah—even though Abraham was 99 years old and Sarah was way too old to have children. God promised He would make Abraham the father of many nations and that he would have millions of descendants. This is when God renamed him Abraham and renamed his wife Sarah as well (she was called Sarai before that).

In time—after Abraham and Sarah hatched a plan to produce a son through Sarah's servant, Hagar (you can read this story in Genesis 16)—God kept His promise. Genesis 17 says that Sarah became pregnant and gave birth to the son God had promised them. They named him Isaac, as God had told them to, and he later became the founder of the nation God had promised Abraham and his family.

This Is Only a Test. . .

Abraham knew beyond all doubt that his son Isaac was the result of God's keeping His promises. But one day, Abraham had to wonder what God could possibly be thinking when He told Abraham to do the unthinkable: sacrifice Isaac on an altar.

Genesis 22 tells the story of Abraham hearing that command and then obediently taking Isaac to a place called Moriah, where he built an altar and prepared to take his son's life. Abraham had placed Isaac on top of the altar, and was about to sacrifice him, when an angel of the Lord stopped him and told him not to harm the young man.

In the end, Abraham sacrificed a ram—caught by its horns in a thicket—instead of his son Isaac.

It was all a test. God wanted Abraham to discover just how deeply he trusted God and just how committed he was to obeying God's every command. Because Abraham proved how faithful he was, God again promised to bless Abraham with countless millions of descendants—all of whom would also be descendants of his son Isaac.

Fun Bible Trivia

The book of Genesis doesn't say what Abraham was thinking as he prepared to sacrifice his son Isaac, but in the New Testament, the book of Hebrews suggests that Abraham believed that if he had actually slain his son, God would have raised Isaac from the dead. (You can look it up in Hebrews 11:17–19.)

More Branches on the Family Tree

After the death of Sarah, Abraham arranged a marriage for Isaac. He sent a servant to his brother Nahor's home to find a wife for Isaac. The servant returned with Nahor's daughter Rebekah. Isaac married Rebekah, and after much prayer—because Rebekah at first couldn't get pregnant—she had twin sons: Esau and Jacob.

Esau was Isaac's favorite son, but when Isaac was very old, Jacob tricked his blind father into giving him the blessing meant for the firstborn child in that culture. (You can read this story in Genesis 27.) That meant that Jacob, not Esau, would become the forefather of the Hebrew people.

Later, Jacob himself was tricked into marrying a woman named Leah—when he really wanted to marry her sister, Rachel. In those days, men were allowed to have more than one wife, so he also married Rachel. Jacob, whom God renamed Israel, became the father of 12 sons, and his family came to be known as the 12 tribes of Israel.

One of those sons was named Joseph, and his story takes up the last 20 chapters of the book of Genesis.

Modern technology allows us to see twins in their mother's womb—but Jacob and Esau were born 4,000 years before ultrasounds!

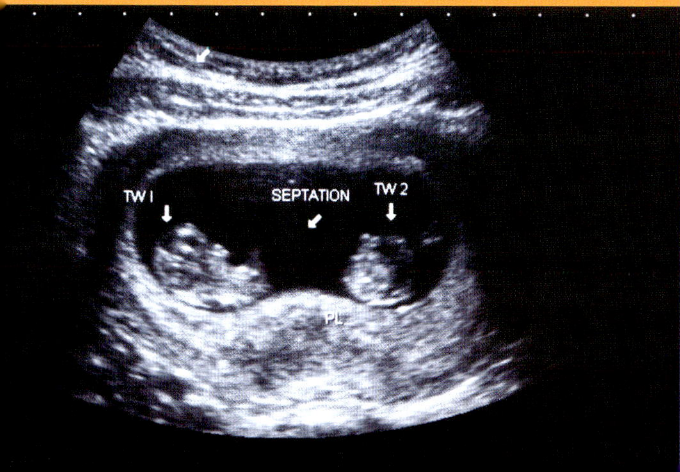

Did You Know. . .?

The name Jacob means "supplanter," which is another word for someone who replaces someone, often by trickery or force. This makes sense because Jacob—with the help of his mother—tricked his father into giving him a birthright meant for his older brother, Esau. Though God doesn't approve of trickery and deception, Jacob's story is an example of how God uses imperfect people to carry out His perfect plans.

That's Some Jacket You're Wearing, Joseph!

Joseph was the second-youngest of 12 sons born to Jacob. You can only imagine the kind of problems he faced being one of 12 boys, but to make matters worse, he was Jacob's favorite, which made the other brothers mad. Not only that, Joseph was a bit of a tattletale, who brought his father bad reports of some of the things the other boys were doing. To top it off, Jacob set Joseph apart by giving him a beautiful robe (called a "coat of many colors" in some Bible versions).

When Joseph's 10 older brothers saw the robe their father had given Joseph, they became very jealous. They disliked him so much that they wouldn't even say anything nice to him. Things only got worse for Joseph when he told his brothers about a couple of strange dreams he had—both of which showed him that his brothers would bow down to him.

A few days later, Jacob asked Joseph to check up on his brothers, who were working in the fields. When the brothers saw him coming, they made plans to kill him. But Reuben, the eldest brother, had another idea: He said they should just throw Joseph into a well and leave him there to die. (Reuben's real plan was to come back later by himself and rescue Joseph.)

After the brothers stripped off Joseph's coat and tossed him into the empty well, a group of men came by on their way to Egypt. That gave Judah, another one of the brothers, an idea. Why not sell Joseph to the men as a slave? That way, the brothers would be innocent of killing him—and they would make a nice profit besides!

So Joseph was off to Egypt, where he was sold to an important man named Potiphar. Meanwhile, Joseph's brothers dipped Joseph's robe in animal blood and took it to Jacob, who believed a wild animal had killed his favorite son.

Joseph started out his life in Egypt as a slave, but because he was faithful to God—and because God blessed him—Joseph became an important person in Egypt. He even got to talk to Pharaoh himself and told him the meaning of some of his dreams.

What's In It for Me?

When you read about how Joseph's brothers treated him—how they sold him to a bunch of strangers—you might be tempted to say, "That's not fair!" But keep in mind that God used what happened to Joseph to help keep the Hebrew race from starving to death. Joseph is an example of how God can use everything that happens in your life—even the tough times you have to go through—for your own good.

One of those dreams meant that there would be a terrible time in the surrounding world when people wouldn't have any food to eat. So Joseph advised Pharaoh to save up lots of food during the good times so people wouldn't starve to death later.

When the hard times came, people came from all over to buy grain from Joseph. That included Joseph's brothers, who bowed to him—just as he had told them they would—because he was such an important person.

Joseph had the authority to have his brothers punished—even put to death—for what they had done to him. But he wasn't about to do that. Instead, he told them not to be afraid of him or angry at themselves for selling him, because God had used what they had done to keep a lot of people from dying.

So Jacob, Joseph's brothers, and their families left Canaan and moved to Egypt to live with Joseph. They had all the food they needed, and their families got bigger and bigger. Because they were Joseph's family, they had the best of everything.

Joseph died in Egypt at the age of 110. But before he died, he promised his brothers that God would one day rescue them and take them back to Canaan. The book of Genesis ends with Joseph's body being placed in a coffin in Egypt.

Now it's time to look ahead about four centuries to see what became of Joseph's descendants in Egypt—and how God made good on Joseph's promise.

Exodus

What It's About: The word *exodus* literally means "departure," and that's what the story in the book of Exodus is all about. The book of Genesis ends with Abraham's descendants living in Egypt as guests of Joseph. After spending more than four hundred years in Egypt, the Hebrews—by now, hundreds of thousands of families—were living in a foreign land as slaves. That all changed when God assigned His own chosen man, Moses, to bring the people of Israel out of Egyptian slavery and set them on their way to the Promised Land of Canaan.

Important Characters/People: Moses, Aaron, Miriam, Pharaoh, Jethro, Joshua

Egyptian taskmasters whip their Hebrew slaves.

What You'll Find in the Book of Exodus

The Israelites had it pretty good in Egypt while Joseph was alive. But after Joseph died, the new pharaoh saw the tribes of Israel not as welcome guests but as a threat to his nation. So Pharaoh made the Israelites slaves in Egypt. God saw what was happening to His chosen people, and He heard their cries for a deliverer. So He called a shepherd named Moses to lead them out of slavery in Egypt.

At first, Moses wasn't sure he was the man for the job. Even though God appeared to him in a miraculous way—out of a bush that looked like it was on fire, even though it wasn't burned up—Moses made excuses about why he couldn't lead the Hebrews out of Egypt. (You can read this story in Exodus 3–4.)

But God wasn't going to have it any other way. Eventually, He convinced Moses that he was the right person to lead the Hebrews, and Moses went to Pharaoh with this demand: "Let my people go" (Exodus 5:1).

Pharaoh knew he had a good thing going with all the free labor provided by the Hebrew slaves, and he wasn't about to let them just walk away—at least not without some heavy persuasion from above! Chapters 7–12 of Exodus tell the story of a series of 10 plagues that God sent on Egypt because Pharaoh wouldn't let the Hebrew nation go free. First it was the water in the Nile River turning to blood, then plagues of frogs, gnats, and flies. Then came the death of the livestock in Egypt, boils breaking out on the people, hail, locusts, and three days of darkness.

Still, Pharaoh wouldn't budge—not until God sent the final plague: the death of all firstborn male children and livestock in Egypt. When Pharaoh saw what had happened, he *begged* Moses and his people to leave Egypt for good. The Egyptian people wanted the Hebrews to leave so much that they let them take anything they wanted with them—as long as they left right away!

Power Words

God replied to Moses, "I AM WHO I AM. Say this to the people of Israel: I AM has sent me to you."

EXODUS 3:14

Who, What, Where?

Where would Moses have been without his big brother, Aaron? When Moses complained that he wasn't a very good speaker, God appointed Aaron as Moses' spokesman, a position he held for almost 40 years. Aaron was also the first priest of Israel and the father of a line of priests that continued for more than 1,000 years.

Time to Hit the Road. . .for the Promised Land!

What a sight it must have been! Hundreds of thousands of people gathering for their exodus from Egypt!

Even though the people of Israel were beginning a journey to the Promised Land, they didn't take the shortest way there—which would have been a straight line through the desert. Instead, they headed toward a place called the Wilderness of Sinai, which is located near the southern tip of the Sinai Peninsula. It was here that God called Moses to the top of Mount Sinai to give him rules to govern the Hebrew people, including the Ten Commandments.

A Mountaintop Experience, the Laws of God. . .and a Calf Made of Gold

Fun Bible Trivia

Ever wonder where in the Bible you can find the Ten Commandments? They're found in Exodus 20:3–17. How many of the Ten Commandments can you remember? Write down the ones that come to mind, and then look them up in your Bible to see how many you got right and how many you missed.

Moses' time with God on the mountain wasn't just a quick visit. In fact, his visit with God is covered in chapters 20–32 of Exodus. The people expected Moses to be back in a short time, and after a while they started to think he had died on the mountain. The people lost their patience and pressured Aaron into building them a golden idol in the shape of a calf.

When Moses returned to the camp and saw the idol, he became so angry that he smashed the stone tablets of the Law. After the idol was destroyed (and after God had restored order), God called Moses back to the mountain and gave him a new copy of the Law.

The last six chapters of Exodus tell the story of the Hebrews' continued journey toward the Promised Land and the construction of the tabernacle, a movable tent used for service and worship to God.

Leviticus

What It's About: Once God had delivered the people of Israel out of slavery in Egypt, He instructed them how to live and how to worship Him. That included a system of sacrifices that would one day be replaced by the onetime sacrifice of Jesus Christ on the cross.

Important Characters/People: Moses, Aaron, Nadab, Abihu, Ithamar, Eleazar

The Writer: Moses (see page 20)

What You'll Find in the Book of Leviticus

The people of Israel lived as slaves in Egypt for more than 400 years. As a result of living among a people who worshipped many false gods, the way the Hebrews viewed God was warped. The words recorded in the book of Leviticus are the words of a God who wanted to bring His people back into fellowship with Him.

The people of Israel were imperfect—just like everyone else—but they were *God's* people, and He provided the words recorded in Leviticus to give them instructions on how to have a relationship with a holy God. That's why you'll see the word *holy* throughout the book of Leviticus. God is holy, and He wants His people to be holy too. And in those days, the only way for that to happen was through sacrifices to pay for the people's sins.

The first seven chapters of Leviticus cover the various offerings and sacrifices that God required from the people. The first three chapters are about what are called *voluntary offerings*, which were meant as worship to God.

God *hated* it when His people worshipped silly idols!

Power Words

"For I am the Lord your God. You must consecrate yourselves and be holy, because I am holy."

Leviticus 11:44

What's In It For Me?

Christians don't live under the rules listed in the book of Leviticus. So why should we read this book? When we read Leviticus, we are reminded of what Jesus has done for us! Because Jesus died for us, paying the price once and for all for our sin, we no longer have to offer any of the sacrifices listed in this book.

Chapters 4 and 5 address offerings made to cover people's sins. Chapters 6 and 7 record laws and regulations about the different kinds of offerings.

Chapters 8–10 cover the rules and regulations for the priesthood of that time. Chapters 11–16 explain to the Hebrew people what to do in order to deal with different kinds of "uncleanness." The last 10 chapters are instructions and guidelines for holy living.

Numbers

What It's About: Even though God brought the nation of Israel out of slavery in Egypt—and performed some amazing miracles for everyone to see—the people were ungrateful and unbelieving. As a result, they were forced to wander in the wilderness of Sinai for 40 years.

Important Characters/People: Moses, Aaron, Joshua, Balaam, Eleazar, the 70 elders, Caleb, Korah, Dathan, Abiram, the 12 spies, Gad, Reuben

The Writer: Moses (see page 20)

Power Words

"And if the LORD is pleased with us, he will bring us safely into that land and give it to us. It is a rich land flowing with milk and honey."

NUMBERS 14:8

What You'll Find in the Book of Numbers

At the beginning of the book of Numbers, God instructs Moses to count all the young men of Israel—which is how the book got its name. God told Moses and his brother, Aaron, along with leaders of the 12 tribes, to do the counting.

Moses sent 12 men to "spy out" the Promised Land.

Most of the events in the book of Numbers take place in the wilderness between Egypt and Canaan. The book begins 14 months after the people had left Egypt, and long after they should have entered the Promised Land. But even though they should have completed the journey in less than two weeks, they were still decades away from claiming the land that God had promised to give them. That's because God was punishing them for their constant complaining and rebellion.

The book of Numbers includes probably the best—or the worst—example of the people's rebellion and lack of faith. It happened while the people were camped out at a place called Kadesh, which was located in the Desert of Zin. They were just days away from entering the Promised Land when Moses sent representatives from each of Israel's 12 tribes ahead to check out the land. When they returned, they told the people that everything they had been told about the land was true and that it would be a great place to live and raise their families.

So what was the problem?

Two of the spies—Joshua and Caleb—told the people to get ready to take the land and that there was no way they could fail, because God would be with them. But 10 of the spies told the people about giants living in the land—giants so big that they made the men of Israel look like grasshoppers in comparison.

Sadly, the people of Israel chose to listen to the 10—and they rebelled against Moses and against God and refused to move out to take the land. Because they rebelled, and because they failed to believe God, many of them died at Kadesh. (You can read the whole story in Numbers 13–14.)

Sadly, a whole generation of people who were just days away from enjoying life in a land flowing with milk and honey instead died in the wilderness. Moses had prayed to God for the rebellious people, and God forgave them. But He wasn't going to reward them for their lack of faith and obedience.

Who, What, Where?

Caleb, who was a member of the tribe of Judah, was one of the 12 spies Moses sent to spy out the land of Canaan. He is an example of what can happen in the life of someone who trusts God instead of allowing fear to rule. The Bible says that Caleb trusted God and acted on that trust, so he became an example of the kind of faith God honors and rewards (see Joshua 14:6–15). Do you have that kind of faith in God?

What's In It for Me?

It's not pleasant reading about thousands of people dying in a desert because they refused to believe God but instead focused on a bunch of giants. But the story of what happened at Kadesh is a great reminder to focus on the size of our God and not on the size of the giants in your life. When you do that, you'll be more than willing to do exactly what God asks you to do—and you'll enjoy the good things God has for you as a result!

Ten of the 12 spies said they didn't want to face the giants in the Promised Land!

They would have to wander in the wilderness until everyone over the age of 20 had died.

Even Moses wasn't allowed to enter the Promised Land. But Joshua and Caleb, the two spies who had tried their best to rally the people and get them to claim what God had already given them, were allowed to enter the land of Canaan.

Deuteronomy

What It's About: Moses, who had led Israel out of captivity and slavery in Egypt, speaks to the Hebrew people four times to remind them where they had come from, where they had been, whom they belonged to (God), and how belonging to God should affect their lives.

Important Characters/People: Moses, Joshua, the Canaanites, the Hittites, the Girgashites, the Amorites, the Perizzites, the Hivites, the Jebusites

The Writer: Moses (See page 20)

What You'll Find in the Book of Deuteronomy

Chapters 1–4 of Deuteronomy record Moses' words to his people reminding them of their 40 years in the wilderness. Moses didn't talk to the people about that time just to give them a history lesson. He wanted them to remember *why* they had wandered in the wilderness—because of their disobedience and lack of faith.

In chapters 5–11, you can read about how Moses repeated the Ten Commandments (5:6–21), reminded the people of the importance of doing what God had told them to do, and promised the people they would soon enter the Promised Land.

Moses begins this part of his address by telling the people, "Listen carefully, Israel. Hear the decrees and regulations I am giving you today, so you may learn them and obey them!" (5:1).

What's In It for Me?

God promises that when you come to Him to confess your sin, He will completely forgive you and cleanse you. It's true now, and it was true in the days of Moses. So why would Moses remind the people of what they had done wrong after they left Egypt? So they would remember their mistakes and not make the same ones again! When you think about the things you've done that displease God, don't beat yourself up. Instead, thank God for His forgiveness. . .and for the lessons He has taught you when you made bad decisions.

The book of Deuteronomy is a written record of Moses' spoken sermons to God's people.

Power Words

"And you must love the LORD your God with all your heart, all your soul, and all your strength."

DEUTERONOMY 6:5

Moses sees the Promised Land from far away, in a 19th-century painting by James Tissot.

In chapters 12–26, Moses reminds the Hebrews of the laws and rules that God wants them to obey once they enter the Promised Land. In chapters 27–30, he tells them what kinds of blessings they would receive for obeying those laws

Chapters 31–33 are Moses' final words to the people before his death—his final good-byes. Chapter 34 is the account of Moses' final days, which he spent on Mount Nebo on the plains of Moab. From there, God showed him the Promised Land, which the people of Israel would soon enter.

After Moses' death, Joshua—the same Joshua who years before had so bravely tried to encourage the people of Israel to possess the land—took over as leader of the Hebrew people.

That's what you'll read about in the next chapter!

CHAPTER 3

His Story. . . and Their Story

The History of God's People (Joshua through Esther)

Someone once said that the Bible isn't just history, but that it's "His story," meaning the story of how God relates to the human race.

The first five books of the Bible—the collection called the Pentateuch—are books about beginnings and the Law of Moses. The next 12 are books of history, and they're the ones that tell the story of the rise and fall, and then the rise again, of the nation of Israel.

These books of history cover more than 1,000 years, starting with the appointment of Joshua to lead the Israelites into the Promised Land (around 1452 BC) and ending after the return of the Jews to Israel following what is called the Babylonian Captivity (which you'll read about later in this chapter).

The people of Israel enjoyed some good times during this period, but they also went through some bad times. As you'll see in this chapter—and in the books of the Bible it covers—those bad times happened because of some bad decisions on the part of Israel's leaders and on the part of the people.

As you read through this part of the Bible, you'll learn how the people of Israel moved into the Promised Land, how they became a kingdom with a human king, how Israel was divided into two kingdoms called Judah and Israel, and the good and bad (mostly bad) things the kings who ruled over Judah and Israel did during their reigns.

Joshua

What It's About: After wandering in the wilderness for 40 years, the people of Israel now led by Joshua capture and settle the Promised Land, also known as the land of Canaan.

Important Characters/People: Joshua, Caleb, Rahab, Eleazar, Achan

The Writer: The book of Joshua doesn't name its writer, but most experts agree that Joshua himself wrote most of it. (The last five verses describe Joshua's death and legacy, so someone else would have written those verses.)

Power Words

"This is my command—be strong and courageous! Do not be afraid or discouraged. For the LORD your God is with you wherever you go."

JOSHUA 1:9

What You'll Find in the Book of Joshua

This book picks up where the book of Deuteronomy leaves off. Moses has died, and now it's up to Joshua the "son of Nun" (1:1) to finish what Moses started and lead the people of Israel into the Promised Land.

Before his death, Moses appointed Joshua as the new leader of the Hebrews (see Deuteronomy 34:9). As the book of Joshua begins, God gives Joshua the encouragement and command to "be strong and courageous" (Joshua 1:6–7, 9). Almost all of the rebellious people who had earlier lost out on their chance to enter the Promised Land have died, leaving a group of people who are ready to follow Joshua's lead and take what God had already said was theirs.

The book of Joshua is split into two 12-chapter sections. The first 12 chapters tell the story of the Israelites' conquest of the people and armies that stood in their way; the last 12 chapters tell the story of how the Israelites divided the land of Canaan among the 12 tribes of Israel.

The city of Jericho is the Israelites' first major obstacle under Joshua's leadership. But God demonstrates what He can do when His people obey His commands. God commanded Joshua's army to march outside Jericho. . .blowing trumpets and shouting! When they did that, God knocked the city walls flat, and the Israelites defeated the city. After that, Joshua's armies drove idol-worshipping people such as the Hittites, Amorites, Canaanites, Perizzites, Hivites, and Jebusites from Canaan.

Fun Bible Trivia

Joshua is a Hebrew name that means either "Jehovah is his help," "Jehovah the Savior," or "Jehovah is salvation." The name *Jesus* essentially means the very same thing!

Who, What, Where?

Rahab was a woman in Jericho who played a big part in the Israelites' defeat of the city. When Joshua sent two spies to check out the city before Israel attacked it, Rahab hid them from the king of Jericho. In return for her kindness, the men promised she and her family would be spared if she hung a scarlet cord from her window when Israel attacked. Rahab is mentioned in the New Testament as a woman of great faith (Hebrews 11:31; James 2:25). You can read the story of Rahab in Joshua 2:1–24.

Judges

What It's About: Judges is a book of ups and downs—followed by still more ups and downs. It tells the 350-year story of how the people of Israel strayed away from God, the punishment the people suffered as a result, and their turning back to God. Each time Israel abandoned God, He appointed leaders, called judges, to lead them back to Him.

Important Characters/People: Othniel, Ehud, Shamgar, Deborah, Gideon, Abimelech, Tola, Jair, Jephthah, Ibzan, Elon, Abdon, Samson, Barak, Jael, Micah, the Midianites, the Amalekites, the Philistines, the Ammonites

The Writer: Experts aren't certain who wrote the book of Judges, but most believe it was the prophet Samuel.

Fun Bible Trivia

Some of the judges listed in the book of Judges had very unusual families. For example, Jair had 30 sons (10:4) and Abdon had 40 sons (12:14). Ibzan had 30 sons and 30 daughters (12:9). Jephthah, on the other hand, had only one child, a daughter he foolishly vowed to sacrifice to God in exchange for a military victory (11:30–40).

Jair had 30 sons who rode 30 donkeys.

What You'll Find in theBook of Judges

This book picks up not long after the book of Joshua leaves off. It tells the stories of 13 people—12 men and one woman—who lead the nation of Israel against the enemies who took over because of the Israelites' disobedience.

The stories in the book of Judges aren't pleasant ones. You can read about how the nation of Israel spent almost four centuries falling away from God, suffering the consequences, and then being rescued by one of the 13 judges.

These are the 13 judges listed in this book and where you can read about them:

Othniel (Judges 3:7–11)—Caleb's brother, who delivered Israel from the king of Mesopotamia and judged Israel for 40 years.

Ehud (Judges 3:12-30)—He defeated the oppressing Moabites. Ehud killed Eglon, the king of Moab, with a dagger while pretending to be on a peace mission.

Shamgar (Judges 3:31)—He fought bravely against the Philistines, killing 600 soldiers with an ox goad—a pointed rod used to prod along oxen as they pulled a cart.

Deborah (Judges 4-5)—She was Israel's only female judge and prophetess. Deborah called Barak to lead warriors into battle against a Canaanite army commander, but Barak would fight only if Deborah went with him.

Gideon (Judges 6-8)—God raised him up to lead Israel against the Midianites.

Who, What, Where?

Gideon was the fifth judge of Israel, and probably the best known of all the judges. God appointed Gideon to lead his nation against the Midianites. The angel of the Lord appeared to Gideon when he was hiding from the enemy, told him God was with him, and called him a "mighty man of valor." Gideon had many doubts, but they did not keep him from obeying God. You can read his story in Judges 6-8.

Abimelech (Judges 9)—He was Gideon's son. He killed all but one of his brothers and was made king of Shechem. He was killed when a woman dropped part of a millstone on his head.

Tola (Judges 10:1-2)—He judged Israel for 23 years.

Jair (10:3-5)—He led Israel for 22 years. He was known for having 30 sons who rode 30 donkeys.

Jephthah (Judges 10:6-12:7)—He was Gilead's son, and he judged Israel for six years.

Ibzan (Judges 12:8-10)—He led the nation for seven years. Ibzan sent his daughters abroad and brought in 30 foreign women as wives for his sons.

Elon (Judges 12:11-12)—He judged Israel for 10 years.

Abdon (Judges 12:13-15)—He led the nation of Israel for eight years. He was known for having 40 sons and 30 grandsons who each rode a donkey.

Samson (Judges 13-16)—He was a Nazirite, which meant he had taken a vow not to eat or drink anything from a grapevine, drink alcohol, cut his hair, or eat anything unclean. Samson performed amazing feats of strength, but he had some weaknesses that led to his downfall.

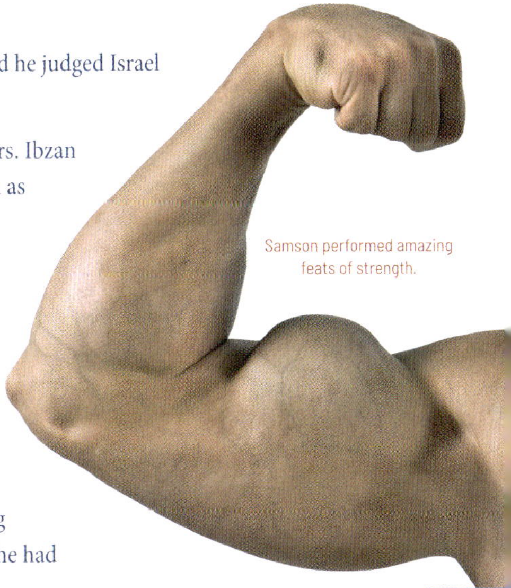

Samson performed amazing feats of strength.

Ruth

What It's About: Ruth was a loyal daughter-in-law of a Hebrew woman named Naomi. After Ruth's husband died, she went on to become an example of faithfulness to God and an object of God's love and care. Ruth and her new husband, Boaz, are the great-grandparents of King David.

Important Characters/People: Ruth, Naomi, Boaz

The Writer: The writer of the book of Ruth isn't named, but some people believe the prophet Samuel wrote the story.

What You'll Find in the Book of Ruth

The story's main character, Ruth, probably lived around 1100 BC, during the time of the judges.

What makes the book of Ruth different from most other Old Testament books is that Ruth wasn't a Hebrew; she was a native of a place called Moab. She married a Jewish man named Mahlon. Mahlon's mother was a Jewish woman named Naomi. Ruth lived with her husband and his family in Moab.

When Naomi's husband, Elimelech, and her two sons (including Ruth's husband) died, Naomi decided to move back to Bethlehem. Naomi told Ruth and her other daughter-in-law, Orpah, to stay in Moab, but Ruth refused to leave Naomi. The two women traveled to Bethlehem, where Ruth gathered leftover barley during the harvest—a practice called gleaning—so that she and Naomi would have enough food to survive.

As Ruth gathered grain one day, Boaz, the wealthy owner of the field where she was working, noticed her and ordered his workers to protect her and to leave some grain behind for her to collect. When Ruth went home that night, she told Naomi about Boaz, and her mother-in-law recognized him as a relative of Ruth's late husband. Naomi encouraged Ruth to pursue Boaz and make herself available to him.

Boaz was flattered by Ruth's attention, and he eventually married her. Together they had a son named Obed, who would one day become the grandfather of King David.

Power Words

Ruth replied, "Don't ask me to leave you and turn back. Wherever you go, I will go; wherever you live, I will live. Your people will be my people, and your God will be my God."

RUTH 1:16

Fun Bible Trivia

Ruth and Boaz are mentioned in the New Testament as ancestors of Jesus. Matthew 1:5 lists them as the parents of Obed, the grandfather of King David.

1 Samuel

What It's About: The 12 tribes of Israel unite under a king. Even though God never wanted His people to live under the rule of a human king, He allows them to set up an earthly kingdom and even chooses the men who would rule over them.

Important Characters/People: Hannah, Eli, Samuel, Saul, David, Jonathan, the Philistines, Abigail

The Writer: The writer of the book of 1 Samuel isn't named, but some experts believe Samuel himself wrote most of it. Some of the history in this book takes place after Samuel's death, and it is not known who wrote the remainder of the book.

What You'll Find in the Book of 1 Samuel

This book tells two stories. First, there's the life of the prophet Samuel, who was Israel's last judge (chapters 1–12). Then there is the life of Saul, Israel's first king (chapters 13–31). It starts out with a miracle birth, as a woman named Hannah prays for a son and promises to dedicate him to God's service. God answers by giving her Samuel.

Samuel was one of Israel's greatest prophets. He spoke out against dishonesty in the priesthood and led the people of Israel to turn away from idolatry and back to their God. Samuel spent his entire life as a judge and prophet in Israel.

This Is Not What God Wanted!

The book of 1 Samuel includes a big change in the nation of Israel. The people ask Samuel for a human king so that they could be just like the other nations around them. Samuel doesn't want Israel to have a king, but he reluctantly prays and tells God what the people want. Even though God warns that having a human king will be disastrous for Israel in the long run, He tells Samuel to appoint a man named Saul as the first king of Israel.

Who, What, Where?

Eli was a priest during the period of the judges at a place called Shiloh, which was about 10 miles north of Jerusalem. After Hannah's miracle son, Samuel, was weaned, she kept a promise to God and brought him to Eli for service and training. One night, Eli realized God had spoken to Samuel and encouraged the boy to listen and respond. In his first prophecy, Samuel spoke out against the dishonesty of Eli's sons, Hophni and Phinehas, who were both priests.

Saul's reign as king starts out well, but later he makes several bad decisions. Because he disobeys God several times, God removes his blessing from Saul and appoints a young shepherd named David as Israel's second king.

Chapter 16 is the story of Samuel's journey to Bethlehem to anoint David as Israel's next king. Chapter 17 covers David's famous battle with a giant Philistine named Goliath. David's victory over Goliath makes him a hero to everyone in Israel except King Saul, who tries several times to kill David. With God's help, David escapes from Saul several times. (You can read the whole story in chapters 19–26.)

In the final chapter of 1 Samuel, Saul's three sons, including Jonathan (a close friend of David's), die in battle with the Philistines, and Saul commits suicide, clearing the way for David to take the throne of Israel.

David, a statue by the Italian artist Michelangelo, was created between the years 1501 and 1504.

Power Words

David replied to the Philistine, "You come to me with sword, spear, and javelin, but I come to you in the name of the LORD of Heaven's Armies—the God of the armies of Israel, whom you have defied."

1 SAMUEL 17:45

2 Samuel

What It's About: This book picks up where 1 Samuel leaves off. David becomes king of Israel. Even though David was far from a perfect man, he becomes Israel's greatest king.

Important Characters/People: David, Joab, Abner, Ishbosheth, Absalom, Michal, Bathsheba, Uriah, Nathan, Hushai

The Writer: Unknown, but it wasn't Samuel, because the events recorded in this book take place after his death. Some suggest that Abiathar the priest was the author (15:35).

What You'll Find in the Book of 2 Samuel

Second Samuel covers about 40 years of Israel's history—the entire reign of David as king of Israel. After King Saul died, David took the throne of the tribe of Judah. Seven years later, after the death of Ishbosheth, the son of Saul and king of the northern tribes, David became king over all Israel.

After capturing Jerusalem from the Jebusites, David made Jerusalem the capital city of Israel. That was the first of many military victories for Israel under King David. After that, Israel became a powerful and rich nation.

One spring, though, David stayed home from battle and committed a terrible sin with Bathsheba, the wife of Uriah, one of his most devoted soldiers. To cover up what he had done, David arranged to have Uriah killed in battle. Even though David repented for his sins and was forgiven, the consequences of what he did affected the rest of his reign—as well as his own family.

David's son Absalom tried to take the throne of Israel from his father. David had to run for his life away from Jerusalem. Eventually, Absalom died in battle, and David returned to Jerusalem to take back the throne. The final three chapters of 2 Samuel tell the story of David's final days.

1 and 2 Kings

What They're About: First Kings starts with the reign of Solomon, David's son, as king of Israel, and 2 Kings ends with both parts of a divided kingdom—the northern kingdom (Israel) and the southern kingdom (Judah)—being defeated and their people taken into captivity. The northern kingdom was defeated by the Assyrians, and the southern kingdom was defeated by the Babylonians.

Important Characters/People: David, Adonijah, Solomon, Rehoboam, Jeroboam, Abijam, Asa, Jehoshaphat, Ahab, Jezebel, Nathan, Ahijah, Elijah, and Micaiah in 1 Kings; Elijah, Elisha, Jehoram, Ben-Hadad, Hazael, Ahaziah, Jehu, Jezebel, Ahab, Joash, Ahaz, Isaiah, Hezekiah, Josiah, and Nebuchadnezzar in 2 Kings

The Writer: First Kings and Second Kings were originally one book in the Hebrew Bible. No writer is mentioned, but tradition teaches that the prophet Jeremiah—the same one who wrote the book of Jeremiah—recorded this time in biblical history.

Power Words

"Give me an understanding heart so that I can govern your people well and know the difference between right and wrong. For who by himself is able to govern this great people of yours?"

1 Kings 3:9

What You'll Find in the Books of 1 and 2 Kings

First Kings covers events from around 970 BC to 850 BC. It begins with the last days of King David, moves through the reign of King Solomon, and ends with the story of Elijah, a powerful prophet of God.

The first 11 chapters of 1 Kings tell the story of the reign of King Solomon, who started his reign as king of Israel very well. He asked for and received wisdom from God, built the temple in Jerusalem, and ruled over Israel as it reached its high point in power and standing in that part of the world.

Solomon had it all—power, riches, and respect from his neighbors. Sadly, though, he didn't finish his time as king of Israel the way he started it. In fact, he led God's chosen people down a terrible path that would end with a divided nation at war with itself.

It's All Downhill from Here—Again

Like his father, David, Solomon had a weakness for women that would eventually bring him and his nation down. After spending seven years constructing the temple for God, Solomon spent the next 13 years building a palace for himself. He also married 700 women, many of whom were foreigners who persuaded him to worship their false gods.

After Solomon's death, his son Rehoboam made some big mistakes that led to the division of the nation of Israel. When all was said and done, the 10 northern tribes formed their own nation under Jeroboam, a former official under Solomon. That nation is called Israel. The two southern tribes made up a nation called Judah.

Who, What, Where?

Both Israel and Judah were led by a series of kings who didn't do what God wanted them to do. There were a few exceptions, though. Three kings of Judah—Asa (1 Kings 15:9–24), Jehoshaphat (1 Kings 22:41–50), and Hezekiah (2 Kings 18–20)—stood out as men who did what pleased God and who encouraged their people to follow Him too.

Who, What, Where?

In the middle of the stories of Israel's and Judah's kings, you can read about two powerful prophets who lived during those times. Elijah is remembered for prophesying that no rain would fall on Israel—which it didn't for three years, until he said it would—and for a showdown at Mount Carmel with the prophets of Baal (1 Kings 18:18–40). Elisha started out as Elijah's student, and he continued the work Elijah had done after Elijah was taken up to heaven in a whirlwind (2 Kings 2:1–15). Both men performed many amazing miracles.

Starting in 1 Kings 12, you can read about the kings (and one queen) of Israel and Judah. Each nation was ruled over by about 20 kings during that time. For the most part, it's not a very positive story. None of the kings of Israel followed God, and only a few of Judah's kings were godly men. They took part in idol worship and encouraged their people to do the same.

Even though God's prophets warned these kings and the people to turn back to God, both countries strayed further and further from Him as time went on. Eventually, God sent judgment in the form of outside invaders, who brought death, destruction, and slavery.

Second Kings ends with the nation of Israel falling to the Assyrians (chapters 16 and 17) in around 722 BC, and Judah falling to the Babylonians (chapters 24 and 25) in about 585 BC.

Second Kings chapter 25 tells how the armies of Babylonian king Nebuchadnezzar surrounded Jerusalem and then destroyed the city and the temple and took everything of value from the temple and the king's palace. The Babylonians also captured thousands of captives and took them away to Babylon, where they stayed for several decades in what is called the Babylonian Captivity.

This "ball and chain" was put on a prisoner's ankle to keep him from trying to run away. The Babylonians probably didn't use balls and chains—but they sure took a lot of prisoners from Jerusalem.

1 and 2 Chronicles

What They're About: These books cover much of the same history you read about in 1 and 2 Samuel and 1 and 2 Kings, but with more emphasis on the spiritual side of the stories you read in those other books. The books of Chronicles were written after the Babylonian Captivity to give the people returning to Israel an understanding of how to worship God.

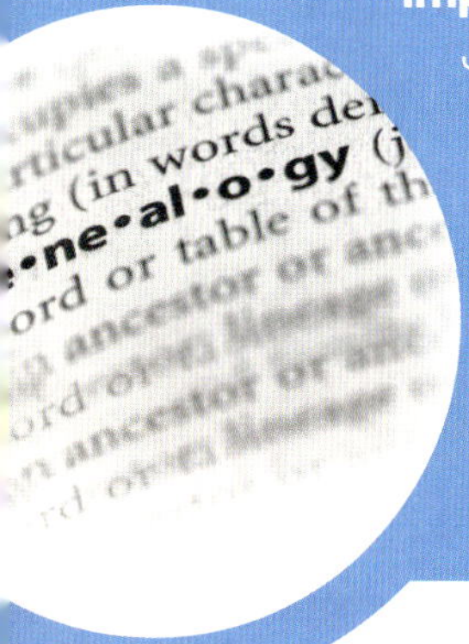

Important Characters/People: Saul, David, Nathan, Gad, Solomon, Joab, Jashobeam, and Eleazar in 1 Chronicles; Solomon, Rehoboam, Jeroboam, Abijah, Asa, Jehoshaphat, Ahab, Jehoram, Ahaziah, Joash, Amaziah, Uzziah, Jotham, Ahaz, Hezekiah, Manasseh, Josiah, and Jehoahaz in 2 Chronicles

The Writer: Like most of the books of the Old Testament, 1 and 2 Chronicles don't name their writers, but centuries of tradition hold that Ezra the priest wrote them.

What You'll Find in the Books of 1 and 2 Chronicles

First Chronicles is a detailed picture of King David's reign over the nation of Israel. It starts with a nine-chapter family history of King David, starting as far back as Adam and his family. Starting with chapter 10, it picks up with David taking the throne of Israel. It ends with Solomon, David's son, taking the throne after his father's death.

We often think of "worship" as a music style. But for the people of Israel, it was a whole way of life.

Did You Know. . .?

The books titled 1 Chronicles and 2 Chronicles in our Bibles today were originally written as one really long book with a title that meant "the words of the days." The book was divided in two in the third century BC, when the Hebrew Bible (also known as the Old Testament) was translated into Greek.

Power Words

He [Solomon] prayed, "O LORD, God of Israel, there is no God like you in all of heaven and earth. You keep your covenant and show unfailing love to all who walk before you in wholehearted devotion."

2 CHRONICLES 6:14

Second Chronicles covers more than 400 years of history. It begins with the construction of Solomon's temple and ends with Cyrus' announcement that the Jews would be allowed to rebuild the temple following the Babylonian Captivity. This book focuses mostly on the southern kingdom of Judah and barely mentions the northern kingdom of Israel. It mentions the invasion of Judah by the Babylonians, but focuses more on the good things that happened there.

Ezra

What It's About: After about 70 years of captivity in Babylon, the Jews return to Israel, where for a time they live lives of obedience and devotion to God.

Important Characters/People: Darius, Cyrus, Artaxerxes, Ezra, Zerubbabel, Zechariah, Haggai

The Writer: The book of Ezra doesn't name its writer, but thousands of years of tradition hold that Ezra himself wrote it. Ezra's name first appears in the book in chapter 7—the same time that the writer changes from writing in the third person to the first person (from "he" to "I").

What You'll Find in the Book of Ezra

This book covers about one hundred years of history, starting in about 530 BC. The book of Ezra begins where the book of 2 Chronicles ends. King Cyrus of Persia declares that the captive Jews will be allowed to return to their homeland, where they will rebuild the temple, which had been destroyed when the Babylonians raided Jerusalem seven decades earlier.

The first six chapters of the book of Ezra tell the story of how a first group of Jews, led by a man named Zerubbabel, left Persia and traveled home to Jerusalem to build the second temple. In between chapters 6 and 7 is a gap of about 58 years, and chapters 7–10 cover the ministry of Ezra, a priest who was accompanied by Israel's religious leaders.

Zerubbabel led a group of people who would build the new temple. Ezra led a group who reestablished what the temple stood for in Jerusalem: a growing relationship with God.

Who, What, Where?

Cyrus was the king of Persia who commanded that the Jewish people be released from captivity so they could return to their home country. He also ordered his people to give donations to help the Jews and returned the temple vessels that Nebuchadnezzar of Babylon had taken when he took the people of Judah into captivity.

What's In It for Me?

The story told in the book of Ezra shows just how willing God is to offer His people second chances. God had punished the people of Judah for their disobedience, but now He is giving them a fresh start in their homeland. Here's the really cool thing you need to remember: The same God who gave those wayward people a second chance is more than willing to do the same thing for you after you've made a bad decision.

Nehemiah

What It's About: The Jewish people, who have just returned to Israel from Babylon, rebuild the walls of the city of Jerusalem.

Important Characters/People: Nehemiah, Artaxerxes, Sanballat, Tobiah, Geshem

The Writer: This book starts out, "The words of Nehemiah" (1:1 NKJV), but according to Jewish tradition, Ezra wrote the book of Nehemiah.

Power Words

"Go and enjoy choice food and sweet drinks, and send some to those who have nothing prepared. This day is holy to our Lord. Do not grieve, for the joy of the LORD is your strength."

NEHEMIAH 8:10 NIV

Who, What, Where?

Nehemiah and the rest of the Jews received plenty of opposition as they worked to rebuild Jerusalem's walls. Three guys, named Sanballat, Tobiah, and Geshem, plotted to attack Jerusalem, which forced the Jews to guard the uncompleted walls. Tobiah and Sanballat hired a man to warn Nehemiah that he would be killed, and Tobiah sent threatening letters to scare Nehemiah.

What You'll Find in the Book of Nehemiah

Nehemiah lived around the same time as Ezra and led the third and final group of Jews from Persia back to their homeland of Judah. He served as Persian King Artexerxes' cupbearer—the man whose job it was to taste the king's food and wine to make sure someone hadn't put poison in them. The king liked Nehemiah, and when Nehemiah heard that the walls around the city of Jerusalem hadn't been rebuilt, Artaxerxes gave him permission to return to Jerusalem.

The temple had been rebuilt, but there were no walls around the city to protect it from its many enemies. Nehemiah wanted to go to Jerusalem and encourage the people to get busy rebuilding the city walls.

The book of Nehemiah tells us how he led a team of builders from Persia to Jerusalem to rebuild the city's walls. With Nehemiah cheering them on—and giving them a little push from behind—the people gave money, supplies, and manpower toward rebuilding the walls. Even though Israel's enemies didn't want the walls rebuilt, the work was completed in just 52 days—a feat that even Israel's enemies saw was the result of God's power.

Not long after the walls were finished, Ezra the priest read the Law of Moses to the people out loud "from early morning until noon" (8:3). That was just the beginning of a spiritual renewal among the people of Israel. Nehemiah also helped reestablish true worship through prayer and encouraged the people to read and obey the Word of God.

Esther

What It's About: Esther, a beautiful Jewish girl who becomes queen of Persia through her marriage to King Ahasuerus (also known as Xerxes), helps save her people from slaughter.

Important Characters/People: Xerxes, Mordecai, Haman, Esther, Hathach

The Writer: The book of Esther doesn't name its author, but one of the most popular traditions is that Mordecai, Esther's cousin, wrote it. Some believe that Ezra or Nehemiah wrote this book.

What You'll Find in the Book of Esther

The story of Esther takes place during the 58-year gap in the book of Ezra (the one between chapters 6 and 7). Many of the Jews who had been held captive all their lives in Persia wanted to stay there. It was, after all, the only place they'd ever known as home.

Fun Bible Trivia

It might surprise you to know this, but the name of God doesn't appear anywhere in the book of Esther. In fact, there are no mentions of service to God of any kind in this book. Yet this story shows the hand of God at work in saving His people from what looked like certain death at the hands of the Persians.

The book of Esther tells the story of how Esther becomes queen of Persia then finds herself and her people threatened by a plot to kill all the Jews in Persia. Esther knew that speaking up to her husband, the king, was dangerous, but she was willing to risk her own life to save the lives of the Jews still living in Persia.

Esther's courage to save God's chosen people is celebrated in the annual Jewish festival of Purim, which is still celebrated today.

CHAPTER 4

Words to Live By

God's Written Wisdom (Job through Song of Solomon)

So far, we've covered books with a lot of history—how things began and what happened after they got their start. Now we're moving on to five books that are often called the Bible's *wisdom literature*.

You can learn a lot about how God wants you to live by reading just about any part of the Bible, but these books are devoted to teaching wisdom for life. In these books are simple instructions for how to maintain your relationship to God, how to get along with other people, and how to be the kind of person God wants you to be.

Out of all the wisdom books, only one—Job—tells someone's story. The rest are mostly collections of thoughts on certain subjects. . .and about God Himself.

Job

What It's About: Job was a good man who loved God but who went through a terrible time of suffering after God allowed Satan to take everything Job had, including his family, his wealth, and his health.

Important Characters/People: Job, God, Satan, Eliphaz, Bildad, Zophar, Elihu

The Writer: Many experts believe that Job is the oldest book in the Bible—even older than Genesis. Jewish tradition says that Moses wrote the book of Job, but the writer isn't known for certain.

Who, What, Where?

Uz was a land east of Judah. Uz was the name of the son of Aram and grandson of Shem (Genesis 10:23; 1 Chronicles 1:17), and many experts believe the land where Job lived was named after him. In Jeremiah's prophecies, Uz is listed among the lands on which God's anger would fall through the conquest of the Chaldean king Nebuchadnezzar.

Power Words

"I came naked from my mother's womb, and I will be naked when I leave. The LORD gave me what I had, and the LORD has taken it away. Praise the name of the LORD!"

JOB 1:21

What You'll Find in the Book of Job

The story of Job takes place during the time of the patriarchs (Abraham, Isaac, Jacob, and Joseph). Job lived with his family—his wife and seven sons and three daughters—in a place called Uz, and he had everything going for him. He owned 7,000 sheep, 3,000 camels, 500 teams of oxen, and 500 female donkeys. In those days, a person's wealth was measured by how many animals he owned, so it's no wonder the Bible calls Job the wealthiest man living in Uz.

But Job's riches aren't the first thing the Bible tells us about him. The very first verse in the book of Job says, "He was honest inside and out, a man of his word, who was totally devoted to God and hated evil with a passion" (Job 1:1 MSG).

Job was such a great example of godliness and character that God bragged on him a little bit when He said to Satan, "He is the finest man in all the earth. He is blameless—a man of complete integrity. He fears God and stays away from evil" (Job 1:8).

Job sounds like just the kind of guy God would protect from suffering and loss, doesn't he? But if you know anything at all about the book of Job, you know that Job went through a time of terrible suffering and loss.

The devil wasn't impressed with what God had to say about Job, and he challenged God to allow him to take away from Job everything he had—his family, his livestock, and his health. When that happened, the devil said, Job would curse God to His face.

God told Satan he could do what he wanted with Job, but with one limit: The devil wasn't allowed to take Job's life.

What followed for Job was suffering on a level that most of us would find hard to imagine. Not only did Job lose his children and his wealth, but he was also covered from head to toe in painful sores called boils. To make matters worse, Job's wife provided no comfort, and when his three best friends came to Uz to "comfort" him, they spent most of their time accusing him of committing some terrible sin against God that led to his suffering.

Most of the book of Job (chapters 3–37) is an account of conversations between Job and his friends—Eliphaz, Bildad, and Zophar—as they try to make sense out of something that made no earthly sense: a good man's horrible suffering, even when he hadn't done anything wrong.

Job cannot understand why all this has happened to him, and finally he calls on God to help him understand. Chapters 38–41 are an account of another conversation—between Job and God.

God confronts Job with question after question about His own character and power. Job has no answer for any of them. In the end, Job realizes that even when he can't make sense of his suffering, he must still remain loyal to the God who had blessed him with so much and then allowed it to be taken away.

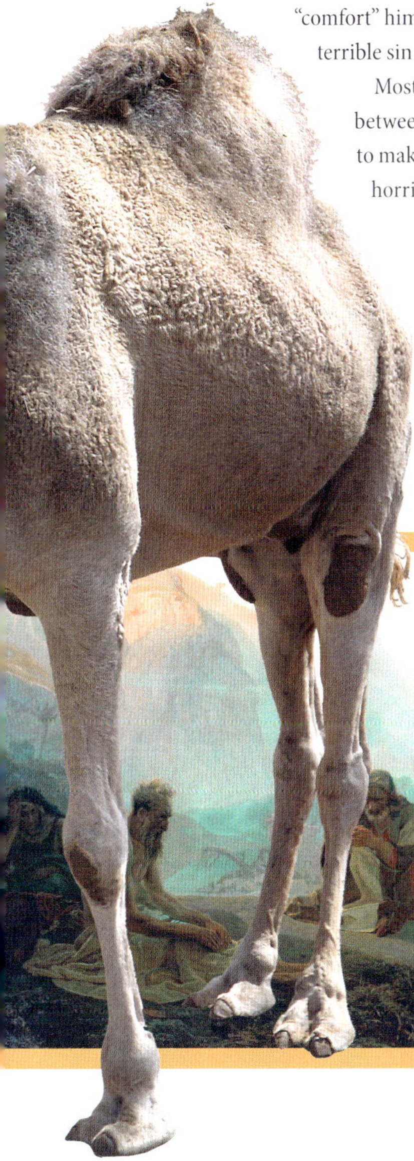

What's In It for Me?

Have you ever gone through a tough time when you wondered if you had done something to deserve it? One of the lessons from the book of Job is that bad things *do* happen to good people, even when they haven't done anything wrong. But don't worry—the Bible promises that God will use everything that happens to you for your own good and for His benefit (see Romans 8:28).

Psalms

What It's About: The book of Psalms is actually a collection of songs, poems, and other writings that showcase the different writers' praise and prayers—and complaints—to God, as well as their thoughts *about* God.

Important Characters/People: David, Asaph, Solomon, the sons of Korah, Moses, Heman, Ethan

The Writers: At least seven different writers contributed to the book of Psalms. Of those, King David is credited with the most—at least 73. Other notable psalmists (people who wrote psalms) include Solomon, Moses (yes, the same Moses who led the people of Israel out of Egypt), Asaph, Ethan, and the sons of Korah. Forty-eight of the 150 psalms are not attributed to a specific writer.

What You'll Find in the Book of Psalms

The book of Psalms includes writings by people who were going through some of the same things you will experience at different times in your life—happiness, sadness, anger, pain, fear, and other strong feelings. Sometimes it's good to read the psalms so you can understand that you're not alone, that other people have felt the same feelings you might be feeling right now.

Fun Bible Trivia

If you were to take your Bible in your hand and try to open it so that you were in the very middle, you'd probably see one of the psalms. The middle chapter of the Bible is Psalm 117 and the middle verse is Psalm 118:8.

The Bible includes 150 psalms. The book of Psalms is by far the longest book in the Bible. It also includes the shortest chapter in the Bible (Psalm 117) and the longest chapter (Psalm 119).

The word *psalm* comes from a Greek word that means "a song sung to the accompaniment of a plucked (or string) instrument." The Jewish people used the psalms as temple hymns during their worship services.

The book of Psalms, which is also called the Psalter, was written over a long time period: from about 1100 BC to around 430 BC. Psalm 90, which was written by Moses, is clearly the oldest of the psalms.

Because the psalms were written as poetry, they use a lot of word pictures to describe what God is like. Here are just a few of the many, many ways God is presented in the psalms:

Creator (8:3–4)
Deliverer (18:2)
Father (68:5–6)
King (93:1–2)
Refuge (46:1)
Shepherd (23:1)
Shield (3:3)
Teacher (25:8–9)
Warrior (35:1–3)

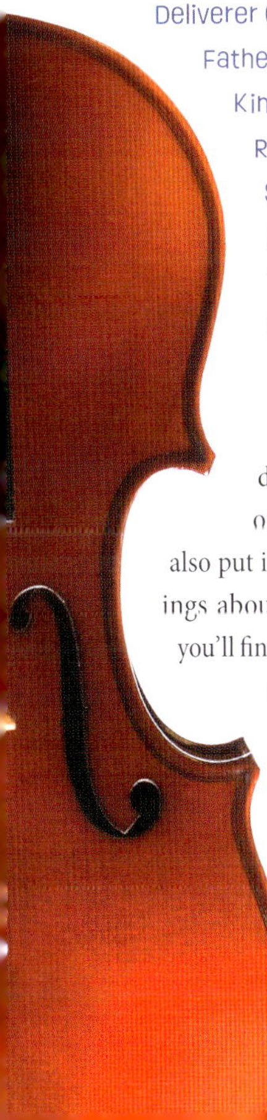

While the psalms describe the many parts of God's character, they also put into words people's feelings about Him. In the psalms, you'll find words of praise for God, confessions of sin to God, and expressions of confidence in God. You'll even find words of disappointment and frustration with God from people who were going through difficult times and wondered if God was really there for them. (Hint: The psalmists usually

Who, What, Where?

The Asaph who wrote Psalms 50 and 73–83 was a descendant of Abraham through Jacob's son Levi. He was one of the key musicians serving in the Jerusalem Temple during the time of King David. David appointed Asaph's descendants "to proclaim God's messages to the accompaniment of lyres, harps, and cymbals" (1 Chronicles 25:1).

Power Words

The LORD is my shepherd; I have all that I need. He lets me rest in green meadows; he leads me beside peaceful streams. He renews my strength. He guides me along right paths, bringing honor to his name.

PSALM 23:1–3

Did You Know. . . ?

The book of Psalms is divided into five smaller collections, based on the time periods in which historians believe they were written or compiled. The five books are as follows:

Book One (Psalms 1–41): Psalms compiled, and mostly written, by David.

Book Two (Psalms 42–72): Psalms written by the sons of Korah and by David; likely compiled while Hezekiah was king of Judah.

Book Three (Psalms 73–89): Psalms written during the reigns of kings Hezekiah and Manasseh, but compiled while King Josiah ruled.

Book Four (Psalms 90–106): Includes the rest of the psalms written prior to the Babylonian Captivity, including one by Moses and a couple by David; the rest are by unknown writers.

Book Five (Psalms 107–150): Psalms written during the Jews' return from the Babylonian Captivity. Books four and five may have been compiled during the time of the prophet Nehemiah.

What's In It for Me?

The very middle verse of many versions of Bible—meaning there are the same number of verses before it and after it—is Psalm 118:8, which says, "It is better to trust in the LORD than to put confidence in man" (NKJV). If God placed that verse in the center of the Bible, what does it tell you about what you should put at the center of your life?

came around to the conclusion that God really was there, even when it seemed He was millions of miles away!) Many of the psalms ask God some really tough questions!

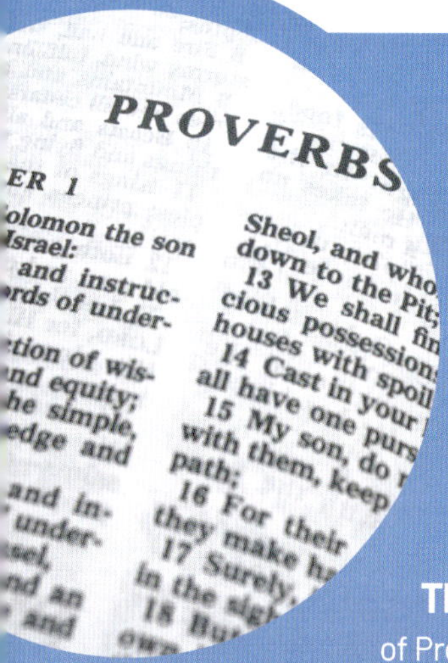

Proverbs

What It's About: This book is mostly a collection of short sayings and thoughts to encourage people of different ages and life situations to follow God and seek out wisdom. The book of Proverbs is different from most other books of the Bible in that it doesn't have a story line, but is instead a collection of practical tips for wise and godly living.

Important Characters/People: Solomon, Agur, Lemuel

The Writers: Most experts agree that the first 29 chapters of the book of Proverbs were written by a man known for his wisdom: King Solomon, the third king of Israel and son of King David. Solomon wrote his proverbs during his reign as king of Israel, which began around 1015 to 1020 BC. Chapter 30 of the book of Proverbs is credited to someone named Agur, who may have been a friend of Solomon's or who may have been Solomon himself writing under another name. Chapter 31 is credited to King Lemuel. It is suggested by some that Lemuel is the name Bathsheba, Solomon's mother, gave to Solomon, so this may be a proverb from Bathsheba.

What You'll Find in the Book of Proverbs

Solomon's purpose for writing the proverbs—as well as the rewards for living by them—is found early in the book, in Proverbs 1:2–6. Solomon writes that he intends for these proverbs to give wisdom, instruction, and understanding to the reader, to teach his readers to live carefully.

God told Solomon that He had given the young king wisdom and understanding (1 Kings 3:12). Later in his life, Solomon didn't apply the wisdom God had given him, and it cost him and his kingdom dearly. But he recorded a lot of wisdom in this book and in the next book of the Bible, Ecclesiastes.

Power Words

Trust in the Lord with all your heart; do not depend on your own understanding. Seek his will in all you do, and he will show you which path to take.

Proverbs 3:5–6

Solomon writes that he intends for these proverbs to give wisdom, instruction, and understanding to the reader, to teach his readers to live carefully.

What's In It for Me?

Many times in the book of Proverbs, Solomon calls his readers "my son." In the Hebrew culture of that time, all male descendants of a king were considered that king's sons, so Solomon wrote to give future kings of Israel wisdom and understanding. The book of Proverbs is still a great source of teaching for all young people. Read the book through once and see what kind of wisdom God might be trying to teach you.

During most of Solomon's reign, the nation of Israel was at an all-time high in a lot of areas. The people worshipped God and lived in a time of prosperity. The surrounding nations treated Israel and its king with amazing respect. Leaders from all over the known world traveled to Israel to hear Solomon speak (see 1 Kings 4:34).

Chapter 31 begins by discouraging the use of strong drink, and continues by describing the perfect wife.

Sometimes the proverbs included together in the same chapter seem completely unrelated to one another, but they all speak to important life issues, such as work, money, relationships, temptation, drinking, laziness, discipline, seeking God, and raising children.

Ecclesiastes

What It's About: "These are the words of the Teacher, King David's son, who ruled in Jerusalem" (1:1). The book of Ecclesiastes points out that life is futile and meaningless when we don't seek and follow God as our top priority.

Important Characters/People: The Teacher, God, wise men, fools

The Writer: The book of Ecclesiastes doesn't name its author, but several verses imply that it was King Solomon. Some experts believe Solomon wrote this book late in his life to help teach others the lessons he had learned from his own wrong choices.

What You'll Find in the Book of Ecclesiastes

Early in his reign as king of Israel, Solomon followed his father's instructions to the letter. He followed God and kept all His commandments. God rewarded Solomon's faithfulness by giving him power, prosperity, popularity, and other earthly blessings. Sadly, later in his life, Solomon abandoned his God and chased after worldly pleasures he had been warned about. The results were disastrous—for Solomon himself and for the kingdom of Israel.

Solomon reigned as king from around 970 BC to about 930 BC. Bible experts believe he wrote the book of Ecclesiastes near the end of his reign—around 935 BC. If Solomon is the author of this book, then it is the reflections of a man who had learned some very hard lessons. He had every earthly blessing a man could want—money, power, and respect, just to name a few—but he understood that none of those things were

Power Words

Don't let the excitement of youth cause you to forget your Creator. Honor him in your youth before you grow old and say, "Life is not pleasant anymore."

Ecclesiastes 12:1

What's In It for Me?

Solomon wrote, "Whatever you do, do well" (Ecclesiastes 9:10). That's great advice. Ask yourself, do you do everything you do to the best of your ability? Are you the best son or daughter you can be? The best brother or sister you can be? Are you the best student you can be?

What's In It for Me?

In the end, after writing about a life of futility and hopelessness apart from God, the Teacher in the book of Ecclesiastes concludes with these wise words: "Fear God and keep His commandments, for this is man's all. For God will bring every work into judgment, including every secret thing, whether good or evil" (12:13–14 NKJV). That's great advice for anyone to follow!

enough to give him a life of joy and happiness. True fulfillment came only when he made God the center of everything he did.

Throughout Ecclesiastes, the word *vanity* (other translations use the word *meaningless*) and the phrase "under the sun" occur repeatedly. The lesson of this book is that everything we can enjoy in this world (under the sun) will one day be left behind; and it all means nothing if we don't make God the center of everything we do, say, and think.

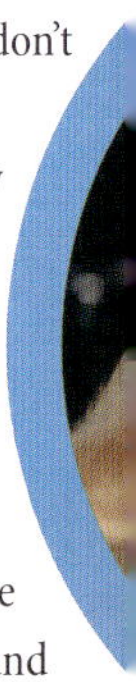

The first seven chapters of this book are the words of a very unhappy man. He has tried to find fulfillment in knowledge, worldly wisdom, riches, work, and other things. But he realizes that these things, though they may bring some pleasure for a while, won't give him the purpose, fulfillment, and happiness that can be found only in eternal things.

The final four chapters of Ecclesiastes are the Teacher's advice on how we should live if we want to find purpose, fulfillment, and happiness. He has left God and tried everything else "under the sun" and has learned (the hard way) that the very best this world has to offer is nothing compared to living a life centered on loving God and keeping His commandments. (Read the Teacher's words in chapter 12.)

Song of Solomon (also known as Song of Songs)

What It's About: Solomon writes about the beauty of married love. Though the name of God is never mentioned in this book, some experts believe the Song of Solomon was written to compare the love of a devoted spouse to the love of God, who is deeply devoted to His people.

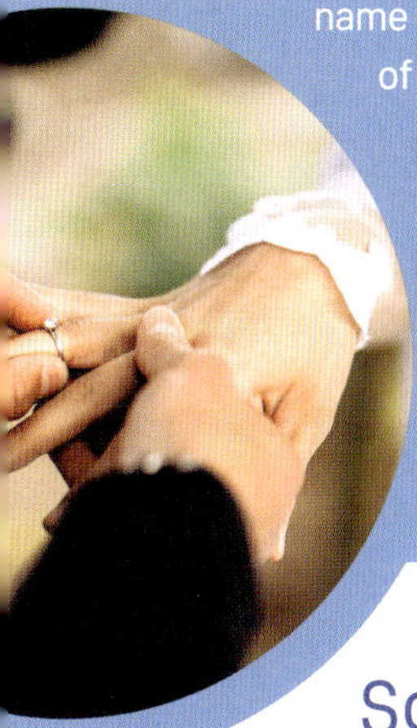

Important Characters/People: The husband and his wife

The Writer: King Solomon wrote more than 1,000 songs, but he calls this his "Song of Songs." Some experts believe it's possible that Solomon didn't write this book but that it was written *about* him.

What You'll Find in the Song of Solomon

The two main characters in this book are Solomon and his wife, the beautiful young Shulamite woman. The words in the poem are those of Solomon, the young woman, and the daughters of Jerusalem.

Power Words

He escorts me to the banquet hall; it's obvious how much he loves me.

SONG OF SOLOMON 2:4

In one of the Bible's weirdest visions, the prophet Ezekiel sees dry, long-dead skeletons being covered with muscles and skin, and coming back to life. This painting, from 1630, is an artist's idea of how Ezekiel 37 might have looked.

CHAPTER 5

God's Messengers

Major and Minor Prophets (Isaiah through Malachi)

The Old Testament includes 17 "prophetic" books—books that warn people of God's judgment and encourage them with promises of forgiveness and restoration if they will turn back to Him.

The Old Testament includes the writings of five "major" prophets and 12 "minor" prophets. The difference isn't that the minor prophets are less important than the others, but that their books are much shorter than those of Isaiah, Jeremiah (who also wrote Lamentations), Ezekiel, and Daniel.

The books of Old Testament prophecy include some of the best-known stories in the Bible. For example, you can read about Daniel in the lions' den and his friends Shadrach, Meshach, and Abednego in the book of Daniel, and you can read about the prophet Jonah finding himself stuck in a giant fish's belly in the book of Jonah.

Isaiah

What It's About: Even though the people of Israel had fallen away from God and would suffer the consequences of their sin, God promises a Messiah to provide forgiveness and save them from their sins.

Important Characters/People: Isaiah, King Hezekiah, the Messiah, kings of Judah and Israel

The Writer: The prophet Isaiah was the son of a man named Amoz, and his ministry to the people of Judah began during the reign of King Uzziah and ended during the reign of King Hezekiah. Isaiah preached during the reigns of four kings. The book of Isaiah was written between 701 and 681 BC.

What You'll Find in the Book of Isaiah

Like the other Old Testament prophets, Isaiah warned the people that they faced God's punishment for their sin. But He also wrote about the coming Messiah, a Savior who would take the punishment for the people's sins and give them peace with God. In fact, chapters 40–66 of Isaiah's long prophecy describe God's restoration of Israel, His promised salvation, and His eternal kingdom.

The prophet Isaiah preached mostly to the kingdom of Judah. At that time, Judah's relationship with God was up and down. There were times when the people stuck close to God, but there were also times when they rebelled against Him.

One interesting fact about the book of Isaiah: It is the Old Testament prophetic book most often quoted in the New Testament (the book of Psalms is the most quoted book overall). The New Testament directly quotes Isaiah 66 times. Also, Isaiah contains more prophecies about Jesus than any other Old Testament book of prophecy.

The book of Isaiah contains literally dozens of prophecies about the life and work of Jesus. These include His virgin birth (7:14), that His ministry would include healing people of sickness and disease (35:5–6), and that He would suffer and die willingly to give people forgiveness and peace with God (53).

Power Words

He was pierced for our rebellion, crushed for our sins. He was beaten so we could be whole. He was whipped so we could be healed. All of us, like sheep, have strayed away. We have left God's paths to follow our own. Yet the LORD laid on him the sins of us all.

ISAIAH 53:5–6

What's In It for Me?

Look up Isaiah 9:1–2 and you'll find a wonderful promise that the Jewish Messiah—Jesus—would come not only for the Jews but for all people. That means that no matter what race or people group you come from, Jesus came to earth and lived, died, and was raised from the dead for you!

Isaiah contains more prophecies about Jesus than any other Old Testament book of prophecy.

Jeremiah

What It's About: The prophet Jeremiah warns the people of Judah of coming punishment and suffering because they have abandoned God.

Important Characters/People: Jeremiah, King Jehoiakim, Hananiah, Baruch

The Writer: Jeremiah was a young boy when God called him to be a prophet (1:6). He was the son of a priest named Hilkiah. His ministry started during the reign of King Josiah (about 617 BC) and ended several years after the Babylonians destroyed Jerusalem, an event he foretold in his writings.

What You'll Find in the Book of Jeremiah

Jeremiah's message to the people of Judah was pretty much all bad news. God had given the people warning after warning through earlier prophets to turn back to Him, but they had refused. Jeremiah warned that God would send the Babylonians to destroy Jerusalem and take the people of Judah into captivity.

The people of Judah—especially the leaders—didn't like what Jeremiah had to say. They made fun of Jeremiah, beat him, and imprisoned him. But Jeremiah's words came true. Chapter 52 of his prophetic book describes the Babylonian invasion of Judah.

Power Words

"O Israel, can I not do to you as this potter has done to his clay? As the clay is in the potter's hand, so are you in my hand."

JEREMIAH 18:6

Who, What, Where?

Baruch was an assistant to Jeremiah who wrote down all the words the prophet received from God and then went to the temple and read those prophecies to the people. When Baruch read the prophecies to the princes of the land, the princes warned him and Jeremiah to hide. After Jehoiakim, the king of Judah, destroyed the first copy of the prophecies, Baruch rewrote it from Jeremiah's dictation.

Lamentations

What It's About: The prophet Jeremiah grieves over the destruction that has come on the city of Jerusalem and the people of Judah—the same destruction he had warned about in the book of Jeremiah.

Important Characters/People: Jeremiah, Zedekiah, the Babylonians

The Writer: Jeremiah the prophet

What You'll Find in the Book of Lamentations

Jeremiah has often been called "the weeping prophet," and the book of Lamentations shows why. It isn't very pleasant to read the words of a godly man who saw the death and destruction in his homeland and mourns over what has happened.

Ezekiel

What It's About: Even though things look hopeless for the people of Judah, who are living in captivity in Babylon, God promises that their nation will one day be restored.

Important Characters/People: Ezekiel, Pelatiah, Jaazaniah, Nebuchadnezzar, Pharaoh

The Writer: Ezekiel was a priest and the son of Buzi. He was about 25 years old when he was among the people of Judah who were taken to Babylon after King Nebuchadnezzar attacked Judah and took many of the people of Jerusalem away. About five years later, while Ezekiel was in Babylon, God came to him in a vision and called him to minister to the rebellious Israelites. The book of Ezekiel was probably written between 593 and 565 BC.

What You'll Find in the Book of Ezekiel

Like Jeremiah, Ezekiel wrote a lot about God's judgment. But he also wrote about God's love and mercy for His people. Yes, God had judged and punished the people of Judah, but He would also forgive them and one day would allow them to return to their homeland.

The book of Ezekiel can be split into four sections. Chapters 1–24 are about the ruin of Jerusalem when the Babylonians attacked, and chapters 25–32 are about God's judgment on the nations around Jerusalem. In chapter 33, Ezekiel records God's call for His people to turn back to him. Chapters 34–48 are chapters of hope for the nation of Israel because they promise that Israel will be restored and rebuilt in the future.

Fun Bible Trivia

The book of Ezekiel includes the story of the fall of Lucifer (also known as the devil), one of the most beautiful and gifted angels God created. Lucifer was kicked out of heaven long ago because of his pride and because he wanted to be like God Himself.

Daniel

What It's About: Daniel—as well as some of his friends—remain true to God while in captivity in Babylon. God blesses their faithfulness, even though they are in a really tough situation.

Important Characters/People: Daniel, Nebuchadnezzar, Darius, Belshazzar, Shadrach, Meshach, Abednego

The Writer: Daniel was a young man when the Babylonians destroyed Jerusalem and took many of the people of Judah captive. During the 70-year Babylonian Captivity, Daniel remained true to God in every way and was rewarded with knowledge, wisdom, and power. The book of Daniel was probably written between 540 and 530 BC.

What You'll Find in the Book of Daniel

During the Babylonian Captivity, the prophet Daniel served in King Nebuchadnezzar's royal court. He also served several rulers who succeeded Nebuchadnezzar. In the book of Daniel, you can read about the prophet's actions and the visions and prophecies he received during this time.

Who, What, Where?

Chapter 3 of the book of Daniel includes an amazing story about three of Daniel's friends—Hananiah, Mishael, and Azariah (also known as Shadrach, Meshach, and Abednego). These three young men refused to worship a gold statue made by King Nebuchadnezzar and were thrown into a fiery furnace as punishment. But God protected them from harm, and amazingly, not a hair on their heads was burned.

Daniel describes and interprets several dreams in this book, including one dream Nebuchadnezzar had about an image of several metals and clay. (You can read the whole story in Daniel 2.) Daniel revealed the meaning of a second dream to Nebuchadnezzar, predicting his downfall until he worshipped God. (That story is found in chapter 4.)

During the reign of King Belshazzar, Nebuchadnezzar's son, Daniel interpreted the meaning of some mysterious handwriting that appeared on the wall during a banquet. As a result, Belshazzar made Daniel the third highest ruler in the kingdom; but later that night, Belshazzar died.

When Darius took over the kingdom of Babylon, he planned to make Daniel one of the most powerful people in the whole kingdom, but other leaders plotted against Daniel. They knew he would never worship anyone but God, and they tricked the king into punishing any person who worshipped anyone but the king. For disobeying this law, Daniel was thrown into the lions' den. But when Daniel came out safely, Darius honored the God who had kept Daniel safe. (You can read the whole story in Daniel 6.)

Daniel's prophecies predicted the coming of several important world figures, including Alexander the Great, Cleopatra, and (most important) Jesus Christ.

Rembrandt's painting *Belshazzar's Feast*

Hosea

What It's About: God calls a prophet to marry an immoral woman named Gomer. When she runs away from Hosea with another man, God tells Hosea to go after her and try to win her back.

Important Characters/People: Hosea, Gomer

The Writer: Hosea served the people of Israel around the time of the reigns of kings Uzziah of Judah (around 792–750 BC), Jotham of Judah (750–735 BC), Ahaz of Judah (735–715 BC), Hezekiah of Judah (715–697 BC), and Jeroboam of Israel (793–753 BC).

What You'll Find in the Book of Hosea

God called Hosea to live a very difficult family life. He commanded Hosea to marry Gomer, a woman Hosea no doubt knew wouldn't be faithful to him. Gomer wasn't faithful to Hosea, but he went after her to try to win her back to himself. God used Hosea's family life to show the people how He loved them despite their unfaithfulness to Him and how He was working to bring them back to Him.

Joel

What It's About: Swarms of grasshoppers descend on the nation of Israel, devouring every living plant in their path. The grasshoppers are an example of God's judgment on a sinful people. In the middle of this plague, God promises salvation to those who turn to Him.

Important Characters/People: Joel, leaders in Jerusalem and Judah

The Writer: Joel, the son of Pethuel (Joel 1:1), was an educated man who knew the words of the earlier prophets. It isn't known for certain when Joel prophesied, but some experts believe it was around the time of the reign of King Joash (835–796 BC). The book of Joel was probably written around that time.

What You'll Find in the Book of Joel

Power Words

"But everyone who calls on the name of the LORD will be saved."

JOEL 2:32

It isn't certain whether swarms of grasshoppers actually devoured all of Israel's crops or if they were part of a story God used to make a point. Either way, however, Joel used the example to warn the people of what would happen if they didn't turn back to God. If they didn't turn back, armies from surrounding nations would invade and "devour" the land, just as the grasshoppers had devoured all the plants there. But if the people did turn back to God, He would forgive them and bless them.

Amos

What It's About: God wanted His people to understand that He wanted them to treat people fairly and justly, not just to observe a bunch of religious rules.

Important Characters/People: Amos, Jeroboam II, Uzziah, Amaziah

The Writer: The prophet Amos was a shepherd and fruit picker from a small village in Judah. He was an uneducated man who ministered during the reigns of King Uzziah of Judah and King Jeroboam II of Israel. This book was probably written around 756 BC.

What You'll Find in the Book of Amos

Amos' message was mostly directed to the nation of Israel. Things were going pretty well in Israel at that time, but the people committed many sins, including idolatry, greed, and mistreatment of poor people. Mostly, the people of Israel ignored Amos' warning of God's judgment for their sins.

The first part of this book includes warnings of judgment on the nations around Israel, and then on the nation of Judah. The second part warns of even worse judgment on Israel. Amos' message is clear: God's judgment is coming soon. The book ends like many other Old Testament books of prophecy—with the promise of better things in the future for some of the people of Israel.

Obadiah

What It's About: God announces that the city of Edom will be judged for taking part in Jerusalem's destruction.

Important Characters/People: Obadiah, Edom's leaders

The Writer: The prophet Obadiah. The Bible says nothing about Obadiah's family or personal life. The book of Obadiah was probably written around 845 BC.

What You'll Find in the Book of Obadiah

Obadiah is the shortest book in the Old Testament—only 21 verses. The prophet Obadiah delivers the message that the nation of Edom will be destroyed because the Edomites celebrated the bad things that had happened to Israel and because they fought against Israel after the Israelites asked for Edom's help against their enemies.

Fun Bible Trivia

The name Obadiah means "serving God." The prophet Obadiah is one of 13 men by that name in the Old Testament.

Jonah

What It's About: A prophet runs the other way when God tells him to go to a city called Nineveh to preach. Because of his disobedience, Jonah is swallowed by a giant fish and stays in its stomach for three days.

Important Characters/People: Jonah, the king of Nineveh, the sailors

The Writer: This is Jonah's story, but it is written in the third person ("he" instead of "I"), so another writer probably recorded the words. This book was written around 760 BC.

Who, What, Where?

Nineveh was a large city located on the eastern bank of the Tigris River. The city was built by a descendant of Noah named Nimrod (Genesis 10:11), who also built the cities of Rehoboth and Calah (see Genesis 10:11). During the time of Jonah, Nineveh was the capital of the Assyrian Empire.

What's In It for Me?

The obvious lesson from the book of Jonah is that it's always the best choice to obey when God tells us to do something. But there's another lesson here, and it's one Jesus taught when He told His followers, "Love your enemies! Pray for those who persecute you!" (Matthew 5:44).

What You'll Find in the Book of Jonah

Jonah lived and preached around the time of King Jeroboam II of Israel. When God called him to travel to Nineveh to preach to the people there, Jonah refused. Being a prophet, Jonah knew that the people of Nineveh would become Israel's mortal enemies. He wasn't about to do anything to help them!

Rather than go to Nineveh, Jonah hightailed it to a port city called Joppa, where he boarded a ship bound for Tarshish—exactly the opposite direction God had told him to go. When a violent storm struck, threatening to sink the ship and kill everyone aboard, Jonah confessed to the sailors that he was running from God, and they threw Jonah overboard.

Jonah was swallowed by a big sea creature, and while inside the animal, he had time to think about his actions—and the fact that he was running from God. After Jonah praised God, the creature vomited him onto dry land. Jonah went to Nineveh, just as God had told him to do, and preached there. Amazingly, the people of Nineveh, led by their king, turned to God, who spared the city.

Micah

What It's About: God announces that Judah (the southern kingdom) and Israel (the northern kingdom) will be judged for worshipping idols instead of God and for their mistreatment and abuse of the poor and needy around them.

Important Characters/People: Micah, Jotham, Ahaz, Hezekiah

The Writer: The prophet Micah was a native of Moresheth in southern Judah who ministered during the reigns of Kings Jotham, Ahaz, and Hezekiah of Judah (750–686 BC). This book was written around 700 BC.

What You'll Find in the Book of Micah

Micah preached against idolatry and cheating the poor and warned that both Judah and Israel would be destroyed by outside invaders.

Like many other prophets, Micah preached a message of God's judgment but also of God's mercy. God would forgive the sins of His people and would not remain angry with them forever—simply because He loves showing mercy.

Power Words

O people, the Lord has told you what is good, and this is what he requires of you: to do what is right, to love mercy, and to walk humbly with your God.

Micah 6:8

Nahum

What It's About: The powerful city of Nineveh, which had repented a century earlier when Jonah preached there, will be destroyed for its evilness.

Important Characters/People: Nahum, the king of Nineveh

The Writer: The prophet Nahum. Nahum lived in a place called Elkosh. He preached to Judah after Assyria had captured Israel. This book was written between 663 and 612 BC.

What You'll Find in the Book of Nahum

This book of prophecy is kind of a sequel (continues a story begun in another book) to the book of Jonah. Even though God had shown mercy on the city after the people repented when they heard Jonah preach, they returned to their old ways. The city was destroyed not long after Nahum preached to the people there.

Habakkuk

What It's About: A prophet questions God—and receives an answer—when he learns that God will allow the evil Chaldeans to destroy the nation of Judah.

Important Characters/People: Habakkuk, the leaders of Judah, Jehoahaz

The Writer: The prophet Habakkuk. Nothing is known of his personal life or his family. He served during the reign of King Josiah of Judah. This book was written around 600 BC.

What's In It for Me?

Ever been in a situation where you just wanted to tell God, "It's not fair!" If you haven't, you most likely will at some point. Then you can follow Habakkuk's example: Talk to God about your situation. Tell Him what you think is unfair about it. Then wait. Even if you don't have an answer, even if things seem more unfair than ever, trust God and allow Him to use your situation for your best.

What You'll Find in the Book of Habakkuk

Being a prophet of God, Habakkuk knew what was ahead for his nation. It was only a matter of time before Judah's mortal enemies, the Chaldeans, attacked and destroyed Judah.

Habakkuk understood that God had to punish his people's sinful, idolatrous behavior. What he couldn't understand was why God would use such an evil, godless people to do it.

In time, Habakkuk had his answer. And even though it wasn't the answer he wanted, he still accepted that God knew what He was doing and why He was doing it the way He was.

Zephaniah

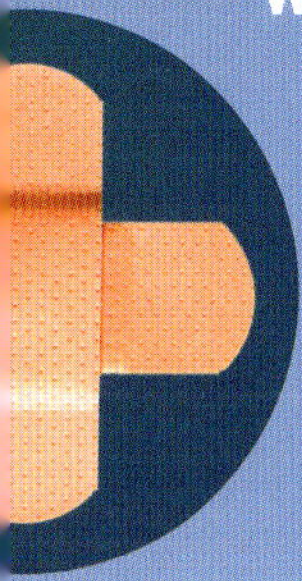

What It's About: God warns of a coming "day of the Lord," when His people will face judgment, but He also promises restoration for the nation of Israel.

Important Characters/People: Zephaniah, Josiah, Nebuchadnezzar

The Writer: Zephaniah was the son of Cushi and great-grandson of King Hezekiah, the godly king of Judah. He preached in the days of King Josiah of Judah (around 640–610 BC). This book was written during that time.

What You'll Find in the Book of Zephaniah

Like Jeremiah, Zephaniah preached of a terrible time of judgment and suffering by the people of Judah because they had moved so far away from their God. Also like Jeremiah, Zephaniah pleaded with the people to seek God before it was too late (Zephaniah 2:1–3).

Zephaniah's book closes with a promising message. Though the prophet agreed that hard times were ahead for his people, he also delivered a message of salvation and restoration (3:8–20).

Power Words

"For the LORD your God is living among you. He is a mighty savior. He will take delight in you with gladness. With his love, he will calm all your fears. He will rejoice over you with joyful songs."

ZEPHANIAH 3:17

Haggai

What It's About: The Jews return to Jerusalem after being held captive in Babylon and are commanded to rebuild God's temple.

Important Characters/People: Haggai, Joshua, Darius, Cyrus, Zerubbabel, Shealtiel

The Writer: The prophet Haggai preached after the Jews had returned from captivity in Babylon to their homeland. The Bible says nothing about his personal life or his family. This book was written in 520 BC, in the second year of Darius the king (1:1).

What You'll Find in the Book of Haggai

What the people saw when they returned to Jerusalem from the Babylonian Captivity broke their hearts. The beautiful temple that King Solomon had built centuries before was nothing but a pile of rubble—thanks to the efforts of King Nebuchadnezzar's men, who had attacked and destroyed the city 70 years earlier.

God had promised that this second temple would be greater than the original temple that Solomon had built. the people had begun the work of rebuilding the temple, but when opposition from surrounding kingdoms arose, the work stopped and the people pursued their own interests.

The unfinished temple sat in place for 16 years before Haggai came on the scene with this simple message: Finish what you've started! When you do, God will give you prosperity.

Power Words

Be strong, all you people still left in the land. And now get to work, for I am with you, says the LORD of Heaven's Armies.

HAGGAI 2:4

Zechariah

What It's About: The Jewish people are commanded to get busy rebuilding the temple—and watch for the arrival of their Messiah.

Important Characters/People: Zechariah, Zerubbabel, Joshua, Darius, Heldai, Tobijah, Jedaiah

The Writer: Zechariah, who is identified in the Bible as the son of Berekiah (1:1), wrote most or all of the book of Zechariah, but some experts believe a second, unnamed writer contributed chapters 9–14. This book was probably written between 520 and 475 BC.

What You'll Find in Zechariah

Like Haggai, Zechariah preached to the people of Judah after their return from Babylon. Also like Haggai, Zechariah's words were written and spoken to encourage the people to dedicate themselves to finishing the new temple.

Zechariah preached a message of encouragement, for the temple would one day be home to the Messiah Himself. The first eight chapters of this prophecy focus on the need to finish the project, while the last six focus on the blessings in store for the Jewish people once the task is completed.

Fun Bible Trivia

Zechariah's prophecy of the Messiah riding a donkey into Jerusalem (9:9) was fulfilled perfectly in Jesus' "triumphal entry" (Matthew 21:1–11). Also, the prophecy "They will look on me whom they have pierced" (12:10) refers to the Roman soldier's spearing of Christ after the Crucifixion (John 19:34).

Malachi

What It's About: God warns the Jewish people to be more careful with their attitude toward Him and what He had told them to do.

Important Characters/People: Malachi, Persian rulers, Jewish religious leaders

The Writer: Other than what is in his book, not a lot is known about the prophet Malachi. He lived during the time of Nehemiah and Ezra, but he is not mentioned in the books of Nehemiah or Ezra. The book of Malachi was written between 440 and 400 BC.

What You'll Find in the Book of Malachi

Power Words

"Bring all the tithes into the storehouse so there will be enough food in my Temple. If you do," says the LORD of Heaven's Armies, "I will open the windows of heaven for you. I will pour out a blessing so great you won't have enough room to take it in! Try it! Put me to the test!"

MALACHI 3:10

The words in the book of Malachi are directed toward the Jews in Jerusalem about 100 years after the end of the Babylonian Captivity. The people were doing what they thought God wanted them to do, but in their hearts they had strayed from God.

Sadly, they were doing the same things and committing the same sins that had led to their captivity in the first place! The men were divorcing their wives to marry foreign women, the people weren't giving of their income the way God had instructed them, and the priests weren't giving God the best when they offered the required sacrifices.

God wanted His people to know how much He loved them, but He wanted them to see that they weren't returning that love. So, speaking through Malachi, God called the people to return to true worship and true love of God.

CHAPTER 6

The Bible's Main Man

The Story of Jesus (Matthew through John)

The time between the writing of the final book of the Old Testament—Malachi—and the birth of Jesus is sometimes called "the silent years," simply because God did not speak through prophets during those 400 years.

But God finally broke the silence with the arrival of the long-awaited Messiah, Jesus Christ. The story of His life is told in what are called the Gospels, the four books you'll read about in this chapter.

As you read through the Gospels, the first four books of the New Testament, you'll notice that they cover many of the same events in the life of Jesus. Even so, from one book to the next, the events may look very different—at least at first. Some of the Gospels include information you won't find in the others. Likewise, some Gospels leave out events that are included in one or more of the other Gospels.

That's because the Gospels were written by men with different life experiences and different ways of looking at things. What was really important to one writer may not have been as important to the others. When they wrote their Gospels, they focused on the things about Jesus' life they thought were most important—or most important to their readers.

Now, let's take a look at what you'll find in the four Gospels, starting where the New Testament starts: with the Gospel of Matthew.

Did You Know. . . ?

The four Gospels included in the Bible (Matthew, Mark, Luke, and John) were not the only stories of the life and ministry of Jesus written during the first and second centuries. Far from it! Dozens and dozens of "gospels" were written during that time, and Christian leaders discussed—and often disagreed about—which ones were accurate accounts and which were not. The four Gospels in the Bible today were approved for inclusion at meetings—called councils—of Christian leaders in the fourth century.

The Gospel of Matthew

What It's About: The apostle Matthew writes about the things Jesus did and the words He spoke—and how they fulfilled Old Testament prophecies.

Important Characters/People: Jesus, Mary and Joseph, the wise men from the East, John the Baptist, Herod, the centurion, the 12 apostles

The Writer: Most Bible experts agree that the writer of the Gospel of Matthew was Matthew (also known as Levi), one of Jesus' 12 original disciples. Luke 5:27–28 tells us that Matthew left everything to follow Jesus when Jesus called him. Some experts believe that Matthew wrote his Gospel between AD 60 and 65, but others believe he wrote it as many as 20 years later.

Power Words

"Love your enemies! Pray for those who persecute you! In that way, you will be acting as true children of your Father in heaven. For he gives his sunlight to both the evil and the good, and he sends rain on the just and the unjust alike."

MATTHEW 5:44–45

Who, What, Where?

If you were going to pick someone to write the story of Jesus' life and ministry here on earth, it probably wouldn't be a guy like Matthew. Before Jesus called him to be a disciple, Matthew was a tax collector for the hated Roman government—a job that most Jews despised because the tax collectors worked for the Romans and engaged in dishonest business practices.

What You'll Find in the Gospel of Matthew

The Gospel of Matthew contains a lot of great messages for any Christian, but it was written specifically for the Jewish people of Matthew's time, especially to the first Jewish Christians.

For centuries, the Jews had suffered under foreign rule, and many of them were more than ready for their Messiah to come. Though Jesus wasn't exactly what most of the people expected, He was everything the Old Testament prophets said He would be.

Many times over, Matthew points out to his readers the things that Jesus did or said that fulfilled Old Testament prophecies about the coming Messiah. His Gospel quotes about 60 references to Old Testament prophecies and directly quotes the Old Testament about 40 times.

As you read the Gospel of Matthew, you'll notice that he uses the word *fulfilled* many times. Here are a few examples:

- "Joseph obeyed. He got up, took the child and his mother under cover of darkness. They were out of town and well on their way by daylight. They lived in Egypt until Herod's death. This Egyptian exile *fulfilled* what Hosea had preached: 'I called my son out of Egypt'" (2:14 MSG).
- "That evening a lot of demon-afflicted people were brought to him. He relieved the inwardly tormented. He cured the bodily ill. He *fulfilled* Isaiah's well-known revelation: He took our illnesses, He carried our diseases" (8:16 MSG).
- "All Jesus did that day was tell stories—a long storytelling afternoon. His storytelling *fulfilled* the prophecy: I will open my mouth and tell stories; I will bring out into the open things hidden since the world's first day" (13:34 MSG).

Power Words

"Keep on asking, and you will receive what you ask for. Keep on seeking, and you will find. Keep on knocking, and the door will be opened to you. For everyone who asks, receives. Everyone who seeks, finds. And to everyone who knocks, the door will be opened."

Matthew 7:7–8

- "All this was done that it might be *fulfilled* which was spoken by the prophet, saying: 'Tell the daughter of Zion, "Behold, your King is coming to you, lowly, and sitting on a donkey, a colt, the foal of a donkey"'" (21:4–5 NKJV).
- "Then they crucified Him, and divided His garments, casting lots, that it might be *fulfilled* which was spoken by the prophet: 'They divided My garments among them, and for My clothing they cast lots'" (27:35 NKJV).

In a nutshell, Matthew's message for his audience was this: "Brothers and sisters, Jesus—the man I spent more than three years of my life with—is the Messiah we have been waiting for. But don't just take my word for it. Look at scripture and you'll see that His words and actions, as well as the things that happened to Him, prove who He is!"

The Gospel of Matthew starts out by referring to Jesus as "the son of David" (the first fulfillment of prophecy that Matthew points out) and then traces Jesus' family tree from Abraham all the way through the centuries (and 14 generations) to Jesus' earthly father, Joseph. It then records the story of Jesus' birth and childhood (1:18–2:23), the ministry of John the Baptist (3:1–12), Jesus' baptism (3:13–17), His temptation by the devil (4:1–11), the calling of some of His disciples (4:12–22), and the beginning of His earthly ministry.

The Best Sermon Ever Preached!

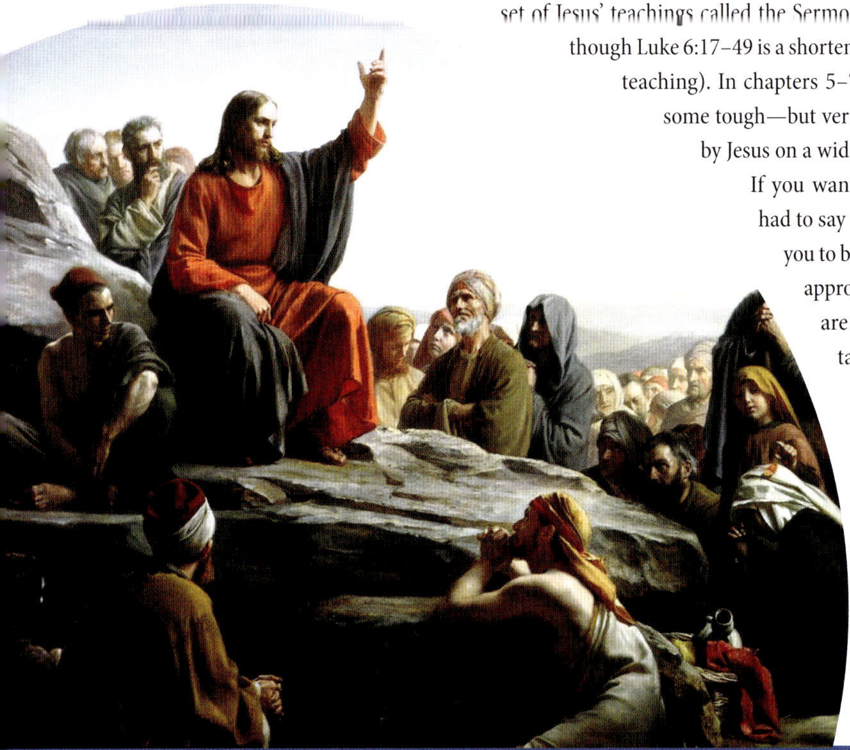

Matthew is the only Gospel to include a fairly long and very detailed set of Jesus' teachings called the Sermon on the Mount (even though Luke 6:17–49 is a shortened version of the same teaching). In chapters 5–7, you can read about some tough—but very practical—teachings by Jesus on a wide variety of subjects.

If you want to know what Jesus had to say about what God wants you to be, how He wants you to approach Him, and how you are to treat other people, take some time to read Matthew 5–7. And don't miss out on what Jesus had to say about prayer in Matthew 7:7–12.

What's In It for Me?

The Sermon on the Mount starts out with eight statements called Beatitudes, which means "statements of blessing":

"Blessed are the poor in spirit, for theirs is the kingdom of heaven" (Matthew 5:3 NKJV).
"Blessed are those who mourn, for they shall be comforted" (verse 4 NKJV).
"Blessed are the meek, for they shall inherit the earth" (verse 5 NKJV).
"Blessed are those who hunger and thirst for righteousness, for they shall be filled" (verse 6 NKJV).
"Blessed are the merciful, for they shall obtain mercy" (verse 7 NKJV).
"Blessed are the pure in heart, for they shall see God" (verse 8 NKJV).
"Blessed are the peacemakers, for they shall be called sons of God" (verse 9 NKJV).
"Blessed are those who are persecuted for righteousness' sake, for theirs is the kingdom of heaven" (verse 10 NKJV).

The Gospel of Mark

What It's About: This Gospel tells how Jesus proved that He is the Savior of all people, not just the Jews, by serving others, by suffering, by dying, and by being raised from the dead.

Important Characters/People: Jesus, John the Baptist, Herod, Pontius Pilate, the 12 apostles, the women who followed Jesus, the Pharisees

The Writer: The Gospel of Mark does not name its writer, but it is generally agreed that the writer was John Mark, who wasn't one of the original 12 disciples but who was a close associate of the apostle Peter. It is believed that John Mark received from Peter an eyewitness account of everything that appears in this Gospel. The Gospel of Mark was probably written around AD 57, making it one of the oldest books—if not *the* oldest book—of the New Testament.

What You'll Find in the Gospel of Mark

The Gospel of Mark is the shortest of the four Gospels. That's because Mark left out a lot of details you'll find in the other Gospels—especially Matthew and Luke. For example, Mark doesn't mention anything at all about Jesus' family tree, and he doesn't mention anything about the virgin birth. Also missing is any part of the famous Sermon on the Mount, which is covered in three chapters in Matthew and one in Luke.

Even though this book tells basically the same story as Matthew, one of the things you might notice is that it doesn't focus on how Jesus fulfilled Old Testament prophecies. In fact, Mark quotes the Old Testament only twice. This is because Mark wasn't writing to a Jewish audience the way Matthew was. Instead, he was writing to Gentile (non-Jewish) Christians, who wouldn't have been as concerned about Old Testament prophecies as their Jewish brothers and sisters.

Power Words

Jesus called out to them, "Come, follow me, and I will show you how to fish for people!"

Mark 1:17

Fun Bible Trivia

Mark 14:51–52 tells us that on the night when Jesus was arrested in the garden of Gethsemane, a young follower of his escaped naked from the scene after having a linen garment pulled off him. Some experts believe that young man was John Mark, the writer of the Gospel of Mark.

Mark understood what Jesus taught during His time on earth—and what the Old Testament prophecies about Jesus said: that Jesus was the Messiah (or Savior), not just for the Jews but for people of all races.

As you read this book, you'll see that Jesus didn't just talk about serving others and sacrificing Himself for them—He put actions behind those words. After introducing his readers to Jesus with an account of His baptism by John the Baptist in the Jordan River, Mark writes about Jesus' life, death, and resurrection. Mark includes some of Jesus' teaching—including some of the parables—but he focuses more on the things Jesus did.

Starting in chapter 11, Mark's Gospel tells the story of Jesus' arrival in Jerusalem, where He would spend most of the last week of His life on earth. Chapters 11–13 cover Jesus' teaching and actions in the city of Jerusalem before His arrest and crucifixion. During that time, He also dealt with people who didn't like what He was doing and teaching and who wanted to kill Him because of His words and actions. He also taught His disciples about the things that would happen in the future (chapter 13).

Chapters 14 and 15 tell the story of Jesus' suffering and death, and chapter 16 covers His resurrection and some of the things He did and said before He returned to heaven to be with His Father.

The Gospel of Luke

What It's About: Luke writes about how God's offer of salvation through Jesus is available to all people, not just the Jews. The Gospel of Luke focuses on Jesus as a perfect man—as the one who was fully God but also fully human. . . and perfect as both. In Luke, we can see Jesus as a man of amazing love and compassion for people around Him.

Important Characters/People: Jesus, Mary and Joseph, Zacharias and Elizabeth, the shepherds, Anna, Simeon, the 12 disciples, the Pharisees, Pilate, Herod

The Writer: Luke was a physician, historian, writer, and missionary who accompanied the apostle Paul on his third of three missionary journeys. Luke was not one of Jesus' original disciples or even an eyewitness to His life here on earth. It isn't known for certain when he became a Christian. Luke is the only Gentile (non-Jew) to write a book of the Bible—in fact, he wrote two: the Gospel of Luke and the book of Acts. Luke probably wrote his Gospel between AD 58 and 65.

What You'll Find in the Gospel of Luke

Luke's Gospel is the only one of the four that is written *chronologically*, meaning in the order that everything happened. It is written to someone named Theophilus (his name means "lover of God"). Luke begins his Gospel by explaining to Theophilus that he had investigated all the accounts written in the book.

Luke was apparently quite the historian, because his Gospel includes a lot of information not included in the other Gospels. For example, Luke gives his readers a detailed story of Jesus' birth—as well as the birth of John the Baptist. Many of the stories you hear told around Christmastime come from Luke's Gospel—including the angel's announcement to the shepherds that their Messiah had been born. (You can read that story in Luke 2:8–20.)

Luke also is the only Gospel writer to include anything about Jesus' childhood. In Luke, you can read about Jesus' circumcision, His presentation at the temple, His visit with a godly man named Simeon and a prophetess named Anna, and the way He amazed Jewish religious scholars with His understanding when he was only 12 years old. (You can read these stories in Luke 2:21–52.)

Who, What, Where?

The angel named Gabriel, who appeared to Mary to tell her she would be the mother of the Messiah (see Luke 1:26–38), is also mentioned in Daniel 9. Gabriel and Michael are the only angels mentioned by name in the Bible. Gabriel's name means "champion of God."

Power Words

"Seek the Kingdom of God above all else, and he will give you everything you need."

LUKE 12:31

Who, What, Where?

Golgotha, also known in Latin as "Calvary," is mentioned in Luke 23:33 as the place where the Romans executed criminals. Jesus was crucified there. Golgotha, which means "skull," is not far outside the city of Jerusalem.

Luke's Gospel includes 25 parables—stories Jesus told to illustrate important truths about the kingdom of God—including 17 that appear only in his Gospel. Two of Jesus' most famous parables—the good Samaritan (10:25–37) and the prodigal son (15:11–32)—appear only in Luke. He also records seven miracles of Jesus that aren't found in the other three Gospels.

Luke presents Jesus as a man who showed compassion to all people, including some the Jewish people of that time wanted nothing to do with. That includes the poor (6:20), Roman soldiers (7:1–10), widows (7:11–17), the "sinful" (7:36–50), the sick (8:43–48), Samaritans (10:33), lepers (17:11–19), and many others—including a dying thief on a cross beside Him (23:40–43).

Jesus is also seen in Luke as a man who valued women in His ministry. For example, in chapter 1, Mary and Elizabeth play important roles in the story, and in chapter 10, He visits the home of Mary and Martha of Bethany.

Like the other three Gospel writers, Luke wrote about Jesus' death and resurrection. He also added detailed accounts of Jesus' appearances to two believers on the Emmaus road and the 11 remaining disciples. At the end of Luke's Gospel, Jesus ascends to heaven to be with His Father.

The Gospel of John

What It's About: Jesus is God in the flesh—the Son of God—and the Savior of all people.

Important Characters/People: Jesus, John the Baptist, the Samaritan woman at the well, Mary Magdalene, Lazarus, Mary and Martha of Bethany, Pilate

Who Wrote It: The writer of the fourth Gospel is the apostle John, the brother of the apostle James. (Don't get him mixed up with John the Baptist.) John and James were the sons of a fisherman named Zebedee, and they were two of Jesus' original 12 disciples. In his Gospel, John refers to himself as "the disciple whom Jesus loved." John's Gospel was the last one of the four written. It was completed between AD 80 and 100. Experts believe John wrote his Gospel when he was very old, while he lived in a Greek city called Ephesus, where he served as a leader of the Ephesian church.

What You'll Find in the Gospel of John

The apostle John wastes no time in telling his readers what his Gospel is all about: "In the beginning was the Word, and the Word was with God, and the Word was God" (John 1:1 NKJV). The "Word" whom John wrote about is Jesus, and John wanted his readers to know that Jesus was no ordinary man and that He wasn't just a great teacher—He was God in the flesh!

The Gospel of John is different from the other three (Matthew, Mark, and Luke, which are called "synoptic Gospels" because they focus on many of the same events) in several important ways. John left out all of Jesus' parables and recorded only seven of His miracles.

John's Gospel focuses more on the spiritual part of Jesus' life and works. John records Jesus' explanation for coming to earth and His discussion of His relationship with God. As you read the Gospel of John, you'll notice that Jesus is often quoted as telling people that God had sent Him and that God was His Father.

John didn't include any of Jesus' parables in his Gospel, but he included some of Jesus' best-known miracles. In chapter 2, you can read the account of Jesus turning water into wine at a wedding in a place called Cana. Chapter 9 includes the story of Jesus healing a man who had been born blind and His teaching about that healing, and chapter 11 tells the story of Jesus raising His good friend Lazarus from the dead.

More than half of John's Gospel is devoted to the events of Jesus' life and teaching during His final week on earth. John records that, just hours before Jesus' arrest, He spoke to the disciples and gave them some final words of encouragement. Jesus told them:

- They should not be troubled by what was happening but to trust in Him (14:1–4).
- They were to trust in Him as the one whom God had sent (14:5–14).
- They were to continue obeying Him—with the help of the Holy Spirit (14:15–31).
- They were to "abide" (remain) in Him (15:1–8).

Fun Bible Trivia

John and his brother James, along with Peter, were part of what is called Jesus' "inner circle" of disciples. These three men were the closest to Jesus and often accompanied Him to places and events the others weren't allowed to see. For example, they were the only three allowed to be with Jesus at an event called the Transfiguration. (You can read that story in Matthew 17:1–9; Mark 9:2–10; and Luke 9:28–36.)

Power Words

"For this is how God loved the world: He gave his one and only Son, so that everyone who believes in him will not perish but have eternal life."

JOHN 3:16

- They were to love one another just as He had loved them (15:9–17).
- He would ask the Father to send the Holy Spirit to them (15:26–16:16).
- Their sadness would be turned to joy (16:17–28).

Like the other three Gospels, John's includes the story of the apostle Peter's denial that he was one of Jesus' followers after Jesus was arrested. But John is the only Gospel writer to include the scene where Jesus spoke to Peter, forgave him, and invited him to continue following Him. (You can read that story in John 21:15–23.)

Now that we've covered the four written accounts of Jesus' life, let's take a look at the men who took His message to the world after Jesus returned to heaven. You'll find their stories in the next book in the Bible: the Acts of the Apostles, or simply Acts.

Who, What, Where?

Jesus spoke the words of John 3:16—probably the best-known verse in the whole Bible—to a Jewish religious leader named Nicodemus, who visited Him late one night to find out more about Him. While most of the religious leaders of that time opposed Jesus, Nicodemus stood up for Him when they hatched the plan to arrest Him. Nicodemus also provided the expensive spices used on Jesus' body when He was buried.

Did You Know. . . ?

Even though the Gospel of John is now many Christians' favorite Gospel, there was a time when church leaders questioned whether it should have been included in the Bible. Some even thought that John's Gospel included false teaching! But it was eventually accepted as part of the canon of scripture, even though many didn't believe it belonged there.

CHAPTER 7

How the Church Got Its Start

(Acts of the Apostles)

The first four books of the New Testament—Matthew through John—tell the wonderful story of how Jesus came to earth from heaven, was born to a virgin girl named Mary in a town called Bethlehem, lived and ministered among the Jewish people of that time, died on a cross, and was raised from the dead.

That sounds like a great ending to the story, doesn't it? But there's more. Lots more!

When we continue on from the end of John's Gospel and begin in the next New Testament book, the Acts of the Apostles (Acts for short), we read about how God started what is called "the church" with a group of 120 believers gathered in Jerusalem, and then used some brave, dedicated men and women to spread the good news of Jesus throughout the known world of that time.

Let's take a look at the book of Acts and the amazing story it has to tell.

Acts

What It's About: Jesus' promise of the Holy Spirit comes true, and believers receive the power He told the apostles they would receive. The church gets its start in Jerusalem and then spreads all over the known world.

Important Characters/People: Peter, John, Gamaliel, Stephen, Philip, Aquila and Priscilla, Paul, Barnabas, Herod, Agrippa, Festus, Apollos, Silas, Lydia, Luke, Timothy

The Writer: The book of Acts was written by Luke, the same writer who wrote the Gospel of Luke. Just as he did with his Gospel, Luke wrote Acts to a man named Theophilus (but the Bible gives us no other information about Theophilus).

What You'll Find in the Book of Acts

Power Words

"You will receive power when the Holy Spirit comes upon you. And you will be my witnesses, telling people about me everywhere—in Jerusalem, throughout Judea, in Samaria, and to the ends of the earth."

ACTS 1:8

Power Words

"Each of you must repent of your sins and turn to God, and be baptized in the name of Jesus Christ for the forgiveness of your sins. Then you will receive the gift of the Holy Spirit."

ACTS 2:38

Did You Know. . . ?

The word *apostle* comes from a Greek word meaning "one sent forth"—specifically to be a representative for the message of salvation through Jesus.

Acts picks up almost exactly where the Gospel of Luke leaves off. The risen Jesus appeared to the apostles several times during the 40 days He remained on earth after God raised Him from the dead.

Not long after those 40 days had passed, Jesus appeared to the apostles one more time at a place called the Mount of Olives, which was located just outside the city of Jerusalem. He reminded them of His promise that God would send the Holy Spirit to give them power so that they could boldly tell the world around them about salvation through Jesus. After that, Jesus was "taken up into a cloud while they were watching, and they could no longer see him" (Acts 1:9).

What Now?

After Jesus returned to heaven, that group of 120 believers, including the apostles, continued to meet together, waiting for God to do something amazing. God never disappoints someone who waits for Him, and that first group of believers was no exception!

One day, about seven weeks after Jesus was raised from the dead, while that small group of believers was gathered in a house in Jerusalem, the Holy Spirit came. It was an amazing scene! What looked like tongues of fire appeared and rested on each person in the room. Everyone there was filled with God's Spirit, and they began talking in languages they didn't even know!

Not long after that, Peter—the same Peter who just weeks before was too scared to admit that he even knew Jesus—delivered an amazing sermon. By the time he was finished, that small group of 120 Christians a much bigger group—more than 3,000 people!

This gathering of believers called the church continued to grow in numbers, mostly through the preaching of Peter and John. There were lots of miracles taking place, a few problems to solve, and some of the apostles got themselves in trouble with the local authorities. But through it all, the church continued to grow, with new members being added every day.

Power Words

"There is salvation in no one else! God has given no other name under heaven by which we must be saved."

Acts 4:12

But now it was time for the message of Jesus to spread from the cozy confines of Jerusalem.

You Can't Keep a Good Message Down (Acts 7–8)

As the church continued to grow, both the Jewish religious leaders and the Roman government wondered what this new group was all about. Jesus had told the apostles that Christians would have to suffer terrible treatment because of Him. Up until now, however, the worst that had happened was that some of the apostles had been arrested for preaching about Jesus.

That all changed in a big way one day when a brave Christian named Stephen spoke to a group of Jewish religious leaders and told them things they didn't like to hear. He told them that Jesus was the Messiah they had been waiting for but that they had rejected Him.

The things Stephen said made these religious leaders so angry that they took him outside the city and killed him by throwing rocks at him. As he died, he prayed, "Lord, don't charge them with this sin!" (7:60).

Stephen's death was just the beginning of a time of terrible treatment of Christians in the city of Jerusalem. While some Christians stayed there, a lot more left the city and moved to places they thought would be safer.

What's In It for Me?

While there was nothing good or right about what happened to Stephen, he is an example of how God can take the bad things that happen to a Christian and use them for good. You probably won't have to suffer something like what Stephen suffered, but how do you respond when bad things happen to you?

Fun Bible Trivia

The first time the word *Christians* appears in the Bible is in Acts 11:26, which says that the believers in Antioch were the first to be called Christians. Some experts believe this word may have been used by nonbelievers back then in a negative or mocking way, but it has stuck as a title for people who follow Jesus.

You might think that when the Christians began to suffer it would bring about the end of Christianity in that part of the world; but it turned out to be only the beginning. You see, when the Christians left Jerusalem, they took with them their faith, and many of them preached to people in places like Judea and Samaria.

Paul: Jesus' Most Unlikely Servant

The Christians in Jerusalem suffered through terrible treatment. Some had their property taken away, some were beaten, and some even lost their lives.

One of the men responsible for this persecution was a Jewish religious leader named Saul (later called Paul). In chapter 9 of Acts, we read that Saul was on his way from Jerusalem to a city called Damascus to attack the Christians there. But something happened to Saul on the road to Damascus—something that would lead to the spread of Christianity all over the world.

As Saul neared Damascus, a bright light came from heaven, so intense that it blinded him and caused him to fall to the ground, and a voice said to him, "Saul! Saul! Why are you persecuting me?" (9:4).

It was Jesus talking to Saul!

Jesus told Paul to go to Damascus and wait for further instructions. Three days after Saul arrived in Damascus, he miraculously received his sight back. But more important than that, he received the Holy Spirit. He would never be the same again!

If you think some of the Christians who heard that Saul was God's choice to preach the gospel to the non-Jewish world were a little skeptical, you'd be right! Ananias, who took care of Saul during his first three days in Damascus, could hardly believe his ears when God told him that Saul would preach to Gentiles, kings, and the people of Israel. But Ananias took care of Saul, just as God had told him to do, making him an important part of the story. (You can read the whole story in Acts 9:10–19.)

The Christians in Jerusalem were also a little wary of Saul. In fact, when he first showed up to meet with them in Jerusalem, they were afraid of him! They thought he was only pretending to be a Christian and that he had something up his sleeve. But after they found out how he had met Jesus on the road to Damascus and how he had so courageously preached there afterward, they accepted him as one of their own.

Who, What, Where?

When we first meet Paul in the Bible, he is watching the stoning of Stephen and giving his approval. Later in the book of Acts, we find more details about Paul's life before he started attacking Christians. For example, he was born in a Roman city called Tarsus (22:3), he was a Pharisee and the son of a Pharisee (23:6), he studied Jewish law under a teacher named Gamaliel (22:3), he was a citizen of Rome (22:25–28), and he had a sister who lived in Jerusalem (23:16).

A New Name. . .and a Road Trip

When you get to Acts 13:9, the first thing you will probably notice is that something else had changed about Saul: his name! This is the first time the Bible calls the man formerly known as Saul by the name Paul.

Chapter 13 of Acts records the beginning of the first of three journeys Paul took during his lifetime to preach the message of Jesus. By this time, Antioch, a city in Syria, had replaced Jerusalem as the church's headquarters.

Paul began this trip with a man named Barnabas and with a young assistant named John Mark, who was a relative of Barnabas'. This long road trip took about three years and is covered in Acts 13:1–15:35.

Power Words

"We are here to proclaim that through this man Jesus there is forgiveness for your sins. Everyone who believes in him is made right in God's sight—something the law of Moses could never do."

Acts 13:38–39

What's In It for Me?

Acts 13:13 tells the story of a young man named John Mark, who deserted Paul and Barnabas during Paul's first missionary journey. Quitting and going home wasn't a great way to start out a life of ministry, but John Mark finished strong. He even wrote a book that ended up in the Bible: the Gospel of Mark. If you've ever failed at something or even quit when things got tough, you don't have to let that failure stop you from doing great things for God.

After a time of fasting and prayer, the three men set sail for the island of Cyprus, Barnabas' home, where they traveled from town to town preaching the gospel (13:1–4). From there, they moved on to Perga. It was here that John Mark left them and returned to Jerusalem. After that, Paul and Barnabas traveled to a town called Pisidian Antioch, where they established the world's first Gentile church.

During the rest of the trip, Paul and Barnabas saw a lot of people coming to faith in Jesus, but they also had to run for their lives a few times. In one city, Lystra (14:8–19), Paul and Barnabas were treated as gods after they performed a miracle healing; but then they were nearly stoned to death after people came from other cities and stirred up the crowds against them.

Their last stop was a city called Derbe (14:20–21), where many people came to faith in Jesus. On their return trip to Antioch, they revisited some of the places they'd been before, and this time they appointed leaders in the newly formed churches (14:21–26).

Road Trip, Part 2 (Acts 15:36–18:22)

After hanging out in Antioch for a while, Paul set out on his second missionary journey. This time, he traveled with a new partner, a man named Silas. The plan was to have Paul, Barnabas, and Silas travel together, but when Paul and Barnabas disagreed over whether or not to take John Mark with them again (Paul was against the idea), they separated, leaving only Silas as Paul's traveling companion.

Along the way, Paul and Silas added two new members to their group: Timothy, who joined them while they were in Derbe and Lystra, and Luke, who joined them while they were in Troas, a Roman colony (see the Fun Bible Trivia sidebar on this page).

On one of their stops—a city called Philippi—Paul and Silas were beaten and thrown in jail. (You can read the whole story in Acts 16:13–40.) Then a miraculous earthquake shook the prison, giving the two men a chance to make their escape. Instead, they stayed put. Because they didn't escape, the jailer, who would have been in trouble if they had escaped, became a Christian.

Paul and Silas were beaten and thrown in jail.

Fun Bible Trivia

During Paul's second missionary journey, Luke the physician—the same Luke who wrote the Gospel of Luke and the book of Acts—joined the team. We know this because, starting with Acts 16:10, Luke refers to the team as "we," meaning he was with them everywhere they went.

Did You Know. . . ?

On Paul's second missionary journey, he visited four cities that became homes to churches he later wrote letters to—letters that later became part of the New Testament. Those cities (and the books of the Bible they are named after) are Philippi (Philippians), Thessalonica (1 and 2 Thessalonians), Corinth (1 and 2 Corinthians), and Ephesus (Ephesians).

Power Words

"Believe in the Lord Jesus and you will be saved, along with everyone in your household."

Acts 16:31

Who, What, Where?

Acts 17:11–12 describes the people of Berea as "more open-minded" than the people of Thessalonica and as people who eagerly heard his message and searched the scriptures to see if what he said was true. Many Jews in Berea believed in Jesus as a result of their searching.

After leaving Philippi, Paul and Silas traveled to Thessalonica (17:1–4), Berea (17:10–12), Athens (17:16–33), Corinth (18:1–18), Ephesus (18:19–20), and Jerusalem (18:22). After making those stops, Paul and Silas returned to Antioch, Syria.

In Athens, which is now the capital city of Greece, Paul was sad to see all the idols erected to the Greek "gods." But when he saw one with an inscription that read "To an Unknown God," he took the opportunity to tell the people about a God they could know through Jesus Christ.

Paul and Silas stayed in Corinth for about 18 months. While there, they met Aquila and Priscilla, a married couple who later traveled with Paul. Paul also wrote his two letters to the Thessalonians while he was in Corinth.

The Parthenon of Athens was dedicated to Athena, the Greek goddess of war, civilization, and justice.

Modern-day Athens, Greece

The First Two Trips Were So Good, We're Taking a Third (Acts 18:23–21:14)

Paul's third and final missionary journey was the longest of the three, beginning in about AD 53 and ending around AD 58.

After spending some time in Antioch, Paul set out to the cities in Galatia and Phrygia, including Tarsus and Iconium. He then traveled to Ephesus, where he stayed for almost three years (Acts 19:1–41).

God did a lot of great work through Paul in Ephesus. Paul preached and taught and did many great miracles—including healing the sick and casting out evil spirits (Acts 19:11–12). His work was so amazing that even magicians stopped their evil practices and burned very expensive books they used for their magic (Acts 19:17–20).

Later, Paul was nearly killed when he exposed the dishonesty of men who were in the business of making and selling idols (19:24–27). Even though Paul was a very busy man, he also found time to write his first letter to the Corinthian church and his letter to the Galatians, both of which are now in the Bible.

Paul then traveled to Macedonia and Greece (20:1–3), where he wrote his second letter to the Corinthians. From there he traveled to Troas (20:6–12) and then to Assos (20:13–14) and then back to Ephesus (20:17–35). The final three stops on his third missionary journey were in Tyre (21:3–6), Ptolemais (21:7), and Caesarea (21:8).

Fun Bible Trivia

In Acts 20:35, Paul quotes Jesus as saying, "It is more blessed to give than to receive." But don't try to find a verse that says that in the four Gospels. Even though that quote sounds a lot like something Jesus would have said, and Paul probably heard from one of the apostles that Jesus had said it, you won't find an account of Jesus speaking those words in Matthew, Mark, Luke, or John.

On to Jerusalem and Rome (Acts 21:15–23:15)

Who, What, Where?

Malta, where the apostle Paul and others stayed after their ship wrecked on the way to Rome, is a southern European archipelago (a large group of islands) located in the Mediterranean Sea, about 60 miles south of the southeastern tip of Sicily, Italy.

The last eight chapters of the book of Acts take place after Paul's third and final missionary journey. But that doesn't mean Paul was finished preaching and teaching the good news about Jesus. And it also doesn't mean an end to the threats on his life.

Even though Paul had been warned there would be trouble if he traveled to Jerusalem, he still went there. This time, the Christians in Jerusalem welcomed him, but his reception among the Jews in the city wasn't as friendly. He was arrested in the temple after a riot broke out because of the things he preached (21:26–36).

After Paul learned of a plot to kill him, he was sent to Caesarea, where he stayed two years before he was sent to Rome. On the way to Rome, the ship he was sailing on shipwrecked during a terrible storm, and he ended up on the island of Malta, where he continued preaching. (You can read this story in Acts 27:14–28:10.)

When Paul finally arrived in Rome, he was placed under house arrest. He was allowed to live by himself—with a Roman soldier to guard him. During his two years in Rome, he wrote several more letters that were later included in the Bible: Ephesians, Philippians, two letters to Timothy, and Philemon.

While Paul was in Rome, he continued to preach—"boldly proclaiming the Kingdom of God and teaching about the Lord Jesus Christ. And no one tried to stop him" (28:31).

The Bible doesn't say exactly when Paul died or how. But historians teach that he was killed by the Roman emperor Nero around AD 67.

CHAPTER 8

Letters That Became Books of the Bible

Epistles from Paul, Peter, and the Rest (Romans through Jude)

If you've ever read through your Bible from Genesis to Revelation, right after you finished reading about the life, words, and deeds of Jesus Christ (Matthew through John), you moved on to the adventures of the men He appointed to continue His work in the then-known world (Acts).

If you're like a lot of people who have just finished reading the Gospels and the book of Acts, you might be wondering, *Okay, now that I know a little something about what Jesus and the men who followed Him have done, what does it mean to me?*

The next 21 books of the Bible—books that are called the Epistles—give you an amazing number of answers to that question. In these books, you'll find some very practical instructions on what you are to believe, how you are to live, and how you are to treat other people.

The Bible's epistles are actually personal letters written by men called apostles. At least five (and probably six) men wrote letters that ended up in the New Testament. The apostle Paul wrote most of the epistles included in the New Testament. He is known for certain to have written 13 of the letters (Romans, 1 and 2 Corinthians, Galatians, Ephesians, Philippians, Colossians, 1 and 2 Thessalonians, 1 and 2 Timothy, Titus, and Philemon) and is thought by some to have written Hebrews (more on that later).

Did You Know. . . ?

Though Paul is credited with writing the first 13 epistles in the New Testament, he didn't work alone. Romans 16:22 credits an assistant of Paul's named Tertius with helping the apostle write down his letter to the Roman Christians; and 1 Corinthians 1:1 credits a man named Sosthenes with assisting Paul in his first letter to the Christians in Corinth. Nothing else is known about either man.

Romans

What It's About: The apostle Paul explains to the Roman Christians that everyone born since the days of Adam and Eve comes into this world as a sinner—someone who is not at peace with God. But there is a way of salvation—and only one way—and that's through faith in Jesus Christ.

Important Characters/People: Paul, Phoebe, Priscilla, Aquila, and many others mentioned in Romans 16

The Writer: Paul, with help from Tertius (16:22), wrote this letter in about AD 56, while he was in the city of Corinth.

What You'll Find in the Book of Romans

Power Words

And we know that God causes everything to work together for the good of those who love God and are called according to his purpose for them.

ROMANS 8:28

Romans is different from Paul's letters to the other churches because he wrote it to a church he'd never personally visited. In fact, he had never even seen the city of Rome at the time he wrote this letter. Paul hoped to see the Roman Christians face-to-face when he traveled to Spain (15:23–24). It's not known if Paul ever made it to Spain, but he did end up in Rome at the end of his life.

Some people have called Romans the "Gospel according to Paul" because it gives its readers such a detailed but simple plan for salvation.

The book of Romans starts out by describing in detail the sad condition of all people. In the first two chapters and most of the third, Paul writes about God's anger over human sin. He points out that even the best people in the world don't live the way God wants them to live. Not only that, but he writes that simply following God's written laws isn't enough to make us right with Him.

Modern-day Rome, Italy

It seems like a pretty hopeless situation, but in chapter 3, Paul begins to explain why there is still hope. It's almost as if Paul were saying, "Here's the bad news, but stay with me while I tell you the good news!" Sure, everyone sins and falls short of God's standard (3:23), but God Himself has lovingly provided the way for people to overcome that sin and have peace with Him: "Yet God, in his grace, freely makes us right in his sight. He did this through Christ Jesus when he freed us from the penalty for our sins" (3:24).

Paul wanted the Christians in Rome to understand that it wasn't about being a better person or about making an effort to follow God's rules. It's not that it wasn't a good idea to do those things, but they would never be enough to get a person into heaven. Salvation comes through one simple thing: trusting in Jesus Christ, who died as a sacrifice for our sins.

> **What's In It for Me?**
>
> Paul writes in Romans 8:15 that Christians can call God "Abba, Father." *Abba* is an Aramaic word for the word *father* that implies a really close relationship—kind of like when you call your father "Daddy." Paul uses this very same word to describe our relationship with God in Galatians 4:6.

In chapters 6–8, Paul encourages his readers with the promise that they can live the way God wants them to live because God has given them power through the Holy Spirit. In chapters 9–11, he expands on how God worked His perfect plan to make people at peace with Him. Chapters 12–15 are some practical instructions for the Christian life.

1 Corinthians

What It's About: The people in the church in the city of Corinth weren't living the way Christians should live and weren't treating one another the way they should, so Paul wrote this letter to correct them and encourage them.

Important Characters/People: Paul, Apollos, Priscilla, Aquila, Timothy, Crispus, Sosthenes, Stephanas

The Writer: The apostle Paul, with help from Sosthenes (1:1)

What You'll Find in the Book of 1 Corinthians

Power Words

Three things will last forever—faith, hope, and love—and the greatest of these is love.

1 CORINTHIANS 13:13

What's in It for Me?

Chapter 13 of 1 Corinthians is well known as the "love chapter" of the Bible. Take some time to read this chapter and ask yourself how you can better show your love for your family, friends, people at church, and others around you.

Paul helped establish the Corinthian church during his second missionary journey (Acts 18). But after Paul moved on to Ephesus, he found out that the Corinthians were having some serious problems. There were arguments in the church, ungodly living, and even lawsuits among the Christians there. Chapters 1–6 cover Paul's warnings and encouragements for the Christians at Corinth about unity in the church and right living for Christians.

In 1 Corinthians, Paul teaches on marriage (chapter 7), problems with food and idols (chapter 8), Christian freedom (chapter 9), the Lord's Supper (11:17–34), spiritual gifts (chapters 12–14), the resurrection of the dead (chapter 15), and giving (chapter 16).

2 Corinthians

What It's About: The apostle Paul writes another letter to the Corinthians, this time to defend his ministry.

Important Characters/People: Paul, the Corinthian church leaders, Titus

The Writer: The apostle Paul, with help from Timothy (1:1)

What You'll Find in the Book of 2 Corinthians

The Corinthian Christians had dealt with some of the problems Paul wrote to them about in his first letter to them, but some troublemakers in Corinth questioned Paul's authority and attempted to divide the church. In the first seven chapters of 2 Corinthians, Paul describes his work as an apostle.

Chapters 8 and 9 of this book are Paul's instructions for giving and sharing in the church, including his words "God loves a person who gives cheerfully" (9:7). In the next three chapters, Paul defends his position as an apostle and tells the Corinthians why he writes with the authority he does.

Fun Bible Trivia

In 2 Corinthians 12:7, Paul mentions a "thorn in my flesh" that God used to keep him humble. Paul doesn't say exactly what that "thorn" is, but some believe it might have been a physical problem like bad eyesight, migraine headaches, or epilepsy. Others believe it might have been attacks in the spiritual or human realm.

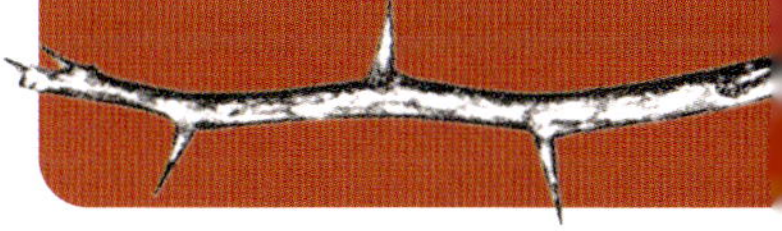

Galatians

What It's About: Paul writes to the Galatian Christians to remind them to trust in only Jesus for their salvation and not in Jewish laws and customs. Paul wanted the Galatians to understand that the Christian life isn't about observing a lot of rules and regulations but about living under the power of the Holy Spirit.

Important Characters/People: Paul, Abraham, Sarah, Hagar, Ishmael, Isaac

The Writer: The apostle Paul. He wrote his letter to the Galatians around AD 50. This letter was actually written to several churches in a larger area called Galatia, which was located in Asia Minor (now Turkey).

What You'll Find in the Book of Galatians

Power Words

Clearly no one who relies on the law is justified before God, because, "the righteous will live by faith."

GALATIANS 3:11 NIV

The Galatian Christians had started their lives of faith in Jesus well, but then a big problem came along. Men called "Judaizers" were trying to convince the Galatians, including the Gentiles, that they needed to observe Jewish rituals and customs in order to be true Christians.

Paul starts out his letter by telling the Galatians that he is shocked that they would turn way from God and His love and mercy (1:6) and follow a different path. He even writes of the Judaizers, "Let God's curse fall on anyone, including us or even an angel from heaven, who preaches a different kind of Good News than the one we preached to you" (1:8).

Paul called the Galatian Christians "foolish Galatians" (3:1) because many of them had tried to take the salvation God had given them freely through Jesus Christ and add Jewish customs and rituals to it.

The main theme of the book of Galatians is *freedom*, and Paul wanted all Christians, including us today, to understand that because we have Jesus, we are free to love God and others without adding rituals, customs, or any human effort to our Christian lives.

Ephesians

What It's About: Paul writes to the church in the city of Ephesus (in Asia Minor) to explain their true identity as Christians and what it should mean to them in their daily lives.

Important Characters/People: Paul, Timothy, Tychicus

The Writer: The apostle Paul

What You'll Find in the Book of Ephesians

If you want to have a good understanding of what God has done for you through Jesus and who He says you are as a Christian, the book of Ephesians is a great place to start.

Paul started the church in Ephesus during his second missionary journey. (You can read the story in Acts 19.) Even though Paul had spent two years in the city, he later wrote to the Ephesians from his prison cell in Rome to explain the meaning of their relationship to Jesus Christ and how it should change their way of living and thinking.

The first three chapters of Ephesians teach what God has done in bringing people to Himself through Jesus. Paul told the Ephesians that through Jesus, God had brought both Jews and Gentiles together to Himself (2:11–18). The final three chapters explain what this new life in Jesus should look like—both in the church and in the home and other places.

Who, What, Where?

Ephesus was the capital city of the Roman province of Asia, in the western part of Asia Minor (now Turkey). The Ephesian church is mentioned in the book of Revelation, where the apostle John wrote God's prophetic message praising the Ephesians for their good deeds but warning them that they had lost their first love (Revelation 2:1–7).

Philippians

What It's About: Paul writes a heartfelt letter of love, friendship, and encouragement to the believers at the church in the city of Philippi.

Important Characters/People: Paul, Epaphroditus, Timothy, Euodia, Syntyche

The Writer: Paul, along with Timothy (1:1)

What You'll Find in the Book of Philippians

When you're going through a hard time and are feeling a little sad, discouraged, or worried, then maybe you should crack your Bible open to the book of Philippians, one of the most positive, upbeat, encouraging books in the whole Bible.

The apostle Paul was probably sitting in a stinky, cold Roman prison cell when he wrote this letter. He had helped establish the Philippian church during his second missionary journey, and this letter shows that he had some very positive, warm feelings for the Christians there.

One of the things you'll notice as you read Philippians is that Paul uses the words *joy* and *rejoicing* over and over. That includes a verse you may have sung as a song at Sunday school: "Rejoice in the Lord always. Again I will say, rejoice!" (4:4 NJKV). Paul knew for himself that no matter what kinds of circumstances he was in, he

Power Words

Don't worry about anything; instead, pray about everything. Tell God what you need, and thank him for all he has done.

PHILIPPIANS 4:6

could always find joy in Jesus. He wanted the Christians in Philippi—and you—to understand that.

One thing Paul never says in this letter is that life is always going to be easy or fun. He was in a bad place himself (he knew his life could be nearing an end), and he warned the Philippians that they could expect to have to suffer for Jesus (1:29–30). Still, he wrote a book filled with words of joy for the life God had allowed him to live and the things God had allowed him to do.

Colossians

What It's About: To fight against false teaching that had arisen in the church in Colossae, Paul writes to the Colossian Christians to remind them that Jesus is higher and greater than everything and everyone.

Important Characters/People: Paul, Barnabas, Aristarchus, Justus

The Writer: The apostle Paul, along with Timothy (1:1)

Did You Know. . . ?

In Colossians 4:16, Paul mentions a letter he wrote to the church in Laodicea. This was one of probably dozens of letters Paul wrote that didn't make it into the Bible as part of the New Testament. Paul also asked that the letter to the Colossians be read to the Christians in Laodicea.

What You'll Find in the Book of Colossians

The Colossian church—like so many others of that time—had been the target of false teaching (or, as Paul calls it in Colossians 2:4, "well-crafted arguments") that had caused some of the Christians in Colossae to add unhelpful things to their Christian faith. When Paul found out about the situation, he wrote this letter to remind the people that Jesus was all they needed—not additional rules and regulations, false thinking, angels, or anything else.

To demonstrate who Jesus is and what He meant to them, Paul reminded the Colossians that Jesus is the image of the invisible God (1:15), is the firstborn over all creation (1:15), is the creator of all things (1:16), is before all things (1:17), holds all things together (1:17), and is the head of the church (1:18).

Power Words

Think about the things of heaven, not the things of earth.

COLOSSIANS 3:2

1 Thessalonians

What It's About: Paul writes to the church in the Macedonian city of Thessalonica to instruct the Christians on living the way God wants them to live and also to assure them that Jesus will one day return to earth.

Important Characters/People: Paul, Silas, Timothy

The Writer: The apostle Paul, along with Silvanus (Silas) and Timothy (1:1). Paul, along with Silas, his traveling companion, had started the church in Thessalonica during his second missionary journey (Acts 17:1–9). He wrote his first letter to the Thessalonians around AD 50.

What You'll Find in the Book of 1 Thessalonians

The first three chapters of this book are Paul's greetings and words of encouragement to a church he knew was growing strong in the faith. In chapter 4, he gives them instructions on living a godly life and encourages them with the promise that Jesus will return and that Christians who have already died will go to heaven when He comes back.

What's In It for Me?

The book of 1 Thessalonians contains many promises for you as a Christian—including the promise that because you are a Christian, you will one day be together in heaven with all your Christian family members and friends (4:13–18).

2 Thessalonians

What It's About: Paul writes a follow-up letter to the Thessalonian church to encourage them not just to wait around until Jesus returns, but to continue the work God has for them to do.

Important Characters/People: Paul, the "man of lawlessness"

The Writer: The apostle Paul, along with Silvanus (Silas) and Timothy (1:1)

What You'll Find in the Book of 2 Thessalonians

Paul wrote this letter to help calm the shaken and troubled (2:2) Thessalonians, who had been told that Jesus had already returned to earth. Some of the Thessalonian Christians had quit their money-earning jobs and stopped doing the work God had for them to do here on earth.

In this letter, Paul assures them that Jesus' second coming is still in the future and that they should continue the work they had been doing before. In chapter 2, Paul tells the Thessalonians not to pay any attention to those who tell them Jesus has already returned and gives them an outline of what will take place in the "day of the Lord." He explains that this day won't come until the "man of lawlessness" is revealed (2:8).

1 Timothy

What It's About: Paul's letter of instruction and encouragement for the church in Ephesus and to a young pastor named Timothy. In this letter, Paul gives Timothy the requirements for church leadership.

Important Characters/People: Paul, Timothy, church leaders, Hymenaeus, Alexander

The Writer: The apostle Paul

What You'll Find in the Book of 1 Timothy

The apostle Paul wasn't just the greatest missionary in the history of Christianity, and he wasn't just the writer of many of the books in the New Testament. Paul was also a teacher and a mentor, and one of his students was Timothy, a young man who had been with Paul on his missionary journeys.

Paul begins his first letter to young Timothy by warning him against some of the false teaching that had made its way around the churches in that part of the world. He encourages Timothy to "fight well in the Lord's battles" and "cling to your faith in Christ, and keep your conscience clear" (1:18–19). In chapter 2, Paul lists some guidelines for the conduct of the church. Then, in chapter 3, he lists the qualifications for pastors and deacons, who were the church leaders of that time.

Chapters 4–6 cover a variety of topics, including more advice for church leaders, including Timothy himself (4:4–16), caring for widows (5:1–21), and avoiding the love of money (6:10–17).

Who, What, Where?

Timothy was a young man who worked side by side with the apostle Paul, who assigned him the tough job of pastoring the church in Ephesus. In his letters to Timothy, Paul addresses him as a loving father would a son.

2 Timothy

What It's About: Paul's final words of encouragement to his much-loved partner and spiritual son, Timothy

Important Characters/People: Paul, Timothy, Demas, Crescens, Carpus, Titus, Luke, John Mark, Alexander

The Writer: The apostle Paul, who wrote this letter in approximately AD 67, shortly before he was put to death in Rome

Power Words

For God saved us and called us to live a holy life. He did this, not because we deserved it, but because that was his plan from before the beginning of time.

2 Timothy 1:9

Did You Know. . . ?

The first nine epistles in the New Testament were written to churches. The next four were written to individuals. Both letters to Timothy and the one to Titus were written to church leaders who had traveled with Paul. That is why they are sometimes called "pastoral epistles."

What You'll Find in the Book of 2 Timothy

Sitting in a Roman prison cell, Paul wrote this letter to Timothy, his young friend and "true son in the faith" (1 Timothy 1:2). Paul knew his life was probably going to end soon, and he might have known that this letter would be his "last words." But even though Paul was in a terrible place, he didn't dwell on his own circumstances but took the time to express his concern for other Christians, especially Timothy.

In this letter, Paul encourages young Timothy to continue loving Jesus passionately and to preserve the truth he had learned from Paul. He pushes him to live the way God wants him to live as an example to Christians around him. Paul also warns Timothy to expect trouble as a result of living for Jesus (3:12) but also encourages him with the promise that God will always be faithful.

Titus

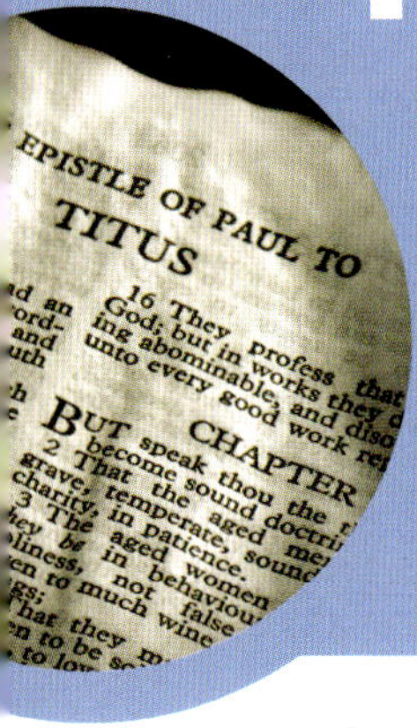

What It's About: Paul instructs Christian leaders on how to live and how to lead their churches.

Important Characters/People: Paul, Titus

The Writer: The apostle Paul

What You'll Find in the Book of Titus

The apostle Paul had left a young traveling companion named Titus on the Mediterranean island of Crete so that Titus could appoint church leaders and correct some of the problems in the new church there.

The people of Crete were known back then for their bad behavior, and they needed a strong leader who would hold them accountable for their actions. Titus was just that kind of leader.

Paul's letter to Titus encourages him to choose godly leaders and to set an example for the Christians on Crete by living the kind of life God wanted him to live. But this book applies to more than just church leaders—it gives good advice for any Christian to follow.

Who, What, Where?

Titus was a Gentile (non-Jewish) friend and helper of the apostle Paul who accompanied Paul and Barnabas on a journey to Jerusalem (see Galatians 2:1) and who was with Paul during his imprisonment in Rome (2 Timothy 4:10). The Bible says he was completely selfless and trustworthy (2 Corinthians 12:18).

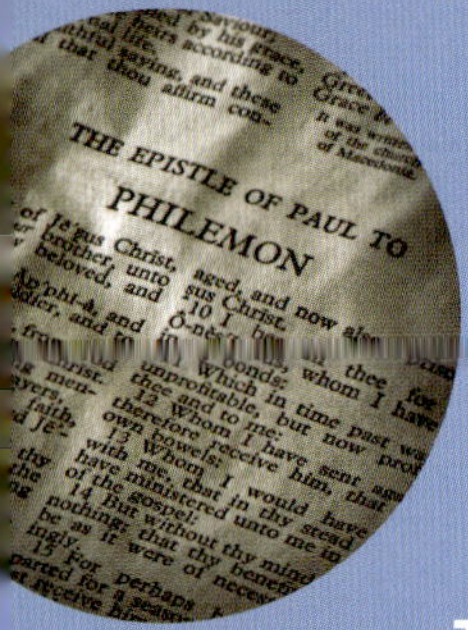

Philemon

What It's About: Paul encourages a slave owner named Philemon to treat his runaway slave like he would any other fellow Christian: with love, compassion, and forgiveness.

Important Characters/People: Paul, Timothy, Philemon, Onesimus

The Writer: The apostle Paul. He wrote his letter to Philemon in about AD 60 while in prison in Rome.

What's in It for Me?

The story of Philemon and his runaway slave is an example of how a Christian should treat someone who has done something wrong. Paul knows Philemon has every right under the law to have Onesimus harshly punished, but Paul begs his friend to treat Onesimus with forgiveness and compassion.

What You'll Find in the Book of Philemon

A slave named Onesimus had robbed Philemon and had run away to Rome, where he met Paul and became a Christian. Paul wanted to keep Onesimus in Rome as a helper, but because Philemon didn't approve, Paul sent Onesimus back to Colossae. Paul then writes a very personal letter in which he asks Philemon to forgive his runaway slave, who faced severe punishment under Roman law for running away from his master.

Hebrews

What It's About: The writer of this letter shows his readers that Jesus is better than any Old Testament sacrifice or ritual. In fact, while those sacrifices and rituals were an imperfect way to approach God, Jesus provided the one and only perfect way to God.

Important Characters/People: Moses, Joshua, Melchizedek, the Hebrew patriarchs, Jesus

The Writer: One of the biggest mysteries in the entire New Testament is this: who wrote the book of Hebrews? It is believed the letter was written around AD 65, but there is no real agreement on who wrote it. Some experts believe the apostle Paul wrote this letter. Others believe the writer was Barnabas, who traveled with Paul on his first missionary journey. Others believe it was a man named Apollos, a Jewish preacher from Alexandria who had been taught by a married couple named Aquila and Priscilla (Acts 18:26).

What You'll Find in the Book of Hebrews

The writer of Hebrews was probably addressing new Jewish Christians (that's why it's called "Hebrews") who might have been tempted to avoid persecution from other Jews and return to the system of sacrifices and other Old Testament–style ceremonies. The writer of Hebrews wanted his readers to understand that Jesus' sacrificial death eliminated the need for those kinds of observances.

In chapter 10, the writer to the Hebrews tells his readers that Jesus was far better than the Old Testament system of sacrifices. For one thing, the sacrificial system required people to make sacrifices once every year through a human priest to cover their sins. The perfect sacrifice of Jesus on the cross was a once-and-for-all sacrifice that allows each individual Christian to approach God without the help of a priest.

The writer of Hebrews encourages Jewish Christians to hold to their faith in Jesus, and also warns them not to neglect their faith (2:1–4), not to fall into unbelief (3:7–4:13), to continue to grow in their faith (5:11–6:20), and to endure persecution and other temptations to give up on their faith (10:32–39).

Fun Bible Trivia

Some Bible experts believe it is possible that a woman named Priscilla (who, along with her husband, Aquila, served the first-century church in Corinth and Ephesus) wrote the book of Hebrews. If that is true, Priscilla would be the only female author of a New Testament book.

Power Words

Fixing our eyes on Jesus, the pioneer and perfecter of faith. For the joy set before him he endured the cross, scorning its shame, and sat down at the right hand of the throne of God.

HEBREWS 12:2 NIV

James

What It's About: The apostle James writes that real Christian faith is shown in a believer's actions, especially in how he or she treats others.

Important Characters/People: James, teachers, church leaders

The Writer: The writer of this letter is believed to be James (also known as James the Just), the earthly brother of Jesus (see Matthew 13:55; Mark 6:3). The Bible tells us that James was not a Christian until after Jesus' resurrection (compare John 7:3–5 with Acts 1:14; 1 Corinthians 15:7; and Galatians 1:19). Once he became a Christian, he served as one of the leaders of the church in Jerusalem (see Galatians 2:9). The book of James is believed to be the oldest book of the New Testament, written as early as AD 45.

What You'll Find in the Book of James

Have you ever heard the saying, "Don't just talk the talk—walk the walk"? That's the message behind the book of James, which encourages Christians to demonstrate their faith in a loving God by loving others through their actions. In a way, it's a more detailed explanation of these words of Jesus: "You should be a light for other people. Live so that they will see the good things you do and will praise your Father in heaven" (Matthew 5:16 NCV).

While Paul taught that Christians are saved by faith alone and not by the good things they do (see Romans 3:28), James teaches that good deeds should follow real faith. That's why he encourages all Christians to focus on living right, watching how they talk, and treating others as valuable in God's eyes—even during difficult times.

Power Words

Come near to God, and God will come near to you.

JAMES 4:8 NCV

1 Peter

What It's About: When a believer suffers for Jesus, he or she should consider it a good thing.

Important Characters/People: Peter, church leaders

The Writer: The apostle Peter, with the assistance of Silvanus (5:12)

What You'll Find in the Book of 1 Peter

Peter wrote this letter to Jewish Christians living all over the Roman Empire to encourage them and challenge them. They needed the encouragement too, because Jewish Christians faced terrible treatment from the Jews and from the Romans.

Peter not only wrote to encourage Christians to endure the bad things that happened to them, but also to rejoice and to see it as a privilege to be mistreated because of their faith in Jesus.

Peter also encouraged Christians to put others ahead of themselves—just like Jesus did. When we do that, we not only become more like Jesus, but we will also receive rewards from God.

Power Words

You are a chosen people. You are royal priests, a holy nation, God's very own possession. As a result, you can show others the goodness of God, for he called you out of the darkness into his wonderful light.

1 PETER 2:9

2 Peter

What It's About: Peter warns believers to watch out for people who are spreading wrong teaching in the church.

Important Characters/People: Peter, prophets, false teachers

The Writer: The apostle Peter. He wrote this letter around AD 66 or 67, near the end of his life.

What You'll Find in the Book of 2 Peter

Power Words

Because of his glory and excellence, he has given us great and precious promises. These are the promises that enable you to share his divine nature and escape the world's corruption caused by human desires.

2 Peter 1:4

Peter was troubled because he knew that men were coming into the churches and spreading wrong teaching about the Christian faith. He encouraged Christians to grow strong in their faith and to focus on his teaching so that they would be able to tell when someone was trying to teach them wrong things.

Peter wrote that some of these false teachers even made fun of the truth that Jesus would return again (3:3–7). Instead of listening to them, he said, hold on to the promise of Jesus' return to earth; that truth will motivate us to live the way God wants us to live (3:14).

1 John

What It's About: Jesus was a real man—just as He was really God—and He set an example for Christians to follow in the way He loved others.

Important Characters/People: John

The Writer: The letters titled 1 John, 2 John, and 3 John don't mention who wrote them, but centuries of tradition hold that it was John, one of Jesus' 12 original disciples, who wrote these three letters around AD 92. John reminds his readers that he and the other disciples knew Jesus personally: "We saw him with our own eyes and touched him with our own hands" (1 John 1:1).

What You'll Find in the Book of 1 John

One of the reasons John wrote this letter was to set believers straight about certain parts of the Christian faith. John knew that false teachers were trying to lead the Christians of that time away from the true Christian faith. The New Testament had not yet been put together into one book, so there was no single book that Christians could read in order to find out whether what they were being taught was true.

In the first two chapters of 1 John, the apostle writes about how a true Christian should live. He writes that people who claim to be Christians but don't live the way God wants them to live aren't really Christians at all (1:8). He also encourages Christians not to hide their sins but to confess them, because God is "faithful and just" to forgive those who confess their sins (1:9).

In chapters 3 and 4, John writes that God loves us so deeply that we should love Him in return and also love others the same way. John encourages his readers to love one another selflessly, even to the point of laying down their lives for one another if necessary (3:16–17).

Power Words

See how very much our Father loves us, for he calls us his children, and that is what we are! But the people who belong to this world don't recognize that we are God's children because they don't know him.

1 John 3:1

John writes that "God is love" (4:8) and that those who really know God will love others as a result. On the other hand, those who don't love don't really know God at all. John says that when we love others, God lives within us (4:12).

In chapter 5, John writes that love and obedience to God are closely tied together and that we can approach God at any time, knowing that He hears us and will answer our prayers.

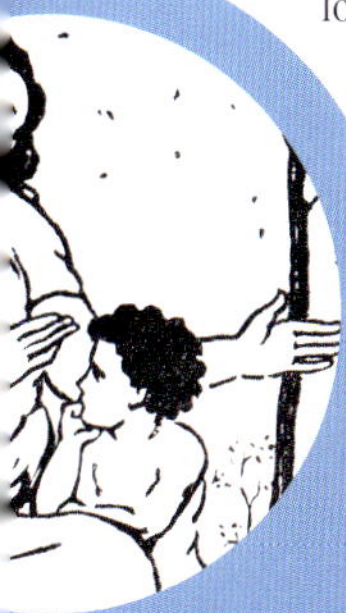

2 John

What It's About: The apostle John warns Christians to watch out for false teachers who don't believe in Jesus' physical life and ministry here on earth.

Important Characters/People: John, "the chosen lady and her children"

The Writer: The apostle John (see page 120)

What You'll Find in the Book of 2 John

The apostle John addressed 2 John to "the chosen lady and to her children." That could have meant a woman of important position in the Ephesian church, or it could have meant the local church.

John wrote this letter to warn Christians against false teachers who taught that Jesus didn't physically rise from the dead, but rose only in a spiritual sense. John warned true believers to completely avoid people who taught that.

3 John

What It's About: True Christian leaders must be humble people who are more concerned about the welfare of others than they are for their own reputation or position.

Important Characters/People: John, Gaius, Diotrephes

The Writer: The apostle John (see page 120)

What You'll Find in the Book of 3 John

John's third epistle was written to a Christian named Gaius (1:1). John wrote of Gaius as a man who demonstrated hospitality to traveling preachers who stopped off in his hometown. He also warns against the kind of leadership practiced by a man named Diotrephes, who was more interested in having power over people than he was in serving them.

Jude

What It's About: Jude warns Christians to watch out for those who try to spread wrong teaching.

Important Characters/People: Jude, Enoch

The Writer: The writer of the epistle of Jude identifies himself only as the "brother of James" (1:1). It's possible that Jude was the brother of James, who is identified as the brother of Jesus (see Matthew 13:55), but Jude does not identify himself as Jesus' brother.

What You'll Find in the Book of Jude

The book of Jude was written between AD 60 and 80, and it deals with some of the same problems Peter addresses in his second letter. Jude wanted to warn Christians not to follow the example of false teachers in the church, who were leading people away from the faith, and complainers, who weren't living right.

CHAPTER 9

What's Ahead

John's Vision of the Last Days (Revelation)

By now, you should have a pretty good idea of what the different books of the Bible are about, the key characters and events in each book, and what you can learn from reading each book.

Now we come to the last book of the Bible: Revelation. Though the Old Testament contains a lot of prophecy books, Revelation is the only New Testament book devoted to prophecy. Other New Testament books include *some* prophecy, but Revelation is the only one that is pretty much all prophecy.

Before you read on, there are some things about Revelation that you should know. First of all, this book has confused some of the most dedicated Bible scholars and Christian leaders, and it has led to some big disagreements. That's because the book uses lots of colorful imagery, and people disagree about what these symbols and pictures mean.

Revelation includes some very strange—and sometimes very scary—passages that can be taken many different ways. Some believe that a lot of what we read in Revelation has already taken place and that the writer wrote the way he did in order to confuse Roman leaders who treated first-century Christians very badly. Other people believe that most of Revelation looks forward to events that haven't happened yet.

No matter what you believe about Revelation, it is a book that promises that things will turn out great for people who follow Jesus faithfully. And it also contains some practical words you can apply to your Christian life every day.

Did You Know. . . ?

The book of Revelation has also been called the Revelation of Jesus Christ, the Apocalypse of John, or simply the Apocalypse. The word *apocalypse* is sometimes used to describe worldwide destruction or a disaster, but it actually means an *unveiling* or *revealing*. That is why most people call this book Revelation.

Revelation

What It's About: Jesus will return to earth and reward those who do right and punish those who do wrong. Revelation describes the final conflict between good and evil.

Important Characters/People: John, Jesus, the dragon (Satan), two beasts, the "messenger" angels

The Writer: The book of Revelation was written by John, one of Jesus' original 12 disciples, who also wrote the Gospel of John, 1 John, 2 John, and 3 John. He received the visions he writes about in this book while living on the island of Patmos, which is off the coast of Greece. The Roman government had sent him there as punishment for preaching the good news of Jesus (see Revelation 1:9).

Power Words

"I am the Alpha and the Omega—the beginning and the end," says the Lord God. "I am the one who is, who always was, and who is still to come—the Almighty One."

Revelation 1:8

Who, What, Where?

Revelation 1:9 says that John received the visions he wrote in the book while living as a prisoner on Patmos, an island located in the Aegean Sea, west of Asia Minor (now Turkey). Patmos covers about 13 square miles and is thought to have been an island prison of the Roman Empire. Today, Patmos is part of Greece.

What You'll Find in the Book of Revelation

Revelation starts by telling readers what they are about to read: "The revelation from Jesus Christ, which God gave him to show his servants what must soon take place" (1:1 NIV). John then explains that he received the visions he writes about from an angel whom God had sent.

After greeting his readers, John writes that he heard a very loud voice instructing him to write down everything he was about to hear and see. Then he describes an amazing—and terrifying—vision of someone "like the Son of Man" (1:13). He was dressed in a long robe with a golden sash across his chest, and his head and hair were "white like wool, as white as snow," and his eyes were like "flames of fire" (1:14). "His feet were like polished bronze refined in a furnace, and his voice thundered like mighty ocean waves" (1:15). He held seven stars in his hand, and out of his mouth came a "sharp two-edged sword" (1:16). His face was like the shining sun (1:16).

After hearing and seeing all this, John was so frightened that he fell on his face as if he were dead. But just then, the person in John's vision laid his hand on John's shoulder and told him not to be afraid, because, He said, "I am the First and the Last. I am the living one. I died, but look—I am alive forever and ever! And I hold the keys of death and the grave" (1:17–18).

John knew who was talking to him. It was Jesus! This was the same Jesus with whom John had spent three years when Jesus was alive on earth. But even though it was the same Jesus, He looked and sounded different, because now He had been "glorified," which means He appeared in His heavenly form.

And He had a lot for John to think and write about!

Fun Bible Trivia

The number seven appears many times in the book of Revelation (seven churches, seven horns, seven eyes, seven seals, seven trumpets, seven bowls). The number seven is important in Jewish tradition because it stands for God's perfection as He rested on the seventh day after He had finished creation. (Look it up in Genesis 2:2–3.)

St John the Evangelist at Patmos by Tobias Verhaecht

Seven Messages for Seven Churches

Chapters 2 and 3 of Revelation are Jesus' own words for seven churches in Asia Minor, a place that is now part of the nation of Turkey. He encouraged some of the churches, but He challenged and criticized others.

Here is a quick look at what Jesus said to the seven churches.

1. Ephesus (2:1–7): Jesus praised this church for doing some good things, but He also called them to love Him and one another as they once had.
2. Smyrna (2:8–11): This church had little money or possessions, and they were spoken against by the outside world. But Jesus praised the church for their spiritual riches and encouraged them to "remain faithful even when facing death, [and] I will give you the crown of life" (verse 10).
3. Pergamum (2:12–17): Jesus gave this church high marks for remaining true to Him, even though they were treated terribly. But He also warned them to stop compromising when it came to the teaching they accepted.
4. Thyatira (2:18–21): Jesus noticed this church's love, faith, service, and endurance, but He warned them to get rid of the idolatry and sin that had made their way into the church.
5. Sardis (3:1–6): This church was spiritually asleep, and Jesus called them to wake up!
6. Philadelphia (3:7–13): Jesus praised this church for their faithfulness and perseverance—even though they had faced persecution from "Satan's synagogue," people who said they were Jews but were not.
7. Laodicea (3:14–19): Jesus reserved His toughest words for the Laodicean church because they were "'like lukewarm water, neither hot nor cold'" (3:16). Jesus called the Laodiceans to decide what they wanted to be and told them to "be diligent and turn from your indifference" (verse 19).

What's in It for Me?

Revelation 3:14–22 contains Jesus' words to the church in Laodicea. They sound like harsh words for a church that had grown "lukewarm," but they can be an encouragement for you to make sure you approach your Christian faith with the kind of devotion and enthusiasm it deserves.

In the last four verses of Revelation 3, Jesus calls the churches to a closer relationship with Him and promises them, "Those who are victorious will sit with me on my throne, just as I was victorious and sat with my Father on his throne" (3:21).

Power Words

"Look! I stand at the door and knock. If you hear my voice and open the door, I will come in, and we will share a meal together as friends."

REVELATION 3:20

John's Second Vision (Revelation 4-6)

After hearing the message to the seven churches, John received a second vision. This vision began with a door standing open in heaven and a voice—the same voice he had heard before—inviting him to see a throne room of God.

John saw quite a scene in the throne room. He saw a throne on which was seated a figure "as brilliant as gemstones" (4:3). This was Jesus, the Lamb of God, and His throne was surrounded by 24 more thrones, each with an "elder" sitting on it.

There were also four living creatures in the throne room, and each was covered with eyes from front to back. One looked like a lion, one like an ox, one like a human, and one like an eagle. Day after day, these creatures cried out, "Holy, holy, holy is the Lord God, the Almighty—the one who always was, who is, and who is still to come" (4:8).

In this vision, John also saw in the right hand of the one sitting on the main throne a scroll that was sealed with seven seals that no one on earth could open and read. John wept out loud because no one was worthy to open the scrolls, but one of the elders said, "Stop weeping! Look, the Lion of the tribe of Judah, the heir to David's throne, has won the victory. He is worthy to open the scroll and its seven seals" (5:5).

Then John saw a lamb that looked as if it had been slaughtered but was still standing. It had seven horns and seven eyes, and it was the one that could open the scroll. This was the Lamb of God—Jesus—and as He stepped forward to take the scroll, the 24 elders and four living creatures fell down before him and "sang a new song" (5:9).

The Seven Seals (6:1–8:1)

Fun Bible Trivia

The four riders listed in Revelation 6 have been called the Four Horsemen of the Apocalypse, even though that title doesn't appear in the book of Revelation or anywhere else in the Bible.

AS John watched, the Lamb of God broke the seven seals one by one. When He opened the first seal, a rider on a white horse appeared and "rode out to win many battles and gain the victory" (6:2). When the second seal was broken, another horse appeared—a red one this time. On its back was a rider who was given a sword and the authority to remove peace from the earth and bring war everywhere. When the third seal was broken, a rider on a black horse appeared, holding a pair of scales in his hand. The breaking of the fourth seal brought a rider on a green horse. The rider was called Death.

When the Lamb of God opened the fifth seal, John saw the souls of Christians who had been killed on account of their faith. These souls asked God when He would punish the people who had taken their lives. Then white robes were given to each of the martyred souls, and they were told to be patient.

The sixth seal brought a huge earthquake. The sun turned black, the moon was turned as red as blood, and what looked like stars fell to the earth. All the mountains and islands of the earth disappeared. It was such a terrible scene that people hid themselves in caves and rocks and hoped the mountains would fall on them so they could escape God's judgment.

When the seventh seal was broken, John heard complete quiet in heaven for half an hour—which was just a moment of silence before the second set of God's judgments on the earth.

The Seven Trumpets (8:2–11:19)

In John's next vision, he saw seven angels with trumpets. One at a time, the angels blew their trumpets, bringing a new judgment on the earth. The first trumpet brought "hail and fire mixed with blood" on the earth that burned up a third of the trees and grass.

When the second trumpet sounded, something that looked like a huge mountain of fire was thrown into the sea, killing one-third of all the things that lived there and destroying one-third of the ships. The third trumpet brought what looked like a flaming star out of the sky. When it landed, it polluted one-third of the fresh water on the earth, leading to the deaths of many people.

Who, What, Where?

Revelation 9:11 mentions a king who is "the angel from the bottomless pit," named Abaddon in Hebrew and Apollyon in Greek (which means "the Destroyer"). It's not certain who this king is, but some experts believe it is either the Antichrist or the devil himself.

When the fourth angel blew his trumpet, one-third of the sun and moon were struck, and one-third of the stars went dark. Then John looked up and saw an eagle crying, "Terror, terror, terror to all who belong to this world because of what will happen when the last three angels blow their trumpets" (8:13).

When the fifth trumpet was blown, John saw what looked like a star falling from the sky. The star "was given the key to the shaft of the bottomless pit" (9:1). When he opened it, smoke came out and darkened the sunlight and air with smoke. Then locustlike creatures with stingers came from the smoke and began attacking people who "did not have the seal of God on their foreheads" (9:4).

When the sixth trumpet sounded, an army of 200 million mounted troops wiped out one-third of humankind with "fire and smoke and burning sulfur" (9:18). Still, John wrote, "the people who did not die in these plagues still refused to repent of their evil deeds and turn to God" (9:20).

When the seventh angel blew his trumpet, John heard loud praise from heaven. The 24 elders fell on their faces and spoke praises to God, because "it is time to judge the dead and reward your servants" (11:18). There was lightning, thunder, a huge earthquake, and a hailstorm.

The Arrival of the Antichrist (12–14)

Fun Bible Trivia

The book of Revelation doesn't use the name *Antichrist*, and neither did the apostle Paul when he wrote his second letter to the Thessalonians. He wrote that the day of the Lord (Christ's return) would not come "until there is a great rebellion against God and the man of lawlessness is revealed" (2 Thessalonians 2:3).

Chapters 12–14 of Revelation cover the arrival of "the beast," which has also been called the Antichrist. In chapter 12, John first sees a vision of a large red dragon with 7 heads and 10 horns, who was kicked out of heaven. This was the devil himself.

Chapter 13 actually describes two beasts—one with 7 heads and 10 horns that came out of the sea, and one with two horns and the voice of a dragon that came up out of the earth. This beast was allowed to do pretty much anything it wanted for 42 months (three and a half years)—including declaring war on Christians.

The second of these two beasts had all the power of the first beast and required all people to worship the first beast and to take a mark with the name of the beast or his number (666) on their right hand or forehead (see Revelation 13:16–18). Those who didn't receive this mark were not allowed to do any kind of business. This beast is later called "the false prophet."

The Seven Bowls (15:1–18:24)

John's vision of God's final judgment on the earth continues in Revelation 15. This time, seven angels carry the seven final plagues on the earth, which are called "bowls." Here are the seven "bowl judgments" listed in the book of Revelation:

1. Horrible sores break out on those who have received the "mark of the beast" (16:2).
2. The sea turns to blood (16:3).
3. Fresh water turns to blood (16:4–6).
4. People are scorched by intense heat (16:8–9).
5. Darkness and pain afflict humans (16:10–11).
6. The Euphrates River dries up, and armies gather for the Battle of Armageddon (16:12–16).
7. The earth is shaken with the worst earthquake ever—islands disappear and mountains are flattened, 75-pound hailstones fall from the sky, and a place called Babylon is divided into three sections (16:17–21).

Who, What, Where?

The apostle John uses the word *Armageddon* to describe the final conflict between God and the Antichrist. This word actually means "mount of Megiddo." Megiddo was an ancient city in northern Israel along the Kishon River. This is where many experts believe the final battle between good and evil will take place.

The End of Babylon, the Beast, and the Devil Himself (17–20)

After the seventh and final bowl is poured out on the earth, a loud voice declares, "It is finished!" (16:17). Babylon had been split in three pieces, and the cities of many nations had been leveled. Every island had disappeared into the oceans and seas, and the mountains had been leveled.

Who, What, Where?

The book of Revelation tells us that a city called Babylon will be destroyed by God near the end of time. But what is the Babylon mentioned in this book? Many experts believe "Babylon" is a code word for the Roman Empire, which oppressed Christians at the time John wrote Revelation. Whatever Babylon is in Revelation, it seems to stand for everything evil and ungodly in the world.

Power Words

Then I heard again what sounded like the shout of a vast crowd or the roar of mighty ocean waves or the crash of loud thunder: "Praise the LORD! For the Lord our God, the Almighty, reigns. Let us be glad and rejoice, and let us give honor to him. For the time has come for the wedding feast of the Lamb, and his bride has prepared herself."

REVELATION 19:6–7

Fun Bible Trivia

The 1,000 years during which the devil will be tied up in chains and kept in the lake of fire while those who have served Christ will reign on earth is sometimes called the Millennium.

After this vision, one of the seven angels who poured the bowls of judgment out on the earth appeared to John and announced that Babylon would be destroyed and that the leaders of the nations would cry and grieve when they saw the city burning.

In heaven, on the other hand, there would be celebration that Babylon was finished (18:20).

Later in chapter 19, after John listened to an angel announcing the end of Babylon, he heard what sounded like a huge crowd in heaven praising God. As he continued to listen, he saw heaven open and a white horse with a rider named Faithful and True (19:11). The rider's eyes looked like blazing fire, and He had many crowns on His head and wore a robe dipped in blood. On His robe and on His thigh was the name "KING OF KINGS AND LORD OF LORDS" (19:11–16 NIV).

It was Jesus!

At the same time, the beast gathered his armies for the final battle against God and the armies of heaven. But it wasn't much of a battle. "Both the beast and his false prophet were thrown alive into the fiery lake of burning sulfur" (19:20), and their armies were destroyed.

Then John saw an angel come down from heaven and tie Satan up in chains and throw him into the same lake of fire, where he would stay for

1,000 years. During those 1,000 years, those who had died because of their faith in Christ, as well as the people who hadn't worshipped the beast or taken his mark, "reigned with Christ" (20:4).

At the end of the 1,000 years, the devil was released from the lake of fire and immediately began deceiving people. He gathered an army and surrounded God's people, but he was then thrown into the lake of fire, where he, the beast, and the false prophet would stay forever.

With the devil taken care of for good, everyone who had died before was judged before a "great white throne" (20:11). They were judged for the things they had done when they were alive, and everyone whose name was not found in the Book of Life was thrown into the lake of fire.

A Peek at Heaven (21–22)

The book of Revelation describes some pretty scary visions of judgment on the earth after the people had turned their backs on God. But we can be grateful that the story doesn't leave off there. As terrible as some of these events might seem, what you're about to read makes reading the scary stuff worth it.

The last two chapters of Revelation record John's visions of what is ahead for people who have put their faith in Jesus. Even though chapters 4–20 are very hard to understand, the remaining two chapters of Revelation spell things out so that they are easy to grasp.

These chapters cover how things will one day turn out for you and everyone else who knows Jesus. And it's something you can look forward to!

In with the New

After seeing the devil and death being done away with, John saw in his vision "a new heaven and a new earth, for the old heaven and the old earth had disappeared" (21:1). The sea was also gone, and John saw a "new Jerusalem" coming down from God out of heaven, "like a bride beautifully dressed for her husband" (21:2).

John then heard a voice saying, "God's dwelling palce is now among the people, and he will dwell with them. They will be his people, and God himself will be with them and be their God. He will wipe every tear from their eyes. There will be no more death or mourning or crying or pain, for the old order of things has passed away" (21:3–4 NIV).

Power Words

"Look, I am coming soon, bringing my reward with me to repay all people according to their deeds. I am the Alpha and the Omega, the First and the Last, the Beginning and the End."

REVELATION 22:12–13

But that wasn't all. John heard that same voice saying, "I am making everything new! . . . Write this down, for what I tell you is trustworthy and true. . . . It is finished! I am the Alpha and the Omega—the Beginning and the End. To all who are thirsty I will give freely from the springs of the water of life. All who are victorious will inherit all these blessings, and I will be their God, and they will be my children" (21:5–7).

An angel then showed John the new Jerusalem, an amazing structure where there was no need for a sun or moon because God and His Son provided the light. A river flowed down the city's main street, and on each side of the street was the tree of life, which produced 12 different kinds of fruit—one for each month of the year.

It was from this place that God and His people would rule "forever and ever" (22:5). Nothing would be cursed any longer; God's throne and Jesus' throne would be there, and His servants would worship Him.

The last 14 verses of Revelation—and of the Bible—include Jesus' promise, "I am coming soon" (22:7, 12, 20).

CHAPTER 10

Why You Should Read the Bible for Yourself. . . and How to Do It!

Throughout this book, you've seen little sidebars titled "What's in It for Me?" Those features were included to give you some ideas about what you can get out of certain portions of the Bible.

As you think about reading the Bible yourself, you might be wondering, *What's in it for me?* Lots of things! In fact, you should know that God wants you to desire to know the Bible more today than you did yesterday.

Here are five good reasons you should make reading the Bible a part of your life every day:

1. You can learn about God Himself. The Bible is filled to the brim with the things God has said, the things He has done, and the ways He has related to His people. When you read about those things, you get a good idea of what God is really like—what kind of person He is!

Do you want to know what makes God happy and what makes Him unhappy? Do you want to know what kinds of things people have done that make Him angry? Do you want to know what kind of love He has for you? There's no better way to learn these things than by opening up your Bible and reading what God has done and said.

> **Power Words**
>
> *For the word of God is alive and powerful. It is sharper than the sharpest two-edged sword, cutting between soul and spirit, between joint and marrow. It exposes our innermost thoughts and desires.*
>
> HEBREWS 4:12

2. You can learn what it takes to have a strong and growing relationship with God. When you became a Christian, God didn't just look down at you and say, "Great! Now you're the kind of person I want you to be! Now you can just wait around until it's time to go to heaven!"

No, when you became a Christian, that was just the beginning of the work God wants to do in you. That's what the apostle Paul meant when he wrote, "I am certain that God, who began the good work within you, will continue his work until it is finally finished on the day when Christ Jesus returns" (Philippians 1:6).

Growing in your relationship with God doesn't just happen on its own, any more than your body grows on its own. Just as your body requires proper nourishment and exercise to grow bigger and stronger, your relationship with God requires nourishment and exercise to grow bigger and stronger. And where do you get that nourishment? From the pages of your Bible!

3. You can learn how to be more and more like Jesus. The Bible teaches that our goal as Christians is to become more and more like Jesus every day. That means you should be more like Him tomorrow than you were today—and a lot more like Him next year than you are right now.

Jesus is your perfect example of how to live, how to think, how to love God, and how to treat other people. And the more you're like Him in every way, the more you please God, and the more you let people around you see how amazing He really is!

Okay, so now that you know that God wants you to be more and more like Jesus every day, the question is, how can you learn what Jesus was like? By reading the Bible! You can see what Jesus was really like—how He thought, prayed, lived, and cared for others—by reading the books of the Bible called the Gospels. Remember where they are? If not, turn back in this book to chapter 6 for a quick reminder.

But you don't need to stop at just the Gospels. Remember, Jesus was God in human form, and everything God the Father says, does, and thinks, Jesus says, does, and thinks right along with Him. So you can learn to be more like Jesus by reading from the entire Bible!

Power Words

All Scripture is inspired by God and is useful to teach us what is true and to make us realize what is wrong in our lives. It corrects us when we are wrong and teaches us to do what is right.

2 Timothy 3:16

4. You can learn how God wants you to live. Someone once said that being a Christian isn't about following a bunch of rules; it's about having a real, personal relationship with God through Jesus Christ.

How true that is!

At the same time, though, the Bible includes a lot of really important commands, encouragements, promises, and guidelines for living the Christian life. So if you want to know how God wants you to live, go straight to the source for His instructions: the Bible!

You almost can't open your Bible without finding some of God's commands, encouragements, promises, and guidelines for life. So when you read your Bible, pay close attention to things God might want you to focus on. Hint: Pay *really* close attention when you're reading books like Proverbs, the Gospels, and the New Testament epistles (Romans through Jude).

5. You can learn how God wants you to treat other people. More than anything, the Bible is about how to have a relationship with God. But it also has a lot to say about how to treat other people, especially other Christians.

If there is one statement that tells us how we are to treat others, it is Jesus' words to His disciples just before His death on the cross: "A new command I give you: Love one another" (John 13:34 NIV). The apostle John, who recorded those words from Jesus, also wrote, "Dear friends, let us love one another, for love comes from God" (1 John 4:7 NIV).

But what does it mean for us to love one another? Should we just have warm, fuzzy feelings for other people? Should we just tell people that we love them and let that be good enough? No! The Bible teaches that we show our love through our words and also through our actions.

You can find great guidelines for how to treat people with God's love in many places in the Bible. If you want a good place to start, read Jesus' teaching—and pay close attention to the Sermon on the Mount (Matthew 5–7). You can also find some great guidelines for how to treat others by reading the book of Proverbs and the New Testament epistles.

Show love for one another with your actions.

Now for the "Hows" of Bible Reading and Study

Okay, now you have a pretty good idea of *why* you should read the Bible. But if you're like most Christians, you are probably wondering *how* to do it. If you're not sure about the best way to approach reading and studying the Bible, don't feel bad. Just realize that there are a lot of really good ways to read the Bible so that you can get the very most out of it.

First is the most obvious way: reading it cover to cover, starting with Genesis 1 and ending with Revelation 22. The best thing about reading the Bible from beginning to end is that you get a good idea of the order in which things happened (keeping in mind that the Old Testament prophecy books were written during different times in Israel's history).

It's a good idea for any Christian to read the Bible all the way through at least once. And it's not as hard as you might think, especially since there are so many prepared schedules you can use to get it done in one year. (See appendix A for a one-year Bible-reading schedule.)

But reading through the Bible in a year—or in less time if you're a fast reader—is only the beginning. And truthfully, if you want to get the most out of your Bible reading, it's a good idea to do it in ways other than just cover to cover.

Don't Just Read. . .Study!

Have you ever read something—part of one of your school textbooks, for example—only to forget what you read five minutes later? Some people have a talent for remembering everything they read, but most of us need to put in some extra effort to remember what we read.

That extra effort is called studying. Studying means not just to read something, but to read it over again, think about what you've read, and try to learn as much as you can from what you've read.

The Bible is a great book to study—by yourself, with your family, with your friends. And just as there are all kinds of settings to study the Bible in, there are also all kinds of ways to do it.

Here are some great ways to study your Bible:

Studying In a Certain Book

One of the things you've learned in reading this book—we hope—is that each book of the Bible has its own writer, its own story, its own background, and its own topics and ideas. Obviously, there's no better way to find out those things about a certain book of the Bible than by reading and studying it yourself.

That's where a book like this one can come in really handy. When you decide you want to read and study a book of the Bible, you can look up *that* book in *this* book to learn the basics.

For example, if you want to read and study the Gospel of Matthew, you can take a look at what this book has to tell you about that particular Gospel. You'll learn that it was written by a man named Matthew, that it was originally written to Jewish people, and that it has a lot to say about how Jesus fulfilled Old Testament prophecies about the coming Messiah.

You'll be amazed at just how much knowing things like that will help you as you prepare to read and study a certain book of the Bible. Go ahead and try it!

Studying a Certain Word

Are there words from the Bible you have heard but don't know exactly what they mean—at least what they mean in the Bible? Do you know what the word *grace* means? How about *mercy* or *pardon*? You can learn what the Bible means when it uses those words when you read and study the Bible using key words that appear in the different books.

To do this kind of study, all you need is your Bible and a concordance, a reference book that lists the different words used in the Bible and tells you where you can find them. If you don't have a concordance, then you can use one of several online concordances available on the internet.

When you study the Bible this way, try using different forms of different words—for example, when you want to study God's forgiveness, take the time to look up the words *forgive*, *forgiving*, and *forgiven*. You can also look up different words that mean the same thing (these words are called synonyms). That way, you'll get a better idea of what those words mean in the Bible.

Some good words to start with are *love, grace, mercy, pardon*, and *forgiveness*—simply because these words are so much a part of God's character.

What's in It for Me?

If you want to get the absolute most you can out of your Bible study, it's a good idea to have at least some of these tools to help you out:

Bible: This might seen too obvious to mention, but which Bible you choose will go a long way in determining how much you learn in your Bible study. Choose a translation that is easy for you to understand, and you'll get a lot more out of your Bible study.

Dictionary: A good dictionary is always handy to have when you're studying anything, including the Bible. When you see a word you don't know, you can look it up in your dictionary to see what it means.

Bible Dictionary: There are a lot of good Bible dictionaries out there to help you with your study. You can even find good ones on the internet. A Bible dictionary will explain what certain words and ideas mean in the Bible.

Concordance: Remember, this is a book made up of an alphabetical list of all Bible words.

Bible Commentary: There are a lot of great Bible commentaries written by people who know the Bible cover to cover. A Bible commentary can help you gain insights when you study. You can find good Bible commentaries online, at your library, or at the local bookstore.

Bible Atlas: An atlas is a book of maps that will help you understand where the Bible stories you read took place. It can also help you to understand more about the stories and other passages you read.

Pencil and Paper: Bible study time is a good time to take some notes!

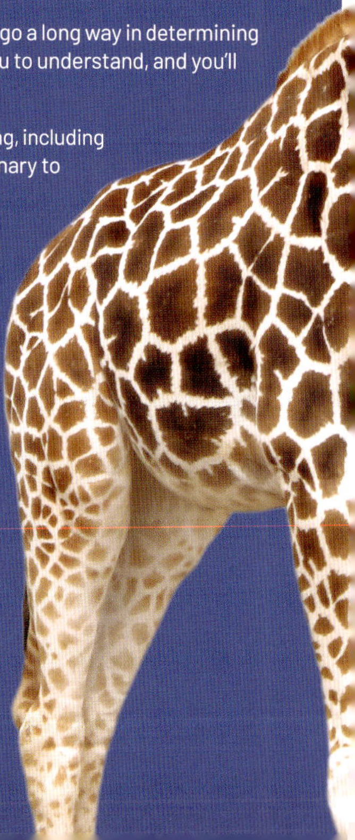

Studying a Certain Subject

If your teacher were to give you an assignment to write a report about a certain animal—let's say a giraffe—how would you research giraffes so that you could write a good report? You probably wouldn't check out a library book about animals that live in Africa and start reading it cover to cover, would you? More than likely, you'd check out that same book and go directly to the section about giraffes. That would save you a lot of time and also allow you to learn more about giraffes because you had spent some time learning all you could about them.

You can study your Bible the same way. Let's say you want to study what the Bible has to say about the subject of God's forgiveness. You'd look up verses and passages in both the Old Testament and the New Testament that had to do with God's forgiveness. Then you would focus on what those verses and passages said, how they were the same or different, and how they applied to you.

By the time you were done doing this kind of study, you'd have a pretty good idea of what God says about any subject you chose.

Studying a Certain Passage (Section)

The Bible is filled with some amazing sections—sometimes called passages—with some great lessons for you today. Another great way to read and study the Bible is to concentrate on one of those sections and see what God is saying to you through it.

As you study a passage of the Bible, pay close attention to the things people do and say, as well as what happened as a result. Don't forget to notice how God responds to the things that people do and say.

There are literally hundreds of great Bible passages to study and learn from. Here are just a few to help you get started with your own study of the Bible:

Genesis 1-2—The creation of the universe, the earth, and humans

Genesis 6:9-8:22—Noah and the flood

Joshua 1—God's instructions and encouragement for Joshua

1 Samuel 17:12-54—David's battle with the giant Goliath

Psalm 1—The blessed man

Daniel 6—The prophet Daniel in the lions' den

Luke 2:1-20—The birth of Jesus

Matthew 5-7—Jesus' Sermon on the Mount

Acts 2—The believers in Jerusalem receive the Holy Spirit

1 Corinthians 13—The "love chapter"

Hebrews 11—Great biblical examples of faith

Studying Certain People, Places, and Things

Who, What, Where?

Do you want a good list to start with as you study the lives of important people in the Bible? Try these names first: Adam and Eve, Noah, Abraham, Joseph, Moses, Joshua, David, Solomon, Jesus (of course!), Peter, the apostle John, and the apostle Paul. Of course, there are hundreds of other people you can study, but this list gives you a good place to start.

The Bible has many examples of how God deals with people—with His own people as well as with people who do not know Him. Another great way to study the Bible is to focus on the people, places, and events of the Bible.

Who are some of the people from the Bible you want to know more about? Adam and Eve? Moses? Joshua? David? Jesus and His disciples? The apostle Paul? Take the time to read all you can about these people (it never hurts to use a Bible dictionary or encyclopedia to help you along), and as you read, pay close attention to their lives—the things they did right, the things they did wrong, and the way God responded to them.

When you focus your attention on a personality from the Bible and learn all you can about him or her, you will find that person's story is filled with great lessons for your own life.

One quick note: When you start a study on a certain person in the Bible, make sure you aren't reading about two or more different people who went by the same name. That's easier to do than you might think. There are 28 men in the Bible named Azariah, 27 named Zechariah, and 25 named Shemaiah. Altogether, there are 23 names connected with 10 or more people.

As for studying places and things, you can apply the same steps you would use if you were studying a person.

Other Things You Can Do with the Bible

Of course, reading and studying your Bible are things God wants you to do. But did you know you can take your reading and studying to another level—or two or three?

As this book draws to a finish, we want you to think about some of the things you can use the Bible for. Some of them might surprise you!

Memorize Bible Verses

Have you ever met someone who seemed to have the ability to quote Bible verses off the top of his or her head? Or maybe noticed that the pastor or teachers at your church can quote verses without looking them up?

Those things don't just happen. Usually, people who can quote Bible passages have spent time memorizing some of the more important verses. It's not as hard as it sounds. All it takes is a little repetition, a little time, and some effort.

What are some of the benefits of memorizing Bible verses? Suppose you had a friend who wanted to know more about your Christian faith. Of course you can tell that person what God has done for you, but when you can remember some important passages from the Bible, you can better explain what the Bible says about becoming a Christian.

Power Words

I have hidden your word in my heart, that I might not sin against you.

Psalm 119:11

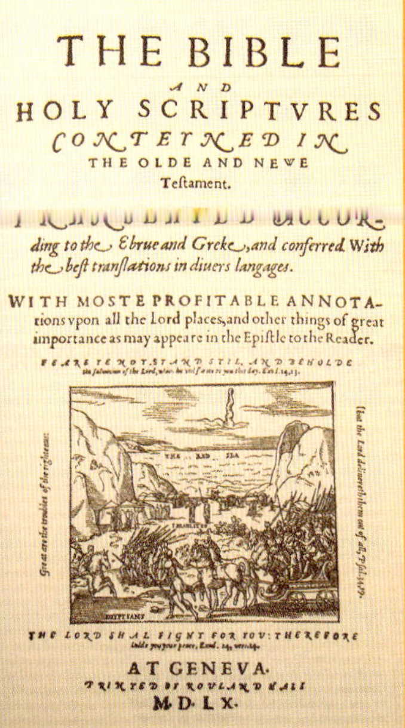
THE BIBLE
AND
HOLY SCRIPTVRES
CONTEYNED IN
THE OLDE AND NEWE
Testament.
TRANSLATED ACCOR-
ding to the Ebrue and Greke, and conferred With the best translations in diuers langages.
WITH MOSTE PROFITABLE ANNOTA-
tions vpon all the hard places, and other things of great importance as may appeare in the Epistle to the Reader.
FEARE YE NOT, STAND STIL, AND BEHOLDE
THE LORD SHAL FIGHT FOR YOU: THEREFORE
AT GENEVA.
PRINTED BY ROVLAND HALL
M.D.LX.

One of the best ways to memorize Bible verses is to simply read them over and over until they are recorded in your memory. And it really helps when you follow these basic Bible memorization steps:

- Pick out a Bible version you like and can most easily understand.
- Pick out the verse or verses you want to memorize.
- Don't try to memorize too much at once.
- Write the verse or verses down. Use flash cards if that helps.
- Work with a friend or family member.

One last thing: It's good to memorize the words of different Bible verses, but it's also really helpful to memorize where they are in the Bible. That means you should also memorize the book, the chapter, and the verse where you found the words you have memorized.

Take It Personally!

Have you ever thought of the words recorded in your Bible as God's personal message to you? Well, you can, because that's exactly what they are! God made sure that every important word, thought, promise, command, and warning made it into the pages of your Bible, and He did that just for you.

One of the best ways to really personalize the Bible is to read a particular passage or verse and then write it down using words like *I* and *me* when the Bible says "you." For example, you can write down Philippians 4:19, which says, "My God shall supply all your need according to His riches in glory by Christ Jesus" (NKJV), like this:

> My God shall supply all MY needs according to His riches in glory by Christ Jesus!

When you read and study the Bible that way, you'll understand more and more every day that the Bible is a book written just for you.

And you'll also see how cool a book it really is.

Did You Know. . . ?

In 1560, the Geneva Bible was printed. It was the first English Bible with a feature that makes Bible memorization easier today: chapter and verse divisions. Three years before that, an Englishman named William Whittingham produced the first English-language New Testament with verse divisions.

APPENDIX A

Through the Bible in a Year

A 365-Day Bible-Reading Schedule

Start your own Bible adventure—read through the whole Bible in a year. It'll only take you about 20 minutes a day!

Day			
Day 1	Genesis 1–2	Matthew 1	Psalm 1
Day 2	Genesis 3–4	Matthew 2	Psalm 2
Day 3	Genesis 5–7	Matthew 3	Psalm 3
Day 4	Genesis 8–10	Matthew 4	Psalm 4
Day 5	Genesis 11–13	Matthew 5:1–20	Psalm 5
Day 6	Genesis 14–16	Matthew 5:21–48	Psalm 6
Day 7	Genesis 17–18	Matthew 6:1–18	Psalm 7
Day 8	Genesis 19–20	Matthew 6:19–34	Psalm 8
Day 9	Genesis 21–23	Matthew 7:1–11	Psalm 9:1–8
Day 10	Genesis 24	Matthew 7:12–29	Psalm 9:9–20
Day 11	Genesis 25–26	Matthew 8:1–17	Psalm 10:1–11
Day 12	Genesis 27:1–28:9	Matthew 8:18–34	Psalm 10:12–18
Day 13	Genesis 28:10–29:35	Matthew 9	Psalm 11
Day 14	Genesis 30:1–31:21	Matthew 10:1–15	Psalm 12
Day 15	Genesis 31:22–32:21	Matthew 10:16–36	Psalm 13
Day 16	Genesis 32:22–34:31	Matthew 10:37–11:6	Psalm 14
Day 17	Genesis 35–36	Matthew 11:7–24	Psalm 15
Day 18	Genesis 37–38	Matthew 11:25–30	Psalm 16
Day 19	Genesis 39–40	Matthew 12:1–29	Psalm 17
Day 20	Genesis 41	Matthew 12:30–50	Psalm 18:1–15
Day 21	Genesis 42–43	Matthew 13:1–9	Psalm 18:16–29
Day 22	Genesis 44–45	Matthew 13:10–23	Psalm 18:30–50

Day 23	Genesis 46:1–47:26	Matthew 13:24–43	Psalm 19
Day 24	Genesis 47:27–49:28	Matthew 13:44–58	Psalm 20
Day 25	Genesis 49:29–Exodus 1:22	Matthew 14	Psalm 21
Day 26	Exodus 2–3	Matthew 15:1–28	Psalm 22:1–21
Day 27	Exodus 4:1–5:21	Matthew 15:29–16:12	Psalm 22:22–31
Day 28	Exodus 5:22–7:24	Matthew 16:13–28	Psalm 23
Day 29	Exodus 7:25–9:35	Matthew 17:1–9	Psalm 24
Day 30	Exodus 10–11	Matthew 17:10–27	Psalm 25
Day 31	Exodus 12	Matthew 18:1–20	Psalm 26
Day 32	Exodus 13–14	Matthew 18:21–35	Psalm 27
Day 33	Exodus 15–16	Matthew 19:1–15	Psalm 28
Day 34	Exodus 17–19	Matthew 19:16–30	Psalm 29
Day 35	Exodus 20–21	Matthew 20:1–19	Psalm 30
Day 36	Exodus 22–23	Matthew 20:20–34	Psalm 31:1–8
Day 37	Exodus 24–25	Matthew 21:1–27	Psalm 31:9–18
Day 38	Exodus 26–27	Matthew 21:28–46	Psalm 31:19–24
Day 39	Exodus 28	Matthew 22	Psalm 32
Day 40	Exodus 29	Matthew 23:1–36	Psalm 33:1–12
Day 41	Exodus 30–31	Matthew 23:37–24:28	Psalm 33:13–22
Day 42	Exodus 32–33	Matthew 24:29–51	Psalm 34:1–7
Day 43	Exodus 34:1–35:29	Matthew 25:1–13	Psalm 34:8–22
Day 44	Exodus 35:30–37:29	Matthew 25:14–30	Psalm 35:1–8
Day 45	Exodus 38–39	Matthew 25:31–46	Psalm 35:9–17
Day 46	Exodus 40	Matthew 26:1–35	Psalm 35:18–28
Day 47	Leviticus 1–3	Matthew 26:36–68	Psalm 36:1–6
Day 48	Leviticus 4:1–5:13	Matthew 26:69–27:26	Psalm 36:7–12
Day 49	Leviticus 5:14–7:21	Matthew 27:27–50	Psalm 37:1–6
Day 50	Leviticus 7:22–8:36	Matthew 27:51–66	Psalm 37:7–26
Day 51	Leviticus 9–10	Matthew 28	Psalm 37:27–40
Day 52	Leviticus 11–12	Mark 1:1–28	Psalm 38
Day 53	Leviticus 13	Mark 1:29–39	Psalm 39
Day 54	Leviticus 14	Mark 1:40–2:12	Psalm 40:1–8
Day 55	Leviticus 15	Mark 2:13–3:35	Psalm 40:9–17
Day 56	Leviticus 16–17	Mark 4:1–20	Psalm 41:1–4
Day 57	Leviticus 18–19	Mark 4:21–41	Psalm 41:5–13

Day 58	Leviticus 20	Mark 5	Psalm 42–43
Day 59	Leviticus 21–22	Mark 6:1–13	Psalm 44
Day 60	Leviticus 23–24	Mark 6:14–29	Psalm 45:1–5
Day 61	Leviticus 25	Mark 6:30–56	Psalm 45:6–12
Day 62	Leviticus 26	Mark 7	Psalm 45:13–17
Day 63	Leviticus 27	Mark 8	Psalm 46
Day 64	Numbers 1–2	Mark 9:1–13	Psalm 47
Day 65	Numbers 3	Mark 9:14–50	Psalm 48:1–8
Day 66	Numbers 4	Mark 10:1–34	Psalm 48:9–14
Day 67	Numbers 5:1–6:21	Mark 10:35–52	Psalm 49:1–9
Day 68	Numbers 6:22–7:47	Mark 11	Psalm 49:10–20
Day 69	Numbers 7:48–8:4	Mark 12:1–27	Psalm 50:1–15
Day 70	Numbers 8:5–9:23	Mark 12:28–44	Psalm 50:16–23
Day 71	Numbers 10–11	Mark 13:1–8	Psalm 51:1–9
Day 72	Numbers 12–13	Mark 13:9–37	Psalm 51:10–19
Day 73	Numbers 14	Mark 14:1–31	Psalm 52
Day 74	Numbers 15	Mark 14:32–72	Psalm 53
Day 75	Numbers 16	Mark 15:1–32	Psalm 54
Day 76	Numbers 17–18	Mark 15:33–47	Psalm 55
Day 77	Numbers 19–20	Mark 16	Psalm 56:1–7
Day 78	Numbers 21:1–22:20	Luke 1:1–25	Psalm 56:8–13
Day 79	Numbers 22:21–23:30	Luke 1:26–56	Psalm 57
Day 80	Numbers 24–25	Luke 1:57–2:20	Psalm 58
Day 81	Numbers 26:1–27:11	Luke 2:21–38	Psalm 59:1–8
Day 82	Numbers 27:12–29:11	Luke 2:39–52	Psalm 59:9–17
Day 83	Numbers 29:12–30:16	Luke 3	Psalm 60:1–5
Day 84	Numbers 31	Luke 4	Psalm 60:6–12
Day 85	Numbers 32–33	Luke 5:1–16	Psalm 61
Day 86	Numbers 34–36	Luke 5:17–32	Psalm 62:1–6
Day 87	Deuteronomy 1:1–2:25	Luke 5:33–6:11	Psalm 62:7–12
Day 88	Deuteronomy 2:26–4:14	Luke 6:12–35	Psalm 63:1–5
Day 89	Deuteronomy 4:15–5:22	Luke 6:36–49	Psalm 63:6–11
Day 90	Deuteronomy 5:23–7:26	Luke 7:1–17	Psalm 64:1–5
Day 91	Deuteronomy 8–9	Luke 7:18–35	Psalm 64:6–10
Day 92	Deuteronomy 10–11	Luke 7:36–8:3	Psalm 65:1–8

Day 93	Deuteronomy 12–13	Luke 8:4–21	Psalm 65:9–13
Day 94	Deuteronomy 14:1–16:8	Luke 8:22–39	Psalm 66:1–7
Day 95	Deuteronomy 16:9–18:22	Luke 8:40–56	Psalm 66:8–15
Day 96	Deuteronomy 19:1–21:9	Luke 9:1–22	Psalm 66:16–20
Day 97	Deuteronomy 21:10–23:8	Luke 9:23–42	Psalm 67
Day 98	Deuteronomy 23:9–25:19	Luke 9:43–62	Psalm 68:1–6
Day 99	Deuteronomy 26:1–28:14	Luke 10:1–20	Psalm 68:7–14
Day 100	Deuteronomy 28:15–68	Luke 10:21–37	Psalm 68:15–19
Day 101	Deuteronomy 29–30	Luke 10:38–11:23	Psalm 68:20–27
Day 102	Deuteronomy 31:1–32:22	Luke 11:24–36	Psalm 68:28–35
Day 103	Deuteronomy 32:23–33:29	Luke 11:37–54	Psalm 69:1–9
Day 104	Deuteronomy 34–Joshua 2	Luke 12:1–15	Psalm 69:10–17
Day 105	Joshua 3:1–5:12	Luke 12:16–40	Psalm 69:18–28
Day 106	Joshua 5:13–7:26	Luke 12:41–48	Psalm 69:29–36
Day 107	Joshua 8–9	Luke 12:49–59	Psalm 70
Day 108	Joshua 10:1–11:15	Luke 13:1–21	Psalm 71:1–6
Day 109	Joshua 11:16–13:33	Luke 13:22–35	Psalm 71:7–16
Day 110	Joshua 14–16	Luke 14:1–15	Psalm 71:17–21
Day 111	Joshua 17:1–19:16	Luke 14:16–35	Psalm 71:22–24
Day 112	Joshua 19:17–21:42	Luke 15:1–10	Psalm 72:1–11
Day 113	Joshua 21:43–22:34	Luke 15:11–32	Psalm 72:12–20
Day 114	Joshua 23–24	Luke 16:1–18	Psalm 73:1–9
Day 115	Judges 1–2	Luke 16:19–17:10	Psalm 73:10–20
Day 116	Judges 3–4	Luke 17:11–37	Psalm 73:21–28
Day 117	Judges 5:1–6:24	Luke 18:1–17	Psalm 74:1–3
Day 118	Judges 6:25–7:25	Luke 18:18–43	Psalm 74:4–11
Day 119	Judges 8:1–9:23	Luke 19:1–28	Psalm 74:12–17
Day 120	Judges 9:24–10:18	Luke 19:29–48	Psalm 74:18–23
Day 121	Judges 11:1–12:7	Luke 20:1–26	Psalm 75:1–7
Day 122	Judges 12:8–14:20	Luke 20:27–47	Psalm 75:8–10
Day 123	Judges 15–16	Luke 21:1–19	Psalm 76:1–7
Day 124	Judges 17–18	Luke 21:20–22:6	Psalm 76:8–12
Day 125	Judges 19:1–20:23	Luke 22:7–30	Psalm 77:1–11
Day 126	Judges 20:24–21:25	Luke 22:31–54	Psalm 77:12–20
Day 127	Ruth 1–2	Luke 22:55–23:25	Psalm 78:1–4

Day 128	Ruth 3–4	Luke 23:26–24:12	Psalm 78:5–8
Day 129	1 Samuel 1:1–2:21	Luke 24:13–53	Psalm 78:9–16
Day 130	1 Samuel 2:22–4:22	John 1:1–28	Psalm 78:17–24
Day 131	1 Samuel 5–7	John 1:29–51	Psalm 78:25–33
Day 132	1 Samuel 8:1–9:26	John 2	Psalm 78:34–41
Day 133	1 Samuel 9:27–11:15	John 3:1–22	Psalm 78:42–55
Day 134	1 Samuel 12–13	John 3:23–4:10	Psalm 78:56–66
Day 135	1 Samuel 14	John 4:11–38	Psalm 78:67–72
Day 136	1 Samuel 15–16	John 4:39–54	Psalm 79:1–7
Day 137	1 Samuel 17	John 5:1–24	Psalm 79:8–13
Day 138	1 Samuel 18–19	John 5:25–47	Psalm 80:1–7
Day 139	1 Samuel 20–21	John 6:1–21	Psalm 80:8–19
Day 140	1 Samuel 22–23	John 6:22–42	Psalm 81:1–10
Day 141	1 Samuel 24:1–25:31	John 6:43–71	Psalm 81:11–16
Day 142	1 Samuel 25:32–27:12	John 7:1–24	Psalm 82
Day 143	1 Samuel 28–29	John 7:25–8:11	Psalm 83
Day 144	1 Samuel 30–31	John 8:12–47	Psalm 84:1–4
Day 145	2 Samuel 1–2	John 8:48–9:12	Psalm 84:5–12
Day 146	2 Samuel 3–4	John 9:13–34	Psalm 85:1–7
Day 147	2 Samuel 5:1–7:17	John 9:35–10:10	Psalm 85:8–13
Day 148	2 Samuel 7:18–10:19	John 10:11–30	Psalm 86:1–10
Day 149	2 Samuel 11:1–12:25	John 10:31–11:16	Psalm 86:11–17
Day 150	2 Samuel 12:26–13:39	John 11:17–54	Psalm 87
Day 151	2 Samuel 14:1–15:12	John 11:55–12:19	Psalm 88:1–9
Day 152	2 Samuel 15:13–16:23	John 12:20–43	Psalm 88:10–18
Day 153	2 Samuel 17:1–18:18	John 12:44–13:20	Psalm 89:1–6
Day 154	2 Samuel 18:19–19:39	John 13:21–38	Psalm 89:7–13
Day 155	2 Samuel 19:40–21:22	John 14:1–17	Psalm 89:14–18
Day 156	2 Samuel 22:1–23:7	John 14:18–15:27	Psalm 89:19–29
Day 157	2 Samuel 23:8–24:25	John 16:1–22	Psalm 89:30–37
Day 158	1 Kings 1	John 16:23–17:5	Psalm 89:38–52
Day 159	1 Kings 2	John 17:6–26	Psalm 90:1–12
Day 160	1 Kings 3–4	John 18:1–27	Psalm 90:13–17
Day 161	1 Kings 5–6	John 18:28–19:5	Psalm 91:1–10
Day 162	1 Kings 7	John 19:6–25a	Psalm 91:11–16

Day 163 1 Kings 8:1–53 John 19:25b–42 Psalm 92:1–9

Day 164 1 Kings 8:54–10:13 John 20:1–18 Psalm 92:10–15

Day 165 1 Kings 10:14–11:43 John 20:19–31 Psalm 93

Day 166 1 Kings 12:1–13:10 John 21 Psalm 94:1–11

Day 167 1 Kings 13:11–14:31 Acts 1:1–11 Psalm 94:12–23

Day 168 1 Kings 15:1–16:20 Acts 1:12–26 Psalm 95

Day 169 1 Kings 16:21–18:19 Acts 2:1–21 Psalm 96:1–8

Day 170 1 Kings 18:20–19:21 Acts 2:22–41 Psalm 96:9–13

Day 171 1 Kings 20 Acts 2:42–3:26 Psalm 97:1–6

Day 172 1 Kings 21:1–22:28 Acts 4:1–22 Psalm 97:7–12

Day 173 1 Kings 22:29–2 Kings 1:18 Acts 4:23–5:11 Psalm 98

Day 174 2 Kings 2–3 Acts 5:12–28 Psalm 99

Day 175 2 Kings 4 Acts 5:29–6:15 Psalm 100

Day 176 2 Kings 5:1–6:23 Acts 7:1–16 Psalm 101

Day 177 2 Kings 6:24–8:15 Acts 7:17–36 Psalm 102:1–7

Day 178 2 Kings 8:16–9:37 Acts 7:37–53 Psalm 102:8–17

Day 179 2 Kings 10–11 Acts 7:54–8:8 Psalm 102:18–28

Day 180 2 Kings 12–13 Acts 8:9–40 Psalm 103:1–9

Day 181 2 Kings 14–15 Acts 9:1–16 Psalm 103:10–14

Day 182 2 Kings 16–17 Acts 9:17–31 Psalm 103:15–22

Day 183 2 Kings 18:1–19:7 Acts 9:32–10:16 Psalm 104:1–9

Day 184 2 Kings 19:8–20:21 Acts 10:17–33 Psalm 104:10–23

Day 185 2 Kings 21–22 Acts 10:34–11:18 Psalm 104:24–30

Day 186 2 Kings 23 Acts 11:19–12:17 Psalm 104:31–35

Day 187 2 Kings 24–25 Acts 12:18–13:13 Psalm 105:1–7

Day 188 1 Chronicles 1–2 Acts 13:14–43 Psalm 105:8–15

Day 189 1 Chronicles 3:1–5:10 Acts 13:44–14:10 Psalm 105:16–28

Day 190 1 Chronicles 5:11–6:81 Acts 14:11–28 Psalm 105:29–36

Day 191 1 Chronicles 7:1–9:9 Acts 15:1–18 Psalm 105:37–45

Day 192 1 Chronicles 9:10–11:9 Acts 15:19–41 Psalm 106:1–12

Day 193 1 Chronicles 11:10–12:40 Acts 16:1–15 Psalm 106:13–27

Day 194 1 Chronicles 13–15 Acts 16:16–40 Psalm 106:28–33

Day 195 1 Chronicles 16–17 Acts 17:1–14 Psalm 106:34–43

Day 196 1 Chronicles 18–20 Acts 17:15–34 Psalm 106:44–48

Day 197 1 Chronicles 21–22 Acts 18:1–23 Psalm 107:1–9

Day 198	1 Chronicles 23–25	Acts 18:24–19:10	Psalm 107:10–16
Day 199	1 Chronicles 26–27	Acts 19:11–22	Psalm 107:17–32
Day 200	1 Chronicles 28–29	Acts 19:23–41	Psalm 107:33–38
Day 201	2 Chronicles 1–3	Acts 20:1–16	Psalm 107:39–43
Day 202	2 Chronicles 4:1–6:11	Acts 20:17–38	Psalm 108
Day 203	2 Chronicles 6:12–7:10	Acts 21:1–14	Psalm 109:1–20
Day 204	2 Chronicles 7:11–9:28	Acts 21:15–32	Psalm 109:21–31
Day 205	2 Chronicles 9:29–12:16	Acts 21:33–22:16	Psalm 110:1–3
Day 206	2 Chronicles 13–15	Acts 22:17–23:11	Psalm 110:4–7
Day 207	2 Chronicles 16–17	Acts 23:12–24:21	Psalm 111
Day 208	2 Chronicles 18–19	Acts 24:22–25:12	Psalm 112
Day 209	2 Chronicles 20–21	Acts 25:13–27	Psalm 113
Day 210	2 Chronicles 22–23	Acts 26	Psalm 114
Day 211	2 Chronicles 24:1–25:16	Acts 27:1–20	Psalm 115:1–10
Day 212	2 Chronicles 25:17–27:9	Acts 27:21–28:6	Psalm 115:11–18
Day 213	2 Chronicles 28:1–29:19	Acts 28:7–31	Psalm 116:1–5
Day 214	2 Chronicles 29:20–30:27	Romans 1:1–17	Psalm 116:6–19
Day 215	2 Chronicles 31–32	Romans 1:18–32	Psalm 117
Day 216	2 Chronicles 33:1–34:7	Romans 2	Psalm 118:1–18
Day 217	2 Chronicles 34:8–35:19	Romans 3:1–26	Psalm 118:19–23
Day 218	2 Chronicles 35:20–36:23	Romans 3:27–4:25	Psalm 118:24–29
Day 219	Ezra 1–3	Romans 5	Psalm 119:1–8
Day 220	Ezra 4–5	Romans 6:1–7:6	Psalm 119:9–16
Day 221	Ezra 6:1–7:26	Romans 7:7–25	Psalm 119:17–32
Day 222	Ezra 7:27–9:4	Romans 8:1–27	Psalm 119:33–40
Day 223	Ezra 9:5–10:44	Romans 8:28–39	Psalm 119:41–64
Day 224	Nehemiah 1:1–3:16	Romans 9:1–18	Psalm 119:65–72
Day 225	Nehemiah 3:17–5:13	Romans 9:19–33	Psalm 119:73–80
Day 226	Nehemiah 5:14–7:73	Romans 10:1–13	Psalm 119:81–88
Day 227	Nehemiah 8:1–9:5	Romans 10:14–11:24	Psalm 119:89–104
Day 228	Nehemiah 9:6–10:27	Romans 11:25–12:8	Psalm 119:105–120
Day 229	Nehemiah 10:28–12:26	Romans 12:9–13:7	Psalm 119:121–128
Day 230	Nehemiah 12:27–13:31	Romans 13:8–14:12	Psalm 119:129–136
Day 231	Esther 1:1–2:18	Romans 14:13–15:13	Psalm 119:137–152
Day 232	Esther 2:19–5:14	Romans 15:14–21	Psalm 119:153–168

Day 233	Esther 6–8	Romans 15:22–33	Psalm 119:169–176
Day 234	Esther 9–10	Romans 16	Psalms 120–122
Day 235	Job 1–3	1 Corinthians 1:1–25	Psalm 123
Day 236	Job 4–6	1 Corinthians 1:26–2:16	Psalms 124–125
Day 237	Job 7–9	1 Corinthians 3	Psalms 126–127
Day 238	Job 10–13	1 Corinthians 4:1–13	Psalms 128–129
Day 239	Job 14–16	1 Corinthians 4:14–5:13	Psalm 130
Day 240	Job 17–20	1 Corinthians 6	Psalm 131
Day 241	Job 21–23	1 Corinthians 7:1–16	Psalm 132
Day 242	Job 24–27	1 Corinthians 7:17–40	Psalms 133–134
Day 243	Job 28–30	1 Corinthians 8	Psalm 135
Day 244	Job 31–33	1 Corinthians 9:1–18	Psalm 136:1–9
Day 245	Job 34–36	1 Corinthians 9:19–10:13	Psalm 136:10–26
Day 246	Job 37–39	1 Corinthians 10:14–11:1	Psalm 137
Day 247	Job 40–42	1 Corinthians 11:2–34	Psalm 138
Day 248	Ecclesiastes 1:1–3:15	1 Corinthians 12:1–26	Psalm 139:1–6
Day 249	Ecclesiastes 3:16–6:12	1 Corinthians 12:27–13:13	Psalm 139:7–18
Day 250	Ecclesiastes 7:1–9:12	1 Corinthians 14:1–22	Psalm 139:19–24
Day 251	Ecclesiastes 9:13–12:14	1 Corinthians 14:23–15:11	Psalm 140:1–8
Day 252	Song of Solomon 1–4	1 Corinthians 15:12–34	Psalm 140:9–13
Day 253	Song of Solomon 5–8	1 Corinthians 15:35–58	Psalm 141
Day 254	Isaiah 1–2	1 Corinthians 16	Psalm 142
Day 255	Isaiah 3–5	2 Corinthians 1:1–11	Psalm 143:1–6
Day 256	Isaiah 6–8	2 Corinthians 1:12–2:4	Psalm 143:7–12
Day 257	Isaiah 9–10	2 Corinthians 2:5–17	Psalm 144
Day 258	Isaiah 11–13	2 Corinthians 3	Psalm 145
Day 259	Isaiah 14–16	2 Corinthians 4	Psalm 146
Day 260	Isaiah 17–19	2 Corinthians 5	Psalm 147:1–11
Day 261	Isaiah 20–23	2 Corinthians 6	Psalm 147:12–20
Day 262	Isaiah 24:1–26:19	2 Corinthians 7	Psalm 148
Day 263	Isaiah 26:20–28:29	2 Corinthians 8	Psalms 149–150
Day 264	Isaiah 29–30	2 Corinthians 9	Proverbs 1:1–9
Day 265	Isaiah 31–33	2 Corinthians 10	Proverbs 1:10–22
Day 266	Isaiah 34–36	2 Corinthians 11	Proverbs 1:23–26
Day 267	Isaiah 37–38	2 Corinthians 12:1–10	Proverbs 1:27–33

Day 268	Isaiah 39–40	2 Corinthians 12:11–13:14	Proverbs 2:1–15
Day 269	Isaiah 41–42	Galatians 1	Proverbs 2:16–22
Day 270	Isaiah 43:1–44:20	Galatians 2	Proverbs 3:1–12
Day 271	Isaiah 44:21–46:13	Galatians 3:1–18	Proverbs 3:13–26
Day 272	Isaiah 47:1–49:13	Galatians 3:19–29	Proverbs 3:27–35
Day 273	Isaiah 49:14–51:23	Galatians 4:1–11	Proverbs 4:1–19
Day 274	Isaiah 52–54	Galatians 4:12–31	Proverbs 4:20–27
Day 275	Isaiah 55–57	Galatians 5	Proverbs 5:1–14
Day 276	Isaiah 58–59	Galatians 6	Proverbs 5:15–23
Day 277	Isaiah 60–62	Ephesians 1	Proverbs 6:1–5
Day 278	Isaiah 63:1–65:16	Ephesians 2	Proverbs 6:6–19
Day 279	Isaiah 65:17–66:24	Ephesians 3:1–4:16	Proverbs 6:20–26
Day 280	Jeremiah 1–2	Ephesians 4:17–32	Proverbs 6:27–35
Day 281	Jeremiah 3:1–4:22	Ephesians 5	Proverbs 7:1–5
Day 282	Jeremiah 4:23–5:31	Ephesians 6	Proverbs 7:6–27
Day 283	Jeremiah 6:1–7:26	Philippians 1:1–26	Proverbs 8:1–11
Day 284	Jeremiah 7:27–9:16	Philippians 1:27–2:18	Proverbs 8:12–21
Day 285	Jeremiah 9:17–11:17	Philippians 2:19–30	Proverbs 8:22–36
Day 286	Jeremiah 11:18–13:27	Philippians 3	Proverbs 9:1–6
Day 287	Jeremiah 14–15	Philippians 4	Proverbs 9:7–18
Day 288	Jeremiah 16–17	Colossians 1:1–23	Proverbs 10:1–5
Day 289	Jeremiah 18:1–20:6	Colossians 1:24–2:15	Proverbs 10:6–14
Day 290	Jeremiah 20:7–22:19	Colossians 2:16–3:4	Proverbs 10:15–26
Day 291	Jeremiah 22:20–23:40	Colossians 3:5–4:1	Proverbs 10:27–32
Day 292	Jeremiah 24–25	Colossians 4:2–18	Proverbs 11:1–11
Day 293	Jeremiah 26–27	1 Thessalonians 1:1–2:8	Proverbs 11:12–21
Day 294	Jeremiah 28–29	1 Thessalonians 2:9–3:13	Proverbs 11:22–26
Day 295	Jeremiah 30:1–31:22	1 Thessalonians 4:1–5:11	Proverbs 11:27–31
Day 296	Jeremiah 31:23–32:35	1 Thessalonians 5:12–28	Proverbs 12:1–14
Day 297	Jeremiah 32:36–34:7	2 Thessalonians 1–2	Proverbs 12:15–20
Day 298	Jeremiah 34:8–36:10	2 Thessalonians 3	Proverbs 12:21–28
Day 299	Jeremiah 36:11–38:13	1 Timothy 1:1–17	Proverbs 13:1–4
Day 300	Jeremiah 38:14–40:6	1 Timothy 1:18–3:13	Proverbs 13:5–13
Day 301	Jeremiah 40:7–42:22	1 Timothy 3:14–4:10	Proverbs 13:14–21
Day 302	Jeremiah 43–44	1 Timothy 4:11–5:16	Proverbs 13:22–25

Day 303	Jeremiah 45–47	1 Timothy 5:17–6:21	Proverbs 14:1–6
Day 304	Jeremiah 48:1–49:6	2 Timothy 1	Proverbs 14:7–22
Day 305	Jeremiah 49:7–50:16	2 Timothy 2	Proverbs 14:23–27
Day 306	Jeremiah 50:17–51:14	2 Timothy 3	Proverbs 14:28–35
Day 307	Jeremiah 51:15–64	2 Timothy 4	Proverbs 15:1–9
Day 308	Jeremiah 52–Lamentations 1	Titus 1:1–9	Proverbs 15:10–17
Day 309	Lamentations 2:1–3:38	Titus 1:10–2:15	Proverbs 15:18–26
Day 310	Lamentations 3:39–5:22	Titus 3	Proverbs 15:27–33
Day 311	Ezekiel 1:1–3:21	Philemon 1	Proverbs 16:1–9
Day 312	Ezekiel 3:22–5:17	Hebrews 1:1–2:4	Proverbs 16:10–21
Day 313	Ezekiel 6–7	Hebrews 2:5–18	Proverbs 16:22–33
Day 314	Ezekiel 8–10	Hebrews 3:1–4:3	Proverbs 17:1–5
Day 315	Ezekiel 11–12	Hebrews 4:4–5:10	Proverbs 17:6–12
Day 316	Ezekiel 13–14	Hebrews 5:11–6:20	Proverbs 17:13–22
Day 317	Ezekiel 15:1–16:43	Hebrews 7:1–28	Proverbs 17:23–28
Day 318	Ezekiel 16:44–17:24	Hebrews 8:1–9:10	Proverbs 18:1–7
Day 319	Ezekiel 18–19	Hebrews 9:11–28	Proverbs 18:8–17
Day 320	Ezekiel 20	Hebrews 10:1–25	Proverbs 18:18–24
Day 321	Ezekiel 21–22	Hebrews 10:26–39	Proverbs 19:1–8
Day 322	Ezekiel 23	Hebrews 11:1–31	Proverbs 19:9–14
Day 323	Ezekiel 24–26	Hebrews 11:32–40	Proverbs 19:15–21
Day 324	Ezekiel 27–28	Hebrews 12:1–13	Proverbs 19:22–29
Day 325	Ezekiel 29–30	Hebrews 12:14–29	Proverbs 20:1–18
Day 326	Ezekiel 31–32	Hebrews 13	Proverbs 20:19–24
Day 327	Ezekiel 33:1–34:10	James 1	Proverbs 20:25–30
Day 328	Ezekiel 34:11–36:15	James 2	Proverbs 21:1–8
Day 329	Ezekiel 36:16–37:28	James 3	Proverbs 21:9–18
Day 330	Ezekiel 38–39	James 4:1–5:6	Proverbs 21:19–24
Day 331	Ezekiel 40	James 5:7–20	Proverbs 21:25–31
Day 332	Ezekiel 41:1–43:12	1 Peter 1:1–12	Proverbs 22:1–9
Day 333	Ezekiel 43:13–44:31	1 Peter 1:13–2:3	Proverbs 22:10–23
Day 334	Ezekiel 45–46	1 Peter 2:4–17	Proverbs 22:24–29
Day 335	Ezekiel 47–48	1 Peter 2:18–3:7	Proverbs 23:1–9
Day 336	Daniel 1:1–2:23	1 Peter 3:8–4:19	Proverbs 23:10–16
Day 337	Daniel 2:24–3:30	1 Peter 5	Proverbs 23:17–25

Day 338	Daniel 4	2 Peter 1	Proverbs 23:26–35
Day 339	Daniel 5	2 Peter 2	Proverbs 24:1–18
Day 340	Daniel 6:1–7:14	2 Peter 3	Proverbs 24:19–27
Day 341	Daniel 7:15–8:27	1 John 1:1–2:17	Proverbs 24:28–34
Day 342	Daniel 9–10	1 John 2:18–29	Proverbs 25:1–12
Day 343	Daniel 11–12	1 John 3:1–12	Proverbs 25:13–17
Day 344	Hosea 1–3	1 John 3:13–4:16	Proverbs 25:18–28
Day 345	Hosea 4–6	1 John 4:17–5:21	Proverbs 26:1–16
Day 346	Hosea 7–10	2 John	Proverbs 26:17–21
Day 347	Hosea 11–14	3 John	Proverbs 26:22–27:9
Day 348	Joel 1:1–2:17	Jude	Proverbs 27:10–17
Day 349	Joel 2:18–3:21	Revelation 1:1–2:11	Proverbs 27:18–27
Day 350	Amos 1:1–4:5	Revelation 2:12–29	Proverbs 28:1–8
Day 351	Amos 4:6–6:14	Revelation 3	Proverbs 28:9–16
Day 352	Amos 7–9	Revelation 4:1–5:5	Proverbs 28:17–24
Day 353	Obadiah and Jonah	Revelation 5:6–14	Proverbs 28:25–28
Day 354	Micah 1:1–4:5	Revelation 6:1–7:8	Proverbs 29:1–8
Day 355	Micah 4:6–7:20	Revelation 7:9–8:13	Proverbs 29:9–14
Day 356	Nahum 1–3	Revelation 9–10	Proverbs 29:15–23
Day 357	Habakkuk 1–3	Revelation 11	Proverbs 29:24–27
Day 358	Zephaniah 1–3	Revelation 12	Proverbs 30:1–6
Day 359	Haggai 1–2	Revelation 13:1–14:13	Proverbs 30:7–16
Day 360	Zechariah 1–4	Revelation 14:14–16:3	Proverbs 30:17–20
Day 361	Zechariah 5–8	Revelation 16:4–21	Proverbs 30:21–28
Day 362	Zechariah 9–11	Revelation 17:1–18:8	Proverbs 30:29–33
Day 363	Zechariah 12–14	Revelation 18:9–24	Proverbs 31:1–9
Day 364	Malachi 1–2	Revelation 19–20	Proverbs 31:10–17
Day 365	Malachi 3–4	Revelation 21–22	Proverbs 31:18–31

APPENDIX B

Timeline of Important Biblical Events

About 4000 BC—The Fall

About 2350 BC—The Flood

About 2235 BC—Dispersion of the races

About 2100–1500 BC—Age of the Patriarchs

About 1950 BC—Amorites conquer Mesopotamia

About 1925 BC—Call of Abraham

About 1720 BC—Joseph becomes governor of Egypt

About 1635 BC—Joseph's death

About 1575 BC—Birth of Moses

About 1500–1200 BC—Exodus and Promised Land conquest

About 1492 BC—Exodus from Egypt

About 1452 BC—Joshua appointed leader of the people of Israel

About 1451 BC—Crossing of the Jordan

About 1451–44 BC—Conquest of Canaan

About 1394–1095 BC—Period of the Judges

About 1095–1055 BC—King Saul, Israel's first monarch

About 1055–1015 BC—King David

About 1050 BC—Philistines settle in southern Canaan

About 1015–975 BC—King Solomon

About 1005 BC—Dedication of the temple

About 975–587 BC—The divided kingdom (Judah and Israel)

About 721 BC—Captivity of Israel

About 587 BC—Babylonian Captivity (Judah)

About 535 BC—Return of the Jews to Jerusalem under Zerubbabel

About 515 BC—Second Temple dedicated

About 458 BC—Ezra leads second wave of Jews back to Jerusalem

About 445 BC—Nehemiah returns to Jerusalem and begins rebuilding city walls

About 37 BC–AD 4—Reign of Herod the Great, Roman-appointed king of Judea

About 4 BC–AD 6—Rule of Herod Archelaus, ethnarch (governor) of Judea, Samaria, and Idumea

About 4 BC–AD 34—Rule of Herod Philip, tetrarch of Iturea and Trachonitis

About 4 BC–AD 39—Rule of Herod Antipas, tetrarch (governor) of Galilee and Perea

About 6–4 BC—Birth of Jesus Christ

About 2 BC—Birth of Saul of Tarsus (later known as the apostle Paul)

About AD 20—Reconstruction of the temple begins

About AD 25–27—Jesus' baptism

About AD 25–28—Ministry of John the Baptist

About AD 26–37—Pontius Pilate, prefect (official who enforces the law) of Judea

About AD 29–30—Christ's crucifixion and resurrection

About AD 31–37—Conversion of Saul of Tarsus (the apostle Paul)

About AD 31–95—Books of the New Testament written

About AD 45–58—The apostle Paul's missionary journeys

About AD 59–60—Paul's first imprisonment begins

About AD 67–68—Paul's final imprisonment and death in Rome

APPENDIX C

Important Dates (and Facts) in Bible Writing, Translation, and Publishing

About 1400 BC— The Ten Commandments delivered to Moses

About 500–400 BC—Completion of Hebrew manuscripts that would become the 39 Old Testament books

Third and second centuries BC—Completion of the Septuagint, a translation of all 39 books of the Old Testament canon and the 14 books of the Apocrypha into Greek

First century AD—Completion of all original manuscripts that make up the 27 New Testament books

About 315—Athanasius, bishop of Alexandria, identifies the 27 books of the New Testament

About 362—Council of Laodicea adopts canon of Old and New Testaments and the Apocrypha

393—Council of Hippo affirms canon of New Testament

397—Council of Carthage affirms canon of New Testament

About 400—Jerome completes the Latin Vulgate, a Greek manuscript containing the 39 books of the Old Testament, the 27 books of the New Testament, and the 14 books of the Apocrypha

995—Anglo-Saxon (early roots of English language) translations of the New Testament

About 1207–28—Archbishop of Canterbury Cardinal Stephen Langton believed to have divided Bible into chapters still used today

About 1246—Cardinal Hugo de Sancto Caro introduces system of Bible chapters

1384—Death of John Wycliffe, who had started the translation of the Bible (the 66 books in the canon of scripture as well as the Apocrypha) into English. The work was completed after his death.

About 1455—German inventor Johannes Gutenberg develops movable-type printing press, allowing for mass production of books. The first book printed is the Gutenberg Bible.

1516—Dutch theologian Desiderius Erasmus produces Greek/Latin parallel New Testament

1522—Martin Luther's German New Testament published

1526—William Tyndale's complete New Testament, the first printed in English

1534—Martin Luther's complete German translation published

1535—Myles Coverdale's Bible, the first complete Bible in English, printed

1537—Matthew-Tyndale Bible, the second complete Bible printed in English. Done by John "Thomas Matthew" Rogers

1539—The Great Bible, the first English-language Bible authorized for public use, printed

1560—The Geneva Bible, the first English-language Bible to include chapter and verse references, printed

1568—The Bishops' Bible printed; revised substantially in 1572; the revised edition was the base text for the King James Version of 1611

1609—The Douay Old Testament and the Rheims New Testament (produced in 1582) are combined to make the first complete English Catholic Bible

1611—The King James Bible, including the Apocrypha, printed; Apocrypha removed in 1885, leaving the 66 books we have today

1782—Robert Aitken's Bible (King James Version), the first English-language Bible printed in America, published

1885—The English Revised Version Bible, the first major revision of the King James Version, published

1900—American publishing company Thomas Nelson & Sons publishes the American Standard Version Old Testament; the following year, the company released the entire Bible, the first major American revision of the King James Bible

1952—The Revised Standard Version published

1965—The Amplified Bible published

1971—The New American Standard Bible and *The Living Bible* published

1978—The complete New International Version (NIV) published

1982—The complete New King James Version published

1996—The complete New Living Translation published

2002—The complete Bible paraphrase, *The Message,* published

2004—Holman Christian Standard Bible published

ART CREDITS

Clipart.com: Page 27, 44, 45, 94, 98, 107, 109, 114, 116, 121

iStockphoto.com: Page 19, 21, 111

Shutterstock.com: Page 7, 9, 10, 12–14, 16, 19, 20, 23–27, 29, 30, 33, 35, 37–42, 44, 46, 48, 49, 51, 53–58, 60–62, 64, 65, 67, 69, 73, 75–85, 87, 89, 91, 93, 94, 96, 97, 99, 100, 102–107, 109, 112–116, 118–120, 122–125, 127–139, 141, 143, 145, 150, 158

Wikimedia: Pages 21, 22, 30–35, 38, 42, 43, 47, 50, 52, 54, 57, 59, 63, 65, 66, 69, 70–72, 74, 75, 79, 80, 86, 90, 92, 95, 97, 111, 117, 119, 124, 128, 129, 142

BONUS GUIDE to GOD'S Creation

What's in This Book

Before You Get Started

Have you ever stopped to think about what the words "In the beginning God created" in Genesis 1:1 really mean? Just when was the beginning, and what did God create back then?

The simple but wonderful answer is that God created *everything*! And while only God knows exactly when the beginning took place, we can know without any doubt that He created a universe so big that people still don't know where it ends—or *if* it ends. He also created all the stars, including the one we call the sun. He created the planets that orbit the sun, including the planet we humans call home—Earth. And He created every living thing that lives here with us: every microbe, every plant, every fish, every bird, every mammal, every insect. . .the list goes on and on.

And of course, He created us humans—the one thing He made in His own image and likeness—and designed us with the special ability to know and communicate with our Maker.

This book is about all the amazing things God created—starting with the heavens and the earth and ending with us humans. It's about the vastness of the universe God created, and it's about the amazing variety of things—things out there in outer space and things here on good old planet Earth—He made during those six days of work He spent creating everything you see. . .and some things you can't see.

Sometimes when we look at the wonder of God's creation, it's hard to fully comprehend that the God who lovingly and thoughtfully made everything—from the biggest galaxies, stars, and

planets all the way down to the tiniest organisms (things you can't see with the naked eye) that live here on Earth—is the same God the Bible says loves each of us deeply and personally.

But the God who loves you is also the God who created everything around you. In fact, He created everything around you *for* you! It's true! Everything God made before He created us humans was with an eye toward preparing a place that would serve as a perfect home for each and every one of us. That's what the six days of creation were all about!

Some of God's creation is big and beautiful beyond description. Some of it is complicated and a little hard to understand. Some of it is funny to look at and think about. Some of it might even seem a little gross to you. But *all* of creation is amazing and wonderful—just like the God who used six days to accomplish all of it.

This book covers all six days of the creation story from the first chapter of Genesis. It gives you a fairly detailed "day-by-day" picture of what God made on each of those creation days. It covers the creation of the universe—or what some people call the *cosmos*—as well as the creation of the earth. . .and everything that lives on it, including an incredible number of plants, animals, and other living things.

Each of the nine chapters in this book includes not only a good overview of the things God made on each creation day, but also some fun, interesting, and sometimes weird special features having to do with the chapter's main subject.

Here is a list of the features you'll enjoy in this book:

- **"That's Weird!"**: Really strange things within different parts of creation—like black holes in space, Venus flytraps (plants that eat meat), and the duck-billed platypus (quite possibly the world's weirdest mammal).
- **"Record Breaking"**: The biggest, the tallest, the farthest, and the most in all of creation!
- **"Exploring the. . ."**: Special experiments or studies you can do outside this book to learn more about the chapter's main topic.
- **"The Way It Used to Be"**: Really strange—and wrong—things people used to believe about different parts of God's creation.
- **"Did You Know. . . ?"**: Fun facts—some of them most people don't know—about the natural world God created.
- **"That's Amazing!"**: Some really astounding tidbits about the universe, the earth, and the natural world that makes its home on our planet.

This book won't teach you everything there is to know about the universe and the world God created for you to live on—or about the living things we share our planet with. For you to learn about every single thing God created, you would need a book many times longer than the one you're holding in your hands right now.

But by the time you're finished reading this book, you will have a pretty good idea how big and wonderful creation really is—and how big and wonderful the God who made it all is too. You also might find yourself wanting to read and study to learn more! When you do that, you'll learn not only about the wonder of God's creation, but you'll also learn a thing or two about God Himself that you might not have known before.

Genesis 1: The Creation Story

1 In the beginning God created the heavens and the earth. 2 The earth was formless and
empty, and darkness covered the deep waters. And the Spirit of God was hovering over
the surface of the waters.

3 Then God said, "Let there be light," and there was light. 4 And God saw that
the light was good. Then he separated the light from the darkness. 5 God called the light
"day" and the darkness "night."

And evening passed and morning came, marking the first day.

6 Then God said, "Let there be a space between the waters, to separate the waters
of the heavens from the waters of the earth." 7 And that is what happened. God made
this space to separate the waters of the earth from the waters of the heavens. 8 God called
the space "sky." And evening passed and morning came, marking the second day.

9 Then God said, "Let the waters beneath the sky flow togetherinto one
place, so dry ground may appear." And that is what happened. 10 God called the dry
ground "land" and the waters "seas." And God saw that it was good. 11 Then God
said, "Let the land sprout with vegetation—every sort of seed-bearing plant, and
trees that grow seed-bearing fruit. These seeds will then produce the kinds of plants
and trees from which they came." And that is what happened. 12 The land produced
vegetation—all sorts of seed-bearing plants, and trees with seed-bearing fruit. Their
seeds produced plants and trees of the same kind. And God saw that it was good.

13 And evening passed and morning came, marking the third day.

14 Then God said, "Let lights appear in the sky to separate the day from the
night. Let them mark off the seasons, days, and years. 15 Let these lights in the sky
shine down on the earth." And that is what happened. 16 God made two great lights—
the larger one to govern the day, and the smaller one to govern the night. He also made
the stars. 17 God set these lights in the sky to light the earth, 18 to govern the day and
night, and to separate the light from the darkness. And God saw that it was good.

19 And evening passed and morning came, marking the fourth day.

20 Then God said, "Let the waters swarm with fish and other life. Let the skies be
filled with birds of every kind." 21 So God created great sea creatures and every living thing
that scurries and swarms in the water, and every sort of bird—each producing offspring
of the same kind. And God saw that it was good. 22 Then God blessed them, saying, "Be
fruitful and multiply. Let the fish fill the seas, and let the birds multiply on the earth."

23 And evening passed and morning came, marking the fifth day.

24 Then God said, "Let the earth produce every sort of animal, each producing
offspring of the same kind—livestock, small animals that scurry along the ground, and
wild animals." And that is what happened. 25 God made all sorts of wild animals, livestock,
and small animals, each able to produce offspring of the same kind. And God saw that
it was good.

26 Then God said, "Let us make human beings in our image, to be like us. They
will reign over the fish in the sea, the birds in the sky, the livestock, all the wild animals
on the earth, and the small animals that scurry along the ground."

27 So God created human beings in his own image. In the image of God he created them; male and female he created them.

28 Then God blessed them and said, "Be fruitful and multiply. Fill the earth and govern it. Reign over the fish in the sea, the birds in the sky, and all the animals that scurry along the ground."

29 Then God said, "Look! I have given you every seed-bearing plant throughout the earth and all the fruit trees for your food.

30 And I have given every green plant as food for all the wild animals, the birds in the sky, and the small animals that scurry along the ground—everything that has life." And that is what happened.

31 Then God looked over all he had made, and he saw that it was very good!

And evening passed and morning came, marking the sixth day.

CHAPTER 1

Day 1, Part I

How It All Started—Heavens, Earth, and Water

In the beginning God created the heavens and the earth. The earth was formless and empty, and darkness covered the deep waters. And the Spirit of God was hovering over the surface of the waters.

GENESIS 1:1–2

Have you ever really thought about the word *nothing*? When you look around you and see all the really cool things God created, it's hard to imagine that there was a time when there was literally nothing around—no Earth, no moon, no stars, no people, no animals, and no plants. There wasn't even a place for God to put all these things! What's more, there wasn't even any light!

The Bible tells us that God's work of creation began in the same place everything else begins: in the *beginning*! Before that day, the only thing that existed was God Himself. And on that first day of creation, He began laying the foundation for everything you see around you—and for a lot of things you can't see.

The Bible tells us "In the beginning, God created the heavens and the earth" (Genesis 1:1). That certainly seems like a good place to start, doesn't it? But the earth God started creating on the first day of creation wasn't at all like the earth you see around you now—at least not at first. The Bible tells us that at the beginning of creation, "the earth was formless and empty" (Genesis 1:2).

What does the phrase "formless and empty" sound like to you? It certainly doesn't sound like the earth would have been a very pleasant place to live back then, does it? In fact, it sounds like the earth was nothing but a huge ball of gases and solid materials that no human, animal, or plant could possibly live on. It sounds like it was more or less a big unformed blob of what God later molded and formed into the amazing planet Earth you live on now.

Some people believe that on the first day of creation, God made what scientists call *matter*. Matter is basically all the materials God would later need to really get the work of creation going.

One of the basic laws of science is that you can't make something out of nothing. But God can! And that's exactly what He did! On that first day of creation, God began an amazing process of putting together everything we see around us—starting with what the Bible calls "the heavens and the earth" (Genesis 1:1).

The Heavens. . .a Huge Area We Call Space

What the Bible calls "the heavens" in Genesis 1, we now call *space* or the *universe* or the *cosmos*. This is a huge area God created on that first day, then later filled with planets, stars, and other amazing things you'll read about later on in chapter 5.

But just how big is the universe? About 500 years ago, people believed the entire universe was only a little bigger than Earth. And it wasn't all that long ago when schoolchildren were taught that the universe is maybe only about 5,000 light-years across—much smaller than scientists have since discovered it really is. Today, when modern technology allows us to see deeper into the universe, we have learned that space is much bigger than anyone in the past could have possibly imagined.

It's hard for most of us to imagine just how big the universe really is. In fact, even the smartest scientists in the world today really don't know the exact size of outer space. Over the past few decades, scientists have come to believe the universe actually had a beginning (just like the Bible says it does) and that it is still growing and expanding. That means we may never know just how big it is—simply because the universe God created is still getting bigger all the time.

For now, scientists know that outer space extends away from Earth by at least 13 billion light-years. A *light-year* is how far light—which travels at about 186,000 miles per second—moves in one year. So you know that the distance between Earth and the farthest objects humans have seen out in space is probably far too huge for you to figure out with a pencil and paper—even if you're really good at arithmetic!

Most everyone has seen a magician make a rabbit appear from an empty hat. But you know it's just a trick. Only God can make something from nothing!

The visible universe covers an area that is about 28 billion light-years across. Scientists know that they are limited in what they can see in space, but they believe it's possible that what they have seen so far could actually make up a small fraction of the whole universe.

Even though the universe is bigger than most people can even imagine, you can know one thing about it for sure: Every inch of it was created by the same God who so carefully and thoughtfully created you and every other person who lives here on Earth, or who has ever lived here on Earth. And He's the same God who made sure during the process of creation that you would have everything you need to live your life here on Earth.

The Hubble Space Telescope floats more than 350 miles above the earth. From that far up, beyond Earth's atmosphere, the Hubble can take clear pictures of deep space objects.

What It's Really Like in Space

What do you think it's like in outer space—thousands or millions of miles away from Earth? Is it really cold out there, or is it really hot? What does outer space sound like? What could you see if you suddenly found yourself floating around in outer space?

When you think of outer space, you probably imagine a huge area filled with stars, planets, asteroids, comets, and other objects zipping around one another at light speed. . .and making lots of noise as they do it. But even though countless numbers of objects like these are out there, outer space isn't really all that crowded. Most of the objects we can see in space are many, many light-years apart, and even those objects that are relatively close to one another very seldom come all that close to one another.

And outer space is anything but noisy. In fact, it's the quietest place in all creation.

Have you ever seen one of those old science-fiction movies where a spaceship explodes and

THAT'S AMAZING!

As of now, the farthest we've seen into space is more than 13 billion light-years away. That tells us that the heavens God created are bigger than most of us can imagine! But as huge as outer space is, the farthest any human being has traveled in space is to our moon, which is about 250,000 miles from Earth. On July 20, 1969, the spacecraft *Apollo 11*, which was commanded by Neil Armstrong, achieved the first manned landing on the moon's surface. Armstrong was the first to set foot on the moon, followed by Buzz Aldrin. After that mission, the United States' National Aeronautics and Space Administration (NASA) carried out five more manned moon landings, the last of which was in 1972.

One of the twelve humans to walk on the moon explores a deep hole called the Plum Crater. Notice the electric-powered "moon buggy" in the background. Look like fun?

gives off a loud *bang*? Outer-space explosions in movies can look and sound pretty cool. But did you know that if a blast like that happened in outer space, it wouldn't give off any sound at all?

In order for sound to travel, it has to have something to travel through. Sound travels by causing tiny particles of air—called *molecules*—to vibrate. Of course, sound can also travel through other kinds of molecules, like water, and even some solid objects like wood and metal. On Earth, where there is air, sound travels to your ears through vibrating air. But since there is no air or atmosphere of any kind in space, sound waves can't travel there.

Light, on the other hand, *can* travel through space. If you want quick proof, all you have to do is look up in the sky at night and see the stars. The light from those stars traveled many millions of miles before it reached Earth. Light can travel through space because it doesn't have to travel through anything like air or other matter. So if you were in outer space and a spaceship exploded, you could see the flash but you wouldn't hear the sound of the explosion.

Dust and hydrogen gas mix form this giant cloud in space. This photo of the Eagle Nebula was taken from the Hubble Space Telescope.

Even though outer space isn't crowded with big objects bumping into one another, it is not really empty, either. Some of the huge gaps between planets and stars and other bodies in space are filled with huge amounts of gas and dust. A lot of that gas and dust is spread very thin in space. Some of it appears only as atoms or molecules. There are also many kinds of radiation in space. The sun gives off many kinds of radiation that make their way through space and arrive here on Earth. Some of the radiation in space is necessary for life on Earth.

The Size and Shape of Planet Earth

The planet you live on might seem pretty big to you, but compared with the rest of the universe God created, Earth is like a tiny speck of sand on a huge, sand-dune-covered beach. The universe is that big!

But just how big is the earth? Actually, that depends on how you measure it. The earth's *diameter* (how wide it is) is about 7,900 miles, and its *circumference* (how big around it is) is about 24,900 miles. The earth's *radius* (the distance between the surface of the earth all the way down to its center) is about 4,000 miles. The earth's total surface area—including both land and water—is almost 197 million square miles.

Earth is huge to us but just a tiny part of the whole universe.

THAT'S AMAZING!

It might amaze you to know this, but people who lived before the time of Jesus had a pretty good idea of the earth's actual size. In about 200 BC, a Greek mathematician named Eratosthenes of Cyrene used the altitude of the sun in the sky on the first day of summer (the summer solstice) in a city called Syene (now Aswan, Egypt) and in Alexandria, Egypt, which was about 490 miles north of Syene, to calculate that the earth's circumference was about 25,000 miles. He was off by less than 100 miles!

Eratosthenes of Cyrene

While you probably didn't know how big around or how wide the earth is, you probably know that the earth is round. Or is it?

Actually, the earth isn't perfectly round. . .even though the globe in your school classroom—or maybe the one you have in your own bedroom—makes it look that way. Scientists call our planet an *oblate spheroid* because it bulges a little bit at the equator, which is the line that circles the earth and separates the Northern Hemisphere from the Southern Hemisphere. The earth is about 42 miles bigger around at the equator than it is when measured around from north to south.

That means that the earth isn't shaped like a fully inflated basketball but more like that same basketball if you let some of the air out of it, put it on the floor, and then lightly press down on it from the top.

THE WAY IT USED TO BE

One of the first things you probably learned in school about the earth is that it is round. But people didn't always believe that. Thousands of years ago, almost everyone believed that the earth was flat like a piece of paper and not round like a basketball. That began to change in the fourth century BC, when Greek scientists and philosophers—including Aristotle, one of the first to provide real evidence that the earth was not flat—began to teach that the earth was a sphere (like a basketball), or at least round in shape.

The Layers of the Earth

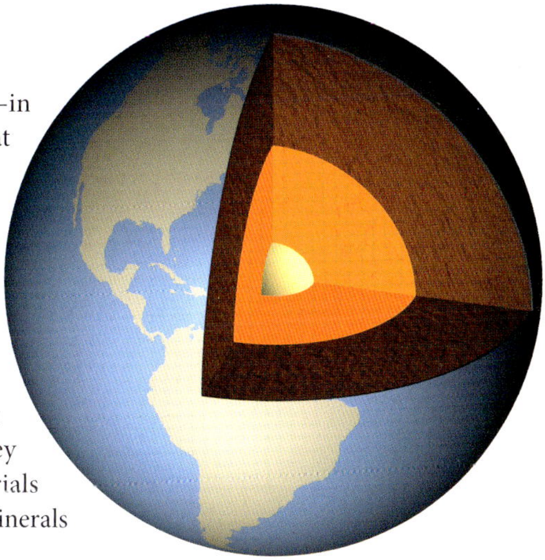

Earth's four layers are seen in this cross-section diagram—the crust, or thin outer layer; the mantle, in brown; the outer core, in orange; and the inner core, in yellow.

If you were to look at a cross section of the earth—in other words, split it in half so you could see what is inside—you'd see that the earth is made of four different layers. . .sort of like the layers of an onion. The outermost layer of the earth is called the *crust*.

The earth's crust is about 25 miles thick underneath land but only about 6.5 miles thick underneath the oceans. The earth's crust is made up of relatively light and brittle materials that can crack during earthquakes. There are about 90 known elements in the earth's crust, and they combine in several natural ways to create materials known as *minerals*. There are about 3,700 known minerals in the earth's crust.

Underneath the earth's crust is what is called the *mantle*. The earth's mantle is the thickest layer of the four. It extends from the bottom of the crust all the way down into the earth about 1,800 miles. The mantle is made up of thick, solid, rocky materials that make up about 85 percent of the earth's weight and mass. Scientists believe the first 50 miles or so of the mantle are made up of very hard rock. The 150 miles after that are made up of very hot (an estimated 4,000 to 6,700 degrees Fahrenheit) rock. The rest of the mantle is made up of very solid, strong, rocky materials.

The next layer of the earth after the mantle is the *outer core*. The outer core is about 3,000 miles beneath the surface. Scientists believe the outer core is made up of very hot (about 6,700 degrees Fahrenheit) liquid metals—mostly iron and nickel. The earth's *inner core* is also very hot (around 6,700 to 8,500 degrees Fahrenheit) and is also made mostly of iron and nickel, but it is under such pressure that it is completely solid.

DID YOU KNOW. . . ?

The earth itself—not counting its atmosphere—is made up of several elements. *Elements* are substances that cannot be broken down by any natural chemical means. They are the basic building blocks of everything around us. The earth is made up of about 34.6 percent iron (most of which is in the inner layers of the earth), 29.5 percent oxygen, 15.2 percent silicon, 12.7 percent magnesium, 2.4 percent nickel, 1.9 percent sulfur, and .05 percent titanium.

The Earth's Surface—a Huge Jigsaw Puzzle

When you look at a map of the earth, you might get the idea that its surface is one solid shell that covers the entire planet. But the earth's crust is not one big solid outer layer. It is actually broken up into several huge, thick plates that sit on top of the earth's mantle. These plates are made of rock, and they are about 50 to 250 miles thick.

The seven largest of these plates are the African plate, the Eurasian plate (under Europe and Asia), the North American plate, the South American plate, the Australian plate, the Antarctic plate, and the Pacific plate. There are also several other smaller plates on the earth's surface, including the Arabian, Nazca, and Philippine plates. The places where the plates meet one another are called *plate boundaries*.

These plates don't just sit in one place. They move both sideways in different directions and up and down. The plates move very slowly—from less than an inch to a few inches every year, depending on which plate it is. Sometimes the plates move away from each other, but sometimes they crash together or brush one another as they move. Most of the earth's volcanoes and earthquakes (what scientists call *seismic activity*) happen when the earth's plates move away from, toward, or into one another.

Scientist Andrea Donnellan uses special equipment to measure California's San Andreas Fault. Earthquakes often happen along the fault, where the North American and Pacific plates meet.

The Gift of Water

Earth is a one-of-a-kind creation because it is the only planet in our solar system—which includes our sun and the other planets that orbit it—known to have liquid water, which is absolutely necessary for the survival of all known life forms.

About 71 percent (almost three-quarters) of our earth's surface is covered with saltwater oceans. Continents and islands—as well as the freshwater rivers, lakes, and streams found on them—make up the rest of the earth's surface.

Scientists estimate that there are more than 326 million *trillion* gallons of water on our planet. That's an awful lot of water! But where do you think all that water is at any given time? If you guessed that most of it is in the oceans, you'd be right! Around 97 percent of the earth's water at any given time is in the oceans, seas, and bays. Less than 3 percent of the earth's water is fresh water, and most of that water is found in ice caps, glaciers, and other frozen forms.

Though you can see the evidence of water in our atmosphere in the form of clouds, the amount of water in the atmosphere (.001 percent) is a very small part of the total water on Earth. It might surprise you to know that the world's freshwater lakes and rivers also account for a very small amount of the total water on Earth.

A scuba diver skims through the clear blue water of the Caribbean Sea.

DID YOU KNOW. . . ?

Even though there is an amazing amount of water on the earth's surface, only a small percentage of it is drinkable. Most of the earth's water is found in seas and oceans—about 97 percent—and is too salty to drink. Another 2 percent is frozen in ice caps and glaciers. That leaves less than 1 percent of all the water on Earth that is fresh and clean enough for humans and animals to drink.

What's So Important about Water?

When God created the earth, He made sure that the people, animals, and plants He created it for would have everything they needed to live, grow, and reproduce. That included the most common—and most important—substance in the world: water!

Without water, life as we know it on Earth simply can't exist. Many kinds of plants and animals live in the water, but they aren't the only ones who need water to live. People, as well as all land animals, plants, and other living things, must have water in order to survive. In fact, we humans can live for weeks without eating food, but we would survive less than seven days without water.

Water is important to all living things because it has the ability to dissolve other substances. That helps water to carry needed nutrients to cells and to carry waste away from them. The bodies of almost all living things are more than half water. Some organisms' bodies are up to 95 percent water. Water makes up about 60 to 70 percent of the weight of your body, and about 83 percent of your blood is water. Even your bones are 25 percent water! The human brain weighs about 3 pounds, but if you squeezed all the water out of your brain, it would weigh only 10 ounces.

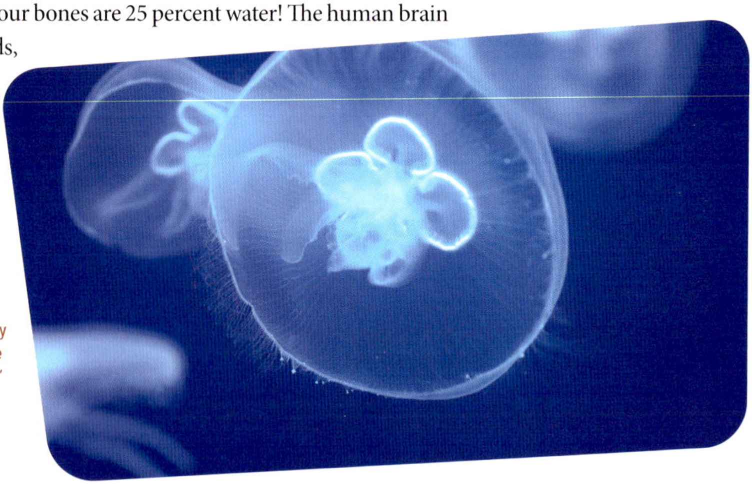

Jellyfish are approximately 95 percent water. This one is called a "moon jellyfish."

The Wonder of Water

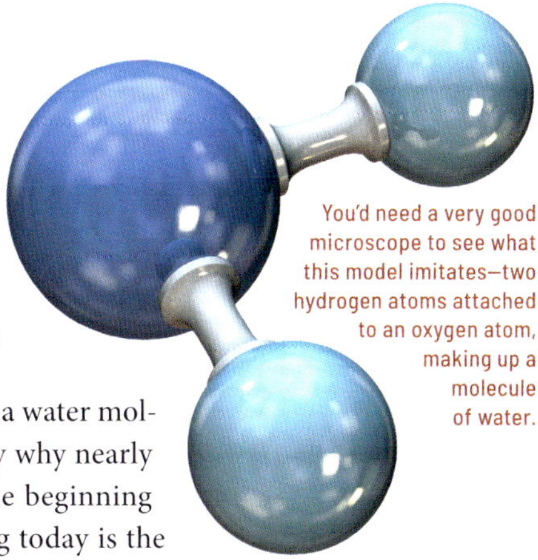

You'd need a very good microscope to see what this model imitates—two hydrogen atoms attached to an oxygen atom, making up a molecule of water.

You've probably heard water called H_2O. Have you ever wondered what that means? When you look at a glass of water, what you're seeing is millions of tiny particles of water called *water molecules*. Each water molecule is made up of two atoms of hydrogen (the H_2 part) and one atom of oxygen (the O part).

When these three atoms come together to form a water molecule, the bond is very hard to break. That is partly why nearly all the water on Earth now has been here since the beginning of creation. That means that the water we are using today is the same water that people all through history used and the same water the animals God first created used. Just think! Someone famous in history may have bathed in the very same water that you brushed your teeth with this morning! (Don't worry. . .all the *impurities*—the gross stuff you wouldn't want to put in your mouth—are long gone, so when you use water from your tap to brush your teeth, you're using just the water.)

Today, we find water on Earth in three forms. Water appears as a *liquid* (just plain water), as a *solid* (ice), and as a *gas* (steam or water vapor). The fact that water can take on these three forms helps the earth to distribute its water through ocean currents, through the movement of ice, and through precipitation (rain and snow).

Water appears in its three forms—liquid, solid, and gas—off Greenland.

In its natural form, water freezes and takes on solid form at 32 degrees Fahrenheit. Water boils and begins to turn to gas at 212 degrees Fahrenheit. But water doesn't have to reach 212 degrees Fahrenheit to be turned to gas or vapor. Water also turns to vapor in the form of clouds and fog when water from the ocean evaporates and forms tiny water droplets. The tiny droplets of water are invisible until they condense enough in the atmosphere to form clouds and fog.

THAT'S WEIRD!

Water really is an amazing substance. You may have learned in school that water is the only material on Earth that exists as a solid, a liquid, and a gas in natural conditions on our planet. But in the right conditions, water can actually take on other forms. When water is cooled down very quickly to colder than around negative 184 degrees Fahrenheit, a weird thing happens: The water turns to the thickness of molasses. At negative 211, the water turns solid but has no crystal structure like normal ice has. Scientists call this phenomenon glassy water—because the frozen water is completely clear, just like glass.

"Altocumulus" clouds are generally dark in the center and puffy white on the edges. . . unless there's a dramatic red sunset behind them!

CHAPTER 2

Day 1, Part II

Let There Be Light!

Then God said, "Let there be light," and there was light. And God saw that the light was good. Then he separated the light from the darkness. God called the light "day" and the darkness "night." And evening passed and morning came, marking the first day.

GENESIS 1:3–5

Can you imagine being in a place where there is absolutely no light? We're not talking about the kind of darkness you can experience on a really dark night away from the city lights when the moon isn't shining overhead. That's dark, but it's not *absolute* darkness because there is always some light. (If you're ever out on a night like that, you'll find that your eyes will adjust and you will be able to see at least a little bit.) We're talking about absolute blackness—the kind where you literally can't see your hand in front of your face.

The Bible says that in the beginning, "darkness covered the deep waters" (Genesis 1:2). This was before God created light of any kind, so it's easy to imagine that creation up to that point was covered in absolute darkness. Not only wasn't there much to be seen (remember, the earth was just a formless mass at that time), there wasn't even any light to see it!

But it wasn't long before God put a stop to that incredible darkness by simply speaking the words, "Let there be light." In an instant, God had taken that first step in preparing the earth as a suitable place for people, plants, and animals to live on. Not only would the light God created allow us humans and the animals to see, but it would also be the basis for all life on planet Earth.

The sun helps plants to grow...
and the plants help you to grow!

Why Light Is Important

How would you answer if someone were to ask you why light is important? Probably the first thing that would come to your mind is that you need light to see! But let's imagine for a moment that every living thing on Earth—including us humans—had every sense we have now. . .except sight. Would light still be important to us? If so, *how* would it be important?

Light, which comes from the sun to the earth, is an absolute necessity for everything that lives here. Without light, nothing could live on Earth. That includes the plants and animals that live above ground, as well as the ones that live underground. And it includes people!

One reason light is important is because plants need it to grow and produce energy—or food. This happens during a process called *photosynthesis*, which you'll read more about in chapter 4. Plants are the foundation of all food here on Earth. All animals on Earth eat either plants or other animals that eat plants. Without light, plants would stop growing and die, and if that happened, all other life here on Earth, including humans, would soon die of starvation.

Light from the sun is also important because it heats the earth. Without the sun's light, there wouldn't be enough energy on Earth to keep us warm enough to live here. God placed our planet just the right distance from the sun to allow its light to heat our atmosphere to just the right temperature.

When God created light, He created the foundation for all the life He would later carefully design to live here on Earth. God thought far enough ahead in His plan of creation to know that before any living things could be placed here on Earth, there had to be light to support them and feed them.

THAT'S WEIRD!

As crazy as it may sound, scientists have proved that light itself can be bent or moved by intense gravity from objects such as stars. Gravity can also change the energy of light. The astrophysicist Sir Arthur Eddington proved the effect of gravity on light during a solar eclipse in 1919. With the sun completely blocked and the sky dark enough to see stars, Eddington photographed the stars that appeared close to the sun in the sky and observed that their light had actually been bent as it passed by the sun.

In a total solar eclipse, the moon almost exactly blocks the sun, leaving only the sun's "crown" (or corona) in view.

What Is Light Really?

Maybe all you really understand about light is that you need it in order to not trip over things when you walk into a room. When you walk into your bedroom at night, the first thing you probably do is reach for a light switch so you can see where you're going.

But there's a lot more to light than just how it allows us to see things. Light is a fascinating creation of God that has some amazing scientific properties—some of which you probably never even thought of before.

Light is sometimes called *radiant energy* or *electromagnetic energy* because it is both electric and magnetic. There are many kinds of light. There is the light you can see, and there is light you can't see—like gamma rays, X-rays, ultraviolet light, and radio waves. While you may not have thought of some of these things as light, by all scientific definitions, they really are forms of light.

Sir Isaac Newton (1642–1727)

For centuries, people argued over whether light travels as a *wave* (like waves in water, only without what scientists call a *medium*) or as *particles* (like tiny pellets from a shotgun blast). In the seventeenth century (about 400 years ago), the great English scientist Sir Isaac Newton studied light and came to the conclusion that it was more or less a stream of particles (he called them *corpuscles*). Around that same time, another great scientist named Christiaan Huygens, who lived and worked in Holland, taught that light traveled in waves.

As it turns out, they were both right!

During the twentieth century, scientists started to believe and teach that light travels as both particles and waves. This idea is called *wave-particle duality*. Scientists began believing this because light behaves like a wave in some ways and like a particle in others. They call the particles of light *quanta*—which is plural for *quantum*—or *photons*.

Christiaan Huygens (1629–1695)

How Light Travels. . . and What It Does When It Gets Here

When you're outside on a sunny day, you probably don't think much about how the sunlight you're enjoying made it through space to Earth. But sunlight doesn't just leave the sun and arrive here on Earth in an instant. In fact, the light and warmth you feel from the sun actually left the sun's surface about 8 minutes, 18 seconds before it reached you.

Light travels through space at about 186,000 miles per second. When light leaves the sun, it travels in a straight line—in all directions. But when it hits something either here on Earth or somewhere else—even air—it starts to act very differently. And you can be thankful that it does!

When it comes to your ability to see things, the most important thing light does when it runs into things is reflect. If it weren't for reflection, you couldn't see anything around you. That's because when light hits something here on Earth—a person, a car, a tree. . .anything you can imagine—it bounces, or reflects, off that object and into your eyes, allowing you to see it. If light were somehow stopped from reflecting off things, they would still be there, but you wouldn't be able to see them.

The speed and direction of light also changes when it runs into materials like water, glass, or plastic. When light waves hit these materials, they slow down and bend. This is called *refraction*. You can see the effects of refraction when you look at someone standing waist-deep in the water in a swimming pool. From where you stand, it looks like the water has changed the angle of the person's legs. But the water hasn't done anything at all to that person; it's just that light bends and changes direction when it hits water, and that makes it look like the person's legs have been bent at the wrong angle.

Humans have made great use of the refraction of light. For example, the lenses of eyeglasses, which are usually made of glass or plastic, are curved enough to refract (or bend) the light that enters a person's eyes and allow him or her to see things more clearly than he or she could without glasses. Refraction is also used in cameras, binoculars, camcorders, and other things designed with lenses.

Light refraction can "enlarge" what you're looking at—which is why Sherlock Holmes used a magnifying glass to look for clues.

Why Is There Color? Because of Light!

One of the coolest things about light is that it allows us to see different colors. But did you know that light itself is actually a big collection of colors! It's true! If there were no colors in light, especially sunlight, you wouldn't be able to see any colors at all.

Here's a quick explanation of how color comes from light.

Light waves come in many different frequencies. The *frequency of light* is the number of light waves that pass through a certain point during a certain time period—usually one second.

Imagine that light waves are like waves in the ocean. Waves in water have a *crest* (a high point) and a *trough* (a low point). Depending on how the wave started, these crests and troughs can be of different sizes and can be farther apart or closer together. The same thing is true of light. In light, the distance between the crests and troughs is called the *amplitude*, and it determines the light's brightness. The distance between the crests of each wave is called the *wavelength*, and it determines the light's color.

If you could see the actual waves of light, you would see that *low frequency* light waves are a lot like slow, rolling waves in water—with more distance between each wave's peaks. *High frequency* light waves are like higher waves in water with less distance between them.

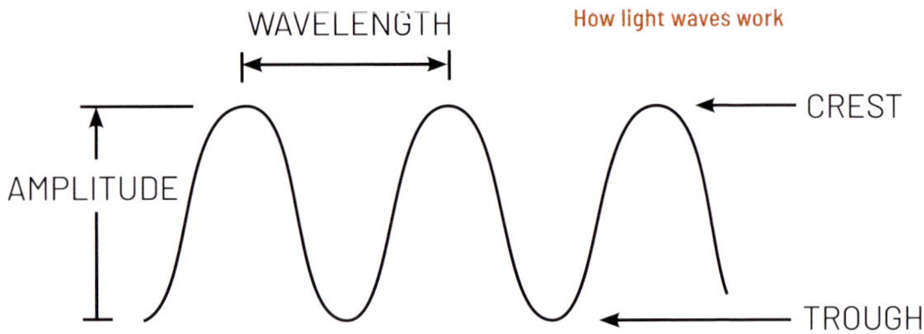

How light waves work

Low frequency light has lower energy, and high frequency light has higher energy. The light with the highest frequency are *gamma rays*, and the light with the lowest frequency are *radio waves*—both of which are invisible to the human eye. The visible light with the highest frequency is *violet light*, and the visible light with the lowest frequency is *red light*.

Your eyes can only see light that is more or less in the middle of the frequency spectrum. This range is called the *visible spectrum* or *visible light*. You can't see infrared light because it is just below the frequency of the visible spectrum, and you can't see ultraviolet light because it is just above the visible spectrum.

Your eye can tell apart around 10,000 different colors or shades of visible light. For example, you can see many different shades of each color. Most of the time, though, the visible spectrum of light is made up of a list of the seven major colors you can see in a rainbow. In order from the longest wavelength to the shortest, these colors are red, orange, yellow, green, blue, indigo, and violet. This list is often referred to as ROY G. BIV (go back and write down the first letter in each color of the rainbow in order, and you'll see why).

THAT'S WEIRD!

All electromagnetic radiation is considered light, but we humans can only see the light that is within a certain frequency or wavelength. But that doesn't mean that light we humans can't see is invisible to every living thing on planet Earth. Scientists have somehow figured out that certain kinds of reptiles can see infrared light and that many fish, reptiles, birds, and insects can see ultraviolet light. Both of these frequencies of light come from the sun, and both are completely invisible to us humans.

A German soldier in Afghanistan is seen through night-vision goggles. These goggles use non-visible light to help people see in the darkness.

God created the rainbow as a promise to never again flood the entire earth. See the whole story in Genesis 9:12–15.

How We See Colors

When you see sunlight on your hand or on some other object, it looks like it's pretty much one color—kind of yellowish white. That is why sunlight is sometimes called *white light*. But in reality, sunlight is made up of all the different colors all mixed together. When you look at a rainbow, what you're seeing is droplets of water splitting sunlight into its different colors by bending (or refracting) different colors of light.

So how do we see different colors here on Earth? Why is an apple red? Why are the leaves on plants green? It has a lot to do with how different things react to sunlight, and it also has to do with how our eyes receive light and color.

When sunlight hits a red apple, the red part of the sunlight is reflected off the apple's peel, while other colors are absorbed into the apple's skin so that you can't see them. On the other hand, if you were to look at the same red apple with sunlight shining on it that had been filtered through a piece of green plastic, the apple wouldn't appear red but would look black or gray. That's because the apple absorbed the green light instead of reflecting it back to you.

Everything on Earth is designed in such a way that it absorbs certain colors of light but reflects others. That's as true of your skin and hair and eyes as it is of green plants, red apples, and anything else on Earth that we see as having a particular color.

THAT'S AMAZING!

The first person to prove that sunlight is a mixture of all colors was Sir Isaac Newton, the great seventeenth-century English scientist. Newton passed sunlight through a glass prism to separate the colors into a rainbow spectrum. He then took a second prism and a lens and combined the two rainbows. You might think that the result was one big rainbow of colors, but you'd be wrong. What Newton produced when he combined the two spectrums was white light. This proved that white light isn't just white but is a mixture of light of many different colors or frequencies.

The First Day and the First Night

The Galileo spacecraft took this picture of earth-half bathed in the light of the sun—from almost four million miles away!

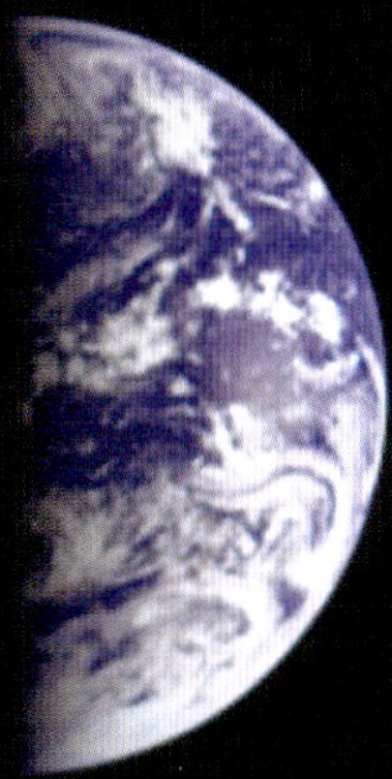

When God created light on that first day of creation, He also separated the times when it was dark outside and when it was light. Another way to say that is to say that God created night and day. Even though God wouldn't make the sun until the fourth day of creation, He started things out on the first day by designing the earth and light so that there would be night and day once about every twenty-four hours.

People use the terms sunrise and sunset to describe the daily appearance and disappearance of the sun. But in reality, the sun doesn't rise or set at all. The sun mostly stays in the same place—at least in relation to the earth—all the time. So when you see the sun appear in the east every morning and disappear in the west every evening, it's because the earth is spinning on an axis as it orbits (or circles) the sun. In other words, it's the earth that is moving in relation to the sun, not the other way around.

When it's dark outside where you live, it's because the sun is shining on the other side of the earth. That means that it's always daylight somewhere on Earth and that while you are sleeping, people on the other side of the world are busy doing some of the same kinds of things you do when it's daytime where you live.

DID YOU KNOW. . . ?

One tradition says that in leap years, a woman can propose marriage to a man. This postcard, from more than 100 years ago, has some fun with that idea.

(in other words, how long a day on Earth lasts), you'd probably answer, "Everyone knows it's 24 hours!" But the earth doesn't rotate quite that long. It actually takes the earth only 23 hours 56 minutes to completely rotate in relation to the sun. But here's another interesting fact: The time it takes the earth to *orbit* (or circle) the sun is actually a little more than a 365-day calendar year. The earth actually orbits the sun once every 365 days plus one-quarter of a day. That's why we have a February 29 once every four years in what is called a *leap year*.

When God Created Time

Even though all Christians agree that God created the earth and everything in and around it, some of them disagree over how long it took God to do it. Some believe the earth is very young—between 6,000 and 10,000 years old—while others believe the earth is very old. . .maybe billions of years old.

People will probably never completely agree on the answer to the question of how old the earth really is—at least not in this lifetime. But one thing we can probably all agree on is that God actually created time as we know it on the first day of creation when He separated day from night.

Has anyone ever asked you to define the word *time*? It's probably not as easy as you think! People mostly think of time in terms of seconds, minutes, hours, days, and years. But those are just *measurements* of time. It's hard to define time, so we'll just say that *time* is the means people use to measure the periods between certain events.

Probably the most basic measurement of time is the day. Since each day has a certain amount of daytime and a certain amount of nighttime, people use 24-hour days to measure time. But time is also measured by years. On Earth, a year is measured by the time it takes for the earth to completely orbit the sun. But even that measurement of time isn't perfect. You see, a year on Earth doesn't last exactly 365 days but about 365 days and 6 hours.

We humans are limited by time. We all begin our time on Earth when we are born, and one day our time on Earth will end. Not so with the God who began the process of making everything around us on that first day of creation. God exists outside the bounds of time. God is eternal. That means that He has always existed and will always exist. And when He created time on the first day, it was just the beginning of the process of showing His own greatness and love through making everything you see around you.

CHAPTER 3

Day 2

Our Earth's Atmosphere

Then God said, "Let there be a space between the waters, to separate the waters of the heavens from the waters of the earth." And that is what happened. God made this space to separate the waters of the earth from the waters of the heavens. God called the space "sky." And evening passed and morning came, marking the second day.

GENESIS 1:6–8

You probably don't give a lot of thought to air when you take a deep breath, but the air you breathe is part of what makes it possible for you—and every other person and every other living thing—to live here on Earth.

Another word for the air you breathe is *atmosphere*. Earth's atmosphere is made up of three main gases: *nitrogen*, *oxygen*, and *argon*. About 78 percent (more than three-quarters) of our atmosphere is made up of nitrogen, with oxygen accounting for about 21 percent. Argon accounts for a little less than 1 percent of our planet's atmosphere, with the remainder made up of carbon dioxide and small traces of other gases. In addition to the gases in our atmosphere, there are also small particles of dust, water, and pollen floating around.

When you breathe in air, you breathe in everything that's in it. Nitrogen and argon are what are called *inert gases*, which means they don't react chemically with other substances. So when the nitrogen and argon enter your lungs when you inhale, they do an about-face and leave your lungs when you exhale. . .without affecting your body in any real way. The same is not true of oxygen—and it's a good thing too!

Oxygen is the life-sustaining part of Earth's atmosphere. Nearly every living thing on Earth needs oxygen to survive. Every cell in your body requires oxygen to work properly. Your body gets the oxygen it needs when you breathe air—or atmosphere—into your lungs.

Oxygen is one of Earth's ninety-four *naturally occurring chemical elements*—meaning a substance that can't be broken down by any natural means on Earth. While nitrogen and argon are inert gases, oxygen reacts easily with many other elements and chemicals. For example, in your body, oxygen reacts with carbon to create carbon dioxide, which leaves your body when you exhale. Oxygen is not only important because most living things breathe it in, but because things on Earth need it to *combust*—or burn.

DID YOU KNOW. . . ?

Have you ever wondered why the sky is blue? Why not red, or green, or yellow. . .or purple? First of all, the sun gives off all different colors of light, and each of those colors comes to Earth in different sizes or wavelengths. Second, the earth's atmosphere is mostly made up of oxygen and nitrogen, two colorless gases that have different effects on the different colors of light that pass through them. An atom of oxygen, it turns out, is about the same size as the wavelength of blue light, which causes oxygen to scatter blue light from the sun in every direction. This is called *Raleigh scattering*, and it's why the sky looks blue in every direction.

How Our Atmosphere Is Put Together

You can think of the earth's atmosphere as a thin layer of air surrounding the entire globe. The atmosphere is held in place by the earth's gravity. The higher you go above the earth's surface, the thinner the atmosphere becomes. That's because gravity pulls the atmosphere down so that it compresses on itself at lower elevations.

The main part of the earth's atmosphere is about 300 miles thick, with smaller parts of the atmosphere extending out about 6,000 miles. Most of the gases and other materials in the atmosphere are found in the first ten miles above the earth's surface.

The air pressure of our atmosphere at sea level is about 14.7 pounds per square inch, which is just about right for people and most other living things to breathe comfortably. This is called *atmospheric pressure*. But the atmosphere's air pressure decreases the higher up you go. At about 18,000 feet, the atmosphere's air pressure can be as low as half what it is at sea level.

If you've ever visited a place that is high above sea level—like on a high mountaintop or in a city like Denver, Colorado—you might have noticed that it was a little harder to breathe. That's because there is less oxygen in the air at higher altitudes, which means your lungs have to work harder to collect enough to keep you going.

The atmosphere not only keeps oxygen where humans and other life forms need it to be, but it also acts like a blanket that insulates the earth and keeps it from becoming extremely hot or extremely cold.

This warning sign on Colorado's Mount Evans warns visitors of the dangers of "thin air."

The Layers of Our Atmosphere

In chapter 1, you read about how the earth is made up of several different layers, each of which was constructed very differently from one another. The same thing is true of the atmosphere that surrounds Earth.

The layer of the earth's atmosphere closest to the ground—the part we live in—is called the *troposphere*. Our troposphere goes up from the earth's surface about 11 miles. The troposphere is where all Earth's weather occurs, and it's also where most of the gases in our atmosphere are concentrated.

The next level of Earth's atmosphere is a thin transitional layer between the troposphere and the stratosphere called the *tropopause*. The *stratosphere* begins about 11 miles from the earth's surface and ends around 31 miles up. This is where the earth's ozone layer is found. *Ozone* is a form of oxygen that is crucial to the survival of life on Earth because it absorbs much of the sun's ultraviolet light, which is very dangerous to people and other living things if they are exposed to it in high doses.

The earth's stratosphere is followed by a layer called the *mesosphere*, which begins about 31 miles above the earth's surface and ends about 50 miles up. Next is the *ionosphere*, which starts between 43 and 45 miles up and continues out about 400 miles. The ionosphere is followed by the *exosphere*, which goes from about 400 miles out to about 800 miles above Earth's surface. The exosphere and part of the ionosphere together make up what is called the *thermosphere*.

Weather. . .an Important Function of the Atmosphere

Take a look outside right now and ask yourself what the weather is like. Is it sunny and warm? Is it cloudy and rainy? Is it windy and cold? We use the word *weather* to describe what our atmosphere is doing around us on a given day—whether it's warm and dry, cool and rainy, or clear and warm. Weather includes factors like cloudiness, *precipitation* (rain, snow, hail, and other kinds of moisture that fall from the sky), windiness, temperature, and *humidity* (how much water vapor is in the air).

Wet, cool weather can sometimes be a disappointment when you want to be outside enjoying yourself. Who wouldn't rather be outdoors on a nice sunny day than stuck inside on a rainy and cold one? But different kinds of weather serve different purposes—and all of them are important for life on Earth. For example, when it rains, water falls on the soil plants grow in and gives them the moisture they need to continue growing. And when the rain stops and the sky clears, those same plants receive an extra shot of sunlight, which is also necessary for them to grow.

Rain is produced when water evaporates and rises up to the sky, forming clouds. When the clouds start moving, the water vapor condenses, forming larger drops of water. When the drops become big and heavy enough, gravity from the earth pulls them downward. When that happens, we have rain!

Snow happens basically the same way, but with a few differences. Snow forms when the temperature in the clouds is cold enough for water vapor to condense and turn into ice. The tiny drops of moisture then start to stick together and become ice crystals. When enough of the ice crystals have gathered together, they begin to fall from the sky (again, getting some help from gravity). If the temperature between the clouds and the ground is cold enough, the ice crystals reach the ground as snowflakes. If not, they reach the ground as rain or a mixture of rain and snow called *sleet*.

Hail also starts as droplets of water. When a strong upward wind from the surface of the earth pushes the drops above the freezing level, the droplets freeze. When they become heavy enough, they start to fall toward Earth. At that point, these balls of ice usually either melt and fall as rain or stay solid and fall as hail. Sometimes, if the upward wind is strong enough, the wind pushes the hailstones back up above the freezing level, where they become bigger hailstones.

These baseball-sized hailstones fell on Wisconsin in 2007.

THAT'S WEIRD!

Late in December of 2006, a couple living in Folsom, California, reported what had to be the strangest weather event they had ever seen. It was *raining fish*! Even if the story seems a little hard to swallow, in truth there are several instances of fish falling from the sky worldwide every year. It can happen when *waterspouts*—tornadoes over water with winds as high as 200 miles per hour—suck fish out of the water and drop them over land. People as far as 100 miles inland have witnessed raining fish.

Like a tornado, a waterspout is made up of whirling winds—which suck up water from lakes or seas.

How Do Clouds Work?

Clouds are actually collections of tiny droplets of water or ice that are small enough for wind to carry them upward from the earth's surface. Most clouds form when water evaporates from the ocean or other big bodies of water, but some clouds can form over land—that is, when there is enough moisture in them.

There are four main types of clouds: cumulus, cirrus, stratus, and nimbus. When you see white, fluffy clouds in the sky—you know, the ones that can sometimes look like animals or people. . . if you use your imagination—you're seeing *cumulus clouds*. But sometimes cumulus clouds can be thick and gray. When you see a big, gray cumulus cloud, then it will probably rain soon. Cumulus clouds are formed when warm air carries water vapor from the ground. When that warm, wet air meets cold air in the sky, the vapor condenses into droplets of water and forms a cumulus cloud.

Cirrus clouds are the thin, wispy clouds you sometimes see high in the sky—even on a very nice day. Cirrus clouds look the way they do because they are made of ice crystals instead of water droplets. Cirrus clouds form high enough in the sky where it is cold enough for water droplets to freeze.

Stratus clouds look like big, gray blankets hanging low in the sky. If you see stratus clouds, then you can be pretty sure that it's going to rain—or snow if it's cold enough outside. Stratus clouds can hang so low from the sky that they touch the ground. That is what we call *fog*.

When you see a *nimbus cloud* headed your way, it's probably a good idea to get inside. That's because nimbus clouds are often the source of thunderstorms—and sometimes tornadoes. Many times when you see a nimbus cloud on the horizon, you can already see that it has rain—or snow, or sometimes hail—falling out of it. You might even be able to see the flashes of lightning too!

There are a few other kinds of clouds, and most of them are combinations of the basic four listed above. There is the *cumulonimbus* cloud, which is a cumulus cloud with rain coming out of it. This cloud can be the source of some really bad weather—even tornadoes. There is also the *stratonimbus* cloud, which is a stratus cloud that looks like a gray blanket with rain falling out of it.

Cumulus clouds

Cirrus clouds

Stratus clouds

Nimbus clouds

What's with the Wind?

Do you like really windy days? Some people like windy days, but some don't like them at all. Some people are even afraid of really strong wind. But wind is an important part of how our earth keeps itself from overheating. That's because wind helps move heat around and equalize it, and also because it moves heat away from the earth's surface and up into the higher parts of the atmosphere.

This barometer measures changes in atmospheric pressure to predict the weather.

Wind happens when air moves from a place where the air pressure—also known as *barometric pressure*—is high to a place where the air pressure is low. How strong the wind blows depends on how big the difference in air pressure is between two places. When there are big differences in air pressure between two places, the wind will be stronger. Sometimes the differences are so great that violent storms like hurricanes and cyclones start. But when the difference isn't too great, the wind will be weaker—maybe even a nice, gentle breeze.

Several different factors can cause the differences in air pressure that result in wind. These factors include heat from the sun. Different parts of the earth receive different amounts of heat and light from the sun. This causes the temperatures to be hot near the equator and cold at the North Pole and South Pole. Extreme heat causes low pressure and extreme cold causes high pressure. That's because hot air tends to rise while cold air tends to stay close to the ground. These extreme differences in temperature cause differences in barometric pressure, which causes wind.

EXPLORING THE WORLD OF WIND

If you're looking for a good illustration of how wind works, try this. Take two balloons that are about the same size. Blow one of them up until it is filled with air—don't tie it off. Blow the other balloon up halfway so that it is still soft and squishy. Now hold each balloon at the bottom, then let them go at the same time. You'll probably notice that the balloon you filled completely flies around the room faster and longer than the one you filled halfway. That's because the balloon you filled completely has higher air pressure inside it so the air comes out of it faster as the air inside the balloon tries to equalize itself with the air outside the balloon.

Climate and Weather: What's the Difference?

There are many factors that determine what kind of weather you see around you. One of those factors is the *climate* you live in. Climate isn't exactly the same thing as weather, but it has everything to do with the kind of weather you usually see where you live.

Weather is what happens in a small area of the world during a short period of time. Weather can and does change often. For example, it might be rainy and cool where you are today, but tomorrow it just might be sunny and warm. Or if it's cold and snowy this week, next week it might be warmer and rainy.

On the other hand, the *climate* of a certain part of the world is usually determined by the kind of weather that area experiences over a long period of time—usually about 30 years. The climates of different parts of the world can be dry or wet, warm or cool—and everything in between. But that doesn't mean that the area won't sometimes experience weather that doesn't exactly fit in with the climate it is known for.

Some parts of the world are known for extreme climates. For example, the Sahara Desert in northern Africa is known for very dry, very hot weather. Antarctica, which is located in the extreme southern part of planet Earth, is known for extremely cold weather—way too cold for people to live there.

Bedouins—people who live in the desert—cross the Sahara with their camels.

Tourists bundle up to watch Antarctic penguins—who watch the people in return.

RECORD BREAKING

Here's the classic image of Death Valley, a bleached cow skull baking on dry, cracked soil.

Most of us are lucky enough not to be living in places where the temperatures get extremely hot or extremely cold. But there are places in the world where records are set. The hottest temperature ever recorded was 134 degrees Fahrenheit on July 10, 1913, in Death Valley, California. The coldest temperature ever was recorded was on July 21, 1983, in Vostok Station in Antarctica (it is winter in Antarctica in July), where it reached negative 128.6 degrees Fahrenheit.

THAT'S AMAZING!

The plants in Washington's Olympic National Park like all that rain—it's one of the wettest places in the United States.

If you don't like rain, then the Atacama Desert in Chile might be the place for you. This area receives an average of about one inch of rainfall a year, but in some spots there has never been measurable rainfall recorded since people started keeping track of weather. Nothing lives in the driest parts of the Atacama Desert, not even cactus plants! On the other hand, if you like rain—*really* like rain—then you would probably like Mawsynram, a village in northeastern India, which receives around 467 inches—almost 39 feet!—of rain each year.

Things that Affect Climate

There are several factors that affect climate in different parts of the world. These factors include an area's distance from the equator, its distance from the ocean, its altitude, and its distance from mountains.

The equator receives more direct sunlight than the rest of the world, so it is warmer. If you were to travel north or south from the equator, you would probably notice that the weather gets cooler and cooler the farther you get from the equator. By the time you reached the North Pole or South Pole, you'd look around you and see that everything is covered in ice and snow.

Coastal areas are usually cooler and wetter than inland areas. That is because clouds form over water when warm air collides with cool air from the sea. Areas close to large bodies of water also tend to be more humid because water from the ocean, sea, or lake evaporates. Generally, the closer you are to the ocean or sea—or other large body of water—the wetter and cooler the air will be where you live. On the other hand, the farther you live from big bodies of water, the drier it will be where you live. That's because moisture from these bodies of water evaporates before it can reach you.

Altitude, meaning how far above sea level a certain place is located, affects climate because places that are farther away from sea level receive less heat and energy from the sun. You can easily see evidence of that fact when you look at a mountain—or a picture of one, if you don't live near a mountain range. Even when the ground is dry, the mountaintop (if it is in a climate where it is possible for snow to fall) is covered in ice and snow. That's simply because it's colder up there!

That seems a little backward, doesn't it? You would think that since higher places are closer to the sun, then they would be warmer. But it doesn't work that way. Actually, the atmosphere isn't warmed directly by the sun's rays. The earth's surface absorbs most of the heat from the sun, and as it warms up, it heats the atmosphere. The lower levels of the atmosphere—the ones close to the earth's surface—absorb and trap most of the heat, leaving very little of it to reach high altitudes.

Mountains can have a huge effect on the climate of the lands around them. In some coastal areas, mountains block rain from reaching inland areas. In situations like that, land on one side of the mountain may be very rainy, but the other side will be drier. In the Pacific Northwest, for example, the Coast Range and the Cascade Mountains each keep inland areas from receiving as much rain as they otherwise would have. That's why it's very rainy on the Oregon and Washington coasts, less rainy in the inland parts of the states, and drier east of the Cascade Mountains.

Skiers are glad that air gets colder as you go up a mountain!

CHAPTER 4

Day 3

The Oceans. . .the Land. . . and the Plants

Then God said, "Let the waters beneath the sky flow together into one place, so dry ground may appear." And that is what happened. God called the dry ground "land" and the waters "seas." And God saw that it was good. Then God said, "Let the land sprout with vegetation—every sort of seed-bearing plant, and trees that grow seed-bearing fruit. These seeds will then produce the kinds of plants and trees from which they came." And that is what happened. The land produced vegetation—all sorts of seed-bearing plants, and trees with seed-bearing fruit. Their seeds produced plants and trees of the same kind. And God saw that it was good. And evening passed and morning came, marking the third day.

Genesis 1:9–13

During the first two days of creation, God laid the groundwork for a world that would look very much like it looks today. From the beginning, God intended that our earth would include oceans and land area that would serve as homes to the amazing number of plants, animals, and other living things He would create just a few days later.

On the third day of creation, God took what had been a fairly shapeless earth and turned it into one with oceans and other bodies of water separating huge pieces of land that would later be home to us humans. Not only that, He also stocked the entire earth with plants—the living things that would later support all life on Earth.

Water, Water Everywhere!

Planet Earth is a one-of-a-kind creation because it is the only planet circling our sun that has oceans. In fact, no other planet known to humans has liquid water, which is necessary for supporting all known forms of life.

The oceans cover about 71 percent of the earth's surface and hold about 97 percent of all water on Earth. The Pacific Ocean is by far the biggest ocean in the world. It covers more than 64 million square miles of the earth's surface and has an average depth of about 14,000 feet. The Pacific is almost twice as big as the second largest ocean, the Atlantic. The Indian Ocean is the third biggest ocean in the world, followed by the Southern Ocean and the Arctic Ocean.

Up until the year 2000, there were four oceans recognized—the Pacific, the Atlantic, the Indian, and the Arctic. That doesn't mean that the earth suddenly developed a new ocean. It means that another area of saltwater was recognized as an ocean. In the spring of 2000, the International Hydrographic Organization recognized the Southern Ocean, which surrounds Antarctica deep in the Southern Hemisphere.

While there are only five oceans in the world, there are more than eighty-five seas. Seas are filled with saltwater, just like oceans, but they are usually smaller than oceans. In fact, many seas are smaller parts of oceans. For example, the Caribbean Sea, which is located southeast of the Gulf of Mexico, is a part of the Atlantic Ocean. The Pacific Ocean has more than thirty seas. Some seas aren't part of oceans but are completely surrounded by land. These are called *landlocked seas*, and they include the Dead Sea and the Caspian Sea.

Salt collects on the shore of the Dead Sea in Israel.

Even though humans have named five different oceans, all the world's oceans are actually connected with one another through currents that flow around the world. The five named oceans are divided up according to continents and other features in the ocean, such as ridges on the ocean floor. This huge body of saltwater is sometimes called the *World Ocean* or *global ocean*. The World Ocean covers about 139 million square miles of the earth's surface and has an average depth of about 12,230 feet.

THAT'S AMAZING!

The deepest water on Earth is called the Challenger Deep, a spot located in the Mariana Islands group at the southern end of the Mariana Trench in the Pacific Ocean—south of Japan, north of New Guinea, and east of the Philippines. No one knows for sure how deep the water there really is, but estimates tell us that it is more than 36,000 feet (almost seven miles) deep! Also amazing is the fact that scientists have found life on the floor of the Mariana Trench, including sea cucumbers, scale worms, shrimps, and other small organisms.

Scientists use underwater machines called "submersibles" to investigate the deeper parts of the ocean. This submersible (at right) has just left an underwater platform.

Why the Oceans Are Important to Us

Even if you don't live near an ocean, the world's oceans play a bigger part in your life than you realize. First of all, oceans are important to all life on Earth because they have a huge effect on weather and temperatures all over the world—even places that are far from any ocean.

Oceans help keep most of the surface of the earth from getting too hot or too cold because they absorb a lot of heat and light from the sun. They influence the entire world's weather by moving the warmth they absorb from the sun around the world through ocean currents and winds.

Oceans are also the source of most rain that falls on land all over the world. When water from the ocean evaporates, it leaves the salt and other materials behind and forms clouds. The clouds that form from the evaporated water then move over land, where the water in them condenses and then falls as life-giving rain.

Oceans are also important to people because they are huge sources of food such as fish, shrimps, crabs, and lobsters. Millions of people worldwide eat food that comes from the sea. That includes about 29 million tons of fish every year.

Another reason oceans are important to people is that many of the world's important goods are moved by ships that travel the ocean between the world's seaports. Those shipped goods include food, petroleum, and other important products you and your family use every day.

A fisherman pulls a net from the Atlantic Ocean, off the West African nation of Sierra Leone.

DID YOU KNOW. . . ?

Have you ever wondered why oceans and other big bodies of water have high tides and low tides every day? Believe it or not, it has to do with gravity. . .from the moon! The moon's gravity pulls at the water in the oceans so that they begin to bulge out in the direction of the moon. If you think that's amazing, then wait till you hear this! The water in the oceans on the side of the earth facing *away* from the moon also bulges out and forms tides. That's because Earth is being pulled toward the moon and away from the water on the opposite side of the earth. High tides and low tides happen twice each day because the earth is rotating, which means that one-half of the earth is always facing away from the moon.

The moon reflects off the Mediterranean Sea over the French Riviera.

THE WAY IT USED TO BE

Up until the late 1400s, many European explorers traveled to other places in Europe and to Africa, but they wouldn't sail into the Atlantic Ocean. And why not? First of all, no one had ever done it, and the explorers didn't want to risk sailing into unknown waters. But they were also afraid of the myths they heard about the Atlantic—that the water far from shore was boiling and filled with horrible sea monsters. That all changed when in 1492, Christopher Columbus and his crew sailed across the Atlantic—without seeing any boiling water or sea monsters.

In the 1600s, when this map was created, some people still imagined monsters lurking in the world's seas.

The Ocean: A Perfect Home for Lots of Living Things

One of the reasons God created the oceans and seas was to provide a home for millions of different forms of life He would be making a few days later. To this day, the oceans are home to an amazing variety of creatures and plants that simply couldn't live anywhere else.

A big part of what makes oceans different from freshwater lakes and rivers is the saltiness of the water. Ocean water is salty because more than 30 different elements, ions, and compounds are dissolved in it. Six of those—chloride, sulfate, sodium (a scientific word for salt), magnesium, calcium, and potassium—make up about 99 percent of the total. The average saltiness of the ocean is about 35 parts per thousand. That means that for every thousand ounces of seawater, 35 of those ounces are made up of "sea salt."

The chemical makeup of saltwater makes it possible for the oceans and most of the seas to support countless kinds of life. Many kinds of animals and plants are designed to live in and near saltwater. That includes tiny creatures called *plankton*, which are food for many other ocean creatures, all the way up to the world's biggest animal, the blue whale. Whales, seals, fish, crustaceans, jellyfish, and many other animals live in the ocean. There are more than 15,000 known species of fish that live in the ocean, with many new kinds of saltwater fish being discovered and named every year. Also, there are more than 200,000 other animals and plants living in the world's oceans.

THAT'S AMAZING!

The Great Barrier Reef is a place where the waters "swarm with fish and other life" (Genesis 1:20).

The Great Barrier Reef, which is located off the coast of Queensland in northern Australia and stretches to a length of 1,616 miles, is such an amazing wonder of nature—and the creativity of God—that it has been called the largest living organism in the world. An amazing 4,000 species of mollusks, 1,500 species of fish (including 125 species of sharks), 400 species of corals, 215 species of birds, 500 species of seaweed, 17 species of sea snakes, and 6 species of sea turtles make their home there. Take the time to look up the Great Barrier Reef and see what kinds of animals and fish live there.

Lots of dry land—in the African nation of Namibia.

Land: The Other Part of the Earth's Surface

About 29 percent (less than one-third) of the earth's surface is dry land. This part of the world is called the *continental area*. Most of the dry land on Earth is joined together in big masses we now call *continents*. Most people recognize seven continents: North America, South America, Africa, Asia, Europe, Australia, and Antarctica. More than two-thirds of the continental area is north of the equator.

Not everyone agrees that there are seven continents on Earth. That's because some continents are joined to one another by land. Some people also believe that Europe and Asia are parts of a huge continent called *Eurasia*. Some even believe that Eurasia and Africa is one continent, which they call *Eurafrasia*. Some believe that North America and South America combined is actually one continent called the *Americas*. And some people believe that Australia is only one part of a larger continent that includes New Zealand and the Pacific Islands. They call that continent *Oceania*.

Asia is by far the largest of the seven most commonly recognized continents. Asia covers more than 17 million square miles, which is almost 30 percent of the world's total land area. Asia is the only continent that borders two other continents—Africa and Europe—which are to the west of Asia. It is bordered to the east by the Pacific Ocean.

RECORD BREAKING

Asia is not only the world's largest continent, it is also home to some other kinds of world records—namely the highest point on Earth and the lowest point on land. The peak of Mount Everest in Asia is the highest place in the world at more than 29,000 feet above sea level. The lowest point on land is the Dead Sea, which is located between Israel and Jordan and sits around 1,370 feet *below* sea level.

Mount Everest, lit by the late afternoon sun

The Great Wall of China is one of Asia's best known landmarks. Here, it crosses mountain tops near Beijing.

Africa is known for its fascinating wildlife. "Safaris"—special trips for tourists—allow people to see animals up close, like these elephants in Tanzania.

Niagara Falls connects the two largest nations of North America—the United States and Canada. Notice the boat in the river below the falls!

A giant statue of Jesus—"Christ the Redeemer"—overlooks one of South America's most important cities, Rio de Janeiro, Brazil.

The Asian continent is so big that it is divided into five subregions: North Asia, Middle East, South Asia, East Asia, and Southeast Asia. Asia is also the continent with the most people living on it. Right now, six out of ten people on Earth live in Asia.

Africa is the world's second biggest continent at more than 11 million square miles, or about 20 percent of the world's total land area. Africa sits on the equator and stretches about 4,970 miles from its most northern point to its most southern tip. At its widest point, Africa is about 4,700 miles wide.

The third largest continent is North America, which includes the United States, Canada, Mexico, and the Caribbean and Central American nations. North America is also home to Greenland, the world's largest island. North America covers more than 9.4 million square miles of the earth's surface and accounts for about 16.5 percent of the world's land.

South America is the world's fourth largest continent, covering more than 6.8 million square miles and making up about 12 percent of the earth's land. South America is home to some amazing natural wonders, including the Amazon River, at more than 3,900 miles long—the second longest river on the planet, as well as the largest tropical rain forest in the world. The Andes Mountains stretch the entire length of the continent.

Antarctica, which is the fifth largest continent by area, accounts for around 9.2 percent of the earth's land mass. Antarctica is almost completely covered year-round by a thick layer of ice. It is the coldest place on Earth, with temperatures in some parts of the continent sometimes dipping all the way down to below negative 100 degrees Fahrenheit! That's why Antarctica is last in total population. No one lives in Antarctica permanently, but a few thousand scientists work there during the summer, with only around 1,000 of them staying through the winter.

Ice, snow, and penguins are among the main features of Antarctica. What you won't find are many people!

Europe is the world's second smallest continent by area, covering just over 3.9 million square miles, or about 6.8 percent of the world's land mass.

The Eiffel Tower in Paris, France, is one of Europe's best-known landmarks. It was built in the late 1880s for a world's fair.

Australia is the smallest continent by area, accounting for about 5.9 percent of the world's land.

Ayers Rock, also called Uluru, is one of Australia's most famous natural landmarks. It's nearly six miles around—that's a big rock!

Where Do Continents End and the Oceans Begin?

Nearly all continents are surrounded from their beaches out toward the ocean by an extension of underwater land in the shallow part of the oceans called the *continental shelf*. The water over the continental shelf is usually not more than 500 to 650 feet deep. How wide a continental shelf is depends on the continent and its geological features. Some areas have almost no continental shelf, while some have continental shelves wider than 250 miles. For areas that do have continental shelves, the average shelf is about 50 miles in width. The largest continental shelf is called the Serbian Shelf. It is located in the Arctic Ocean and stretches 930 miles from shore.

The continental shelf is actually made up of several parts. The first part of the continental shelf starts just outside the shoreline of the continent. As you move from the shoreline out into the deeper parts of the ocean, the shelf slopes smoothly until it reaches what is called the *continental shelf break*. The continental shelf break usually starts in ocean waters about 430 feet deep. After the continental break, the floor of the ocean turns quickly downward. This feature of geology is called the *continental slope*. Farther out from the continental slope is the *continental rise*, which is a deposit of sediments that form as a result of runoff from the continent's streams and rivers. After the continental rise is what geologists call the *abyssal plains*, which is a scientific way of saying the deepest parts of the ocean.

The continental shelf isn't always flat. Some parts of the continental shelf include deep valleys as well as tall mountains and hills. Some of these mountains reach up past the surface of the sea, creating islands. Islands that stand on a continent's continental shelf are considered part of that continent.

The continental shelf is home to most of the kinds of plants and animals that live in the ocean—including fish and other living things that humans harvest and eat. This part of the ocean supports the most kinds of life because it receives more sunlight and because the sediment that washes into the ocean from the continent's rivers and streams provides nourishment for microscopic plants and animals that larger animals—such as fish—feed on. The continental shelf also supports the largest amounts of plants and animals that live on the ocean floor.

The continental shelf is a shallow, underwater plain that makes up a continent's true outer edge. It can be a few miles to more than 200 miles wide, before dropping off quickly to the deep ocean floor.

Islands Big and Small

It might surprise you to hear this, but today one out of every ten people living in the world live on islands. But when you realize that 200 million people live in Indonesia—which is made up entirely of islands—and that more than 60 million live on the island of Great Britain, it's not hard to imagine how so many people live on islands today.

Islands are bodies of land that are surrounded on all sides by water. Continents are also surrounded by water, but they are much larger and are therefore classified as continents. For example, Australia is surrounded by water, but it covers almost three million square miles. That's why Australia is considered a continent. Greenland, which is the world's largest island, is about one-fourth the size of Australia and is therefore considered an island.

It's hard to say how many islands there are in the world. Today, people live on more than 100,000 of the world's islands, and there are many times more islands that people don't live on. The Asian island nation of Indonesia leads the world with a total of 13,667 islands, 6,000 of which are inhabited by people.

There are many kinds of islands in the world. Islands that sit on the continental shelf of a certain continent are called *continental islands*. The nations of Great Britain, Ireland, New Guinea, Barbados, and several others are all considered continental islands. Islands that sit in the ocean away from continental shelf are called *oceanic islands*. Scientists believe that almost all oceanic islands were made as the result of volcanoes. The Hawaiian Islands are examples of volcanic islands.

The smallest island in the world is Bishop Rock, which is located at the southwestern part of the United Kingdom. Actually, Bishop Rock is little more than that: a rock sticking up out of the water. Greenland, on the other hand, covers about 840,000 square miles.

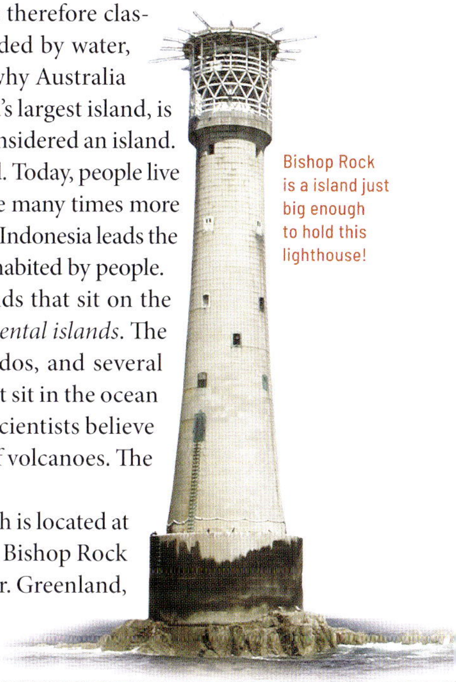

Bishop Rock is a island just big enough to hold this lighthouse!

Red-hot lava bursts out of a volcano called Piton de la Fournaise, on the Indian Ocean island of Réunion.

Here's some good trivia to remember: The second tallest mountain in the world is called K2, or Mount Godwin-Austen. It's near the border of Pakistan and China.

RECORD BREAKING

You probably already know that Mount Everest in Asia is the highest mountain peak in the world. The peak of Everest is an amazing 29,028 feet above sea level. But it might surprise you to know that Everest is not really the world's tallest mountain. That honor goes to Mauna Kea, a dormant volcano in Hawaii. Mauna Kea's peak is 13,796 feet above sea level, less than half the elevation of Everest. But if you measured from the base of Mauna Kea, which is deep on the ocean floor, you'd find it was more than 32,800 feet tall, far taller than Everest.

Observatories—buildings that house large telescopes—sit atop Hawaii's Mauna Kea. It's one of the best places in the world to see the stars.

important to people, animals, and plants because they serve as barriers to weather and because they collect snow in the winter, which runs off the mountain when the weather warms and provides people with fresh water.

There are several kinds of mountains on Earth today. Some mountains were formed when huge plates on the earth's surface pushed against one another and caused the mountains to arise. The Rocky Mountains in North America are examples of those kinds of mountains. Other mountains were formed as the result of molten rock, or *magma*, pushing up from under the earth's crust. Sometimes the magma erupts and piles up on the surface, making what is called a *volcanic mountain*. Mount St. Helens in Washington state is a volcanic mountain.

Some areas of land on Earth have no hills or mountains and receive enough precipitation to make them suitable for farming. These areas are called *plains*. The Great Plains of North America, which are located west of the Mississippi River and east of the Rocky Mountains, produce about 25 percent of the world's wheat, oats, barley, rye, sorghum, and corn.

Some areas of the world receive enough rain and snow each year to support large numbers of plants and

Giant farm machines called combines harvest wheat on the plains.

other life. But other areas are so dry that only certain kinds of plants and animals can live there. *Deserts* are usually defined as areas of land that receive less than ten inches of rain or snow every year.

Camels can go a long time between drinks of water—which allows them to live in desert areas. This one is in China's Gobi Desert.

When God Made the World Come Alive

Imagine if someone set up a terrarium at school one day. He'd add the rocks, the sand, the water—maybe even some natural-looking decorations. Now. . .what do you think is missing? That's right! Plants and animals! No terrarium is complete without living things, even if they're just plants.

Creation wasn't complete until God began adding the living things He prepared Earth for in the first place. He had already finished making planet Earth a suitable home for all animals and other living things, so now it was time to begin the process of giving the earth life by filling it with every kind of living thing you can imagine—and some you can't.

The first living things God created were ones that don't move. . .at least not on their own: plants.

Plants live and grow just about anywhere there is sunlight and water. Plants can be found on land, in oceans, and in fresh water. Not all plants need the same amount of sunlight and water to live and grow. But God designed each and every one of them to be able to live and grow and reproduce in the different kinds of surroundings He placed them in.

There are many different types of plants living on Earth today. There are many kinds each of trees, grasses, flowers, bushes, herbs, ferns, mosses, vines, and algae. Scientists estimate that there are about 350,000 species of plants living on Earth today, but so far almost 288,000 kinds of plants have been identified and named.

The arrival of land animals on Earth wouldn't begin for another few days. But in the meantime, God created living things that were like animals in some ways but very different in others. Plants are different from animals in three important ways.

First, plants have chlorophyll in them. *Chlorophyll* is what makes plants green and also allows them to produce their own food by absorbing sunlight. Second, the cell walls of all plants are made of a very sturdy material called *cellulose*. The cells of animals, on the other hand, don't have rigid walls the way plants do. Third, plants don't move on their own. Sure, they may seem to move as they respond to sunlight—like when a sunflower points toward the sun so that it can absorb more sunlight—but no plant can just get up and move on its own.

Why the Earth Needs Plants

Have you ever stopped and thought about how important plants are to all life on Earth? They're probably more important than you realize. First of all, plants are necessary for food for all animals—even the ones that eat mostly meat. Nearly every living creature that lives on Earth depends on plants to survive. All animals either eat plants or they eat other animals that eat plants.

The ability of plants to produce food is an amazing part of God's design for life on Earth. When He made plants, He gave them the ability to collect energy directly from the sun. In a process called *photosynthesis*, almost all plants use the chlorophyll stored in their leaves to convert the energy they collect from the sun into food. The plants store this energy in the form of natural sugar or *carbohydrates*—which are the basis of all food that animals and people eat. That means there are no naturally produced foods that aren't somehow based on plants.

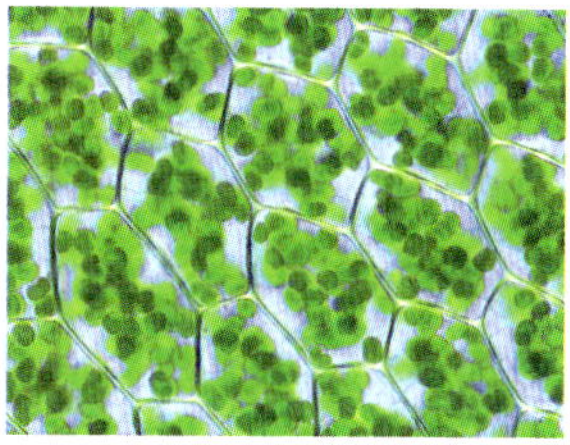

Chloroplasts, the parts of a plant cell that carry on photosynthsesis, show up as green circles in this highly magnified picture.

Plants supply the earth with much more than food. During the process of photosynthesis, plants also absorb carbon dioxide and then release oxygen into the atmosphere. Scientists estimate that plants—from microscopic ones that live in the ocean to the biggest trees growing on land—produce as much as 98 percent of the breathable oxygen in the earth's atmosphere.

All this means that without plants, there would be no life on Earth—at least as we know it today. It also means that God, who created all the earth and everything that lives in it, thought ahead enough to provide all living things with all they needed to live and grow and reproduce here on Earth.

DID YOU KNOW. . . ?

If you've ever been in the produce department at your local supermarket, you've probably noticed that mushrooms are placed in the produce department—along with fruits and vegetables, all of which come from different kinds of plants. But mushrooms aren't plants and don't come from plants. They belong in what is called the fungus kingdom. . .along with spores and molds. That's right! Mushrooms aren't vegetables, even though your grocer puts them in the same department as fruits and vegetables. They are a part of the same kingdom of living things as molds and fungi (the plural of *fungus*).

Would you eat a fungus? If you like mushrooms, you would!

The First Kingdom on Earth: The Plant Kingdom

By the time God was finished creating all the living things on Earth, there were millions and millions of species of plants, animals, and other life forms. Since then, *biologists*—scientists who study living things—have sorted and classified all living things by how they are different and how they are alike.

The largest classes of living things are called *kingdoms*. All living things are classified into one of five different kingdoms, and all plants are placed in the plant kingdom (or as some people call it, *Kingdom Plantae*).

Biologists have broken down the plant kingdom into smaller and smaller divisions based on different things that are true about different kinds of plants. The two largest divisions are between plants that can circulate water and other liquids through their roots, stems, and leaves, and plants that need to absorb all their water from their surroundings.

Spores of a mossy plant

Most plants can circulate water through their roots, stems, and leaves. Biologists call these *vascular* plants. These types of plants are then broken down by how they reproduce. Most plants reproduce through seeds, but some reproduce through spores. Plants that reproduce through seeds are called *spermatophytes*. Plants that reproduce through spores are called *pteridophytes*, and they include some mosses and ferns.

Pine cone

Some plants reproduce through seeds that aren't encased in anything. These plants are called *gymnosperms*. Many of these types of plants are very important to humans because they are a source of wood. That includes different species of cedars, firs, pines, spruces, redwoods, and others. These plants reproduce through seeds, but the seeds are stored in female cones until they are fertilized by the pollen of male cones. After the seeds mature, they are dropped out onto the ground, where they sprout and eventually mature into a fully grown plant.

Apples, showing seed inside

Most plants reproduce through seeds that are encased in things people and animals eat. You know how apples, cucumbers, pears, and other types of fruits and vegetables have seeds inside them? That's so they can reproduce and make more of their own kind. These kinds of plants are called *flowering plants*, or more scientifically, *angiosperms*.

More Reasons to Like Plants with Flowers

Can you remember the last time you saw a beautiful flower? How about the last time you enjoyed a fresh piece of fruit or a juicy, sweet piece of corn on the cob? How about the last time you wore something made of cotton? If you can remember the last time you did one of those things, then you can remember the last time you benefited from a group of plants scientists call the *angiosperms*.

All these types of plants have one thing in common: flowers.

Not all flowers are as colorful or showy as a rose or a daffodil. . .or even a daisy. Many flowers are very small and not all that colorful. Sometimes you wouldn't even think of them as flowers. For example, oak trees, grass, and wheat plants all have flowers, but they aren't much to look at, so you don't really notice them. But all flowers, even the ones that aren't as pretty as others, serve the same purpose: reproduction of the plant.

When you hear the word *flowering*, you probably think of pretty flowers like roses, pansies, daisies, and other kinds of popular flowers. But did you know that most of our food comes from flowering plants? All grains, beans, nuts, fruits, vegetables, and spices come to our dinner tables as a result of the reproduction process of flowering plants. So do drinks like coffee, tea, and cola. Flowering plants also help us in the production of a lot of our clothes. Cotton and linen are produced from the fibers of flowering plants. A lot of the medicines we use are also made from flowering plants.

THAT'S WEIRD!

Look out, fly—you're about to become lunch!

The plant world includes some of the strangest of all God's created things. Did you know that there are plants that eat meat? It's true! Instead of taking all their nourishment through their roots and from sunlight like most plants do, these plants trap and eat insects and sometimes (are you ready for this?) small amphibians, reptiles, birds, and mammals. Probably the best known of the carnivorous plants is the Venus flytrap. But there are several other plants that eat meat. They include bladderworts, butterworts, pitcher plants, sundews, and cobra lilies.

Flowering plants reproduce through a process called *pollination*. Pollination happens when male plant spores (the pollen) combine with the female reproductive cells. Once pollination takes place, the plant begins to produce seeds and fruit. Pollen from a flowering plant is dusty-looking stuff that is most often yellow but can also be black, white, green, orange, or just about any other color you can think of.

Different kinds of flowering plants pollinate in different ways. Some plants need the help of birds and bats, as well as bees and other insects, to pollinate. Other kinds of plants are pollinated when the wind picks up their pollen and spreads it out onto other plants of the same species. A few plants, such as peanut plants, just pollinate themselves.

Pollination is a necessary part of a flowering plant's life cycle. Without pollination, flowering plants can't reproduce. That means they couldn't bear fruit or seeds. If pollination were to suddenly stop, then almost all the earth's plant life would soon begin to die off.

CHAPTER 5

Day 4

Some Great Stuff God Made "Out There"

Then God said, "Let lights appear in the sky to separate the day from the night. Let them be signs to mark the seasons, days, and years. Let these lights in the sky shine down on the earth." And that is what happened. God made two great lights—the larger one to govern the day, and the smaller one to govern the night. He also made the stars. God set these lights in the sky to light the earth, to govern the day and night, and to separate the light from the darkness. And God saw that it was good.

And evening passed and morning came, marking the fourth day.

GENESIS 1:14–19

On the fourth day of creation, God made things that have amazed and confused humans since the beginning of time. On that day, He made the things that aren't really part of the planet Earth but that are still important parts of His creation. That includes the objects we can easily see in the sky, like the sun, the moon, and some of the stars and planets. But it also includes things in outer space that it took thousands of years for people to figure out how to see from here on Earth. All of these things that God made and placed out in space on the fourth day of creation make up what we now call the universe.

When you start to understand some things about what God really did on the fourth day of creation, you'll be amazed. But you'll also begin to understand that even though our planet is very, very big, it is really just a tiny speck in an unbelievably huge universe.

One of the great things about knowing a little something about the stars, planets, galaxies, and other things God made on that fourth day of creation is that it helps you to understand just how big and awesome the God who made all those things really is!

Giant radio antennas in California's Mojave Desert scan the skies, helping scientists learn more about the gigantic universe we live in.

Just How Big Is the Universe Anyway?

Almost since we first noticed the sun, the moon, the stars, and other mysterious objects in the sky, we humans have tried our best to discover what's out there in that enormous universe God created.

Thousands of years ago, people started to get the fact that the universe God created was really big and really amazing and that it included some amazing creations. But it wasn't until the past several hundred years that we started to understand just *how* big it really is.

No one really knows for sure how big the universe is. So far, *astronomers*—scientists who study things in outer space—have located objects as far away from Earth as 10 to 13 billion light-years (for a quick reminder of how far a light-year is, look back at page 15 in chapter 1). Some of these objects are called *quasars*. Scientists believe quasars are formed when two *galaxies* (huge collections of stars, which you'll read about later in this chapter) collide with one another. They believe quasars are probably huge points of light that are fueled by enormous black holes in outer space.

How many miles are in a light year? Let's see. . .

Light travels 186,000 miles a second. . .

There are (x) 60 seconds in a minute. . .

There are (x) 60 minutes in an hour. . .

There are (x) 24 hours in a day. . .

There are (x) 365 days in a year. . .

So light travels about

5,865,696,000,000 miles in a year!

What Stars Are and How They Work

If you've ever been on a camping trip or just been outside during a really dark, clear night, you have probably seen thousands of stars in the sky. But during the day you can see the most important star to us humans: the sun! The stars you see at night look very tiny from Earth, but they are all actually huge balls of burning gas—just like our sun.

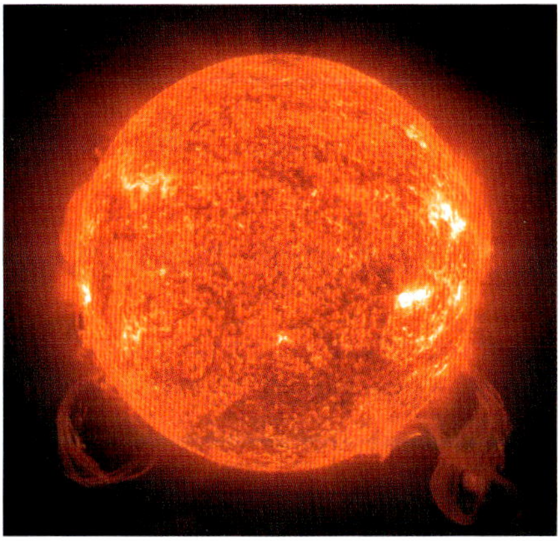

Our sun—photographed by the Solar and Heliospheric Observatory spacecraft—shoots out flares on two sides. Doesn't that look hot?

Even though stars give off huge amounts of heat and light, they don't burn the same way things burn here on Earth. For a fire to start here on Earth, you need three things: fuel, oxygen, and something to ignite the fire. Stars have plenty of fuel in the form of hydrogen, but since there is no oxygen inside stars, they have to burn another way. That way is called *nuclear fusion*, and it happens in stars when gravity from inside the star—which is many, many times as strong as the earth's gravity—pulls hydrogen inward and causes four atoms of hydrogen to fuse together to form one atom of helium. When that happens, part of the mass from the hydrogen atom is left over, and that extra mass is converted into heat and light.

Even though all stars look pretty much the same when you look at them from Earth, there are actually several kinds of stars. Some stars are very small, at least compared to other stars, and some stars are many times bigger than our sun. The smallest stars in the universe are called *neutron stars*. These are actually dead stars that are no wider than a city. The biggest stars in the universe—in fact, the biggest objects of any kind in the universe—are called *supergiant* stars. Some supergiants are more than 1,000 times bigger than our sun.

Most stars fit into a class astronomers call *main sequence stars*. Our sun is a main sequence star. Main sequence stars come in many different sizes, and many of them burn a lot brighter than others. But like our sun, all main sequence stars convert hydrogen into helium in their cores and release amazing amounts of heat and light.

RECORD BREAKING

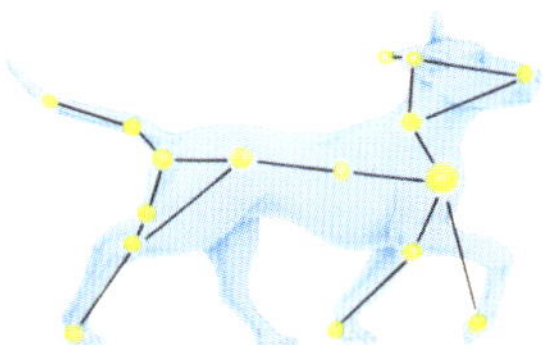

Sirius is often called the Dog Star because it's part of the "big dog" (Canis Majoris) constellation.

The biggest star known to humans is called VY Canis Majoris. It is located in the constellation Canis Majoris, which also includes Sirius, the brightest star in the sky. Scientists estimate that VY Canis Majoris is up to 2,100 times the diameter of our sun and that if it were to replace our sun, it would stretch all the way out to Saturn, the sixth planet in our solar system. VY Canis Majoris is so big that if you could hollow it out, it could hold 7 billion stars the size of our sun inside it.

Constellations: Random Puzzles in the Sky

From Earth, some of the stars in the sky are grouped in a way that makes them look like connect-the-dots puzzles of animals, people, and other things. These are called *constellations*.

There is a total of 88 named constellations. You've probably seen the Big Dipper, the Little Dipper, and other easy-to-find constellations. What constellations you see at night depends on where you live and what time of the year you look. The ones you can see in the Northern Hemisphere are different from the ones you can see in the south. For example, people in the north can see the Big Dipper and people in the south can see the Southern Cross.

Even today, some people believe that where the constellations appear in the sky affects life here on Earth. But in truth, constellations are nothing more than imaginary formations of stars in the sky. Even though the constellations may *look* like pictures of animals, people, or other things, most of them are made up of stars that are many light-years apart in space. One exception to that rule is the Big Dipper. The Big Dipper is made up of stars that really *are* close together—at least when you compare the distance between them with the distances between other stars.

People in North America call this constellation "the Big Dipper"—but in England, they're more likely to say "the Plough."

THAT'S WEIRD!

Here is an artist's idea of how a "black hole" can swallow a star: The star (left) comes within the black hole's extreme gravity and begins to break apart (center), finally swirling into the dark void (right).

Have you ever heard of a black hole? It's an object in space with such strong gravity coming from it that nothing, including light, can escape from it. Scientists believe that black holes are created when massive stars run out of fuel and die. When that happens, the star's gravity pulls its material inward and compresses its core, which creates a supernova explosion. What is left over after the explosion is the star's core. The core's gravitational pull is so strong that not even light can escape it. The object is now a black hole. Although scientists can't really see black holes, they can find them by watching how objects around them are affected.

What Happens When a Really Big Star Dies? A Supernova!

All stars have a certain amount of fuel they can burn to produce light and heat. When the fuel in a really big star runs out, that star begins to die. When that happens, the star explodes and forms what astronomers call a *supernova*. A supernova is a gigantic explosion that makes the star brighter than all the other stars.

When the supernova is finished, what is left is a huge cloud called a *nebula* and a compressed star called a *neutron star*. If the star that exploded is one of the biggest stars in the universe, then it leaves behind a nebula *or* what is called a *black hole*.

Supernovas are very rare events. But every year astronomers see about 300 supernovas in other galaxies. Almost a thousand years ago, astronomers in China, Japan, Korea, and Arabia recorded a supernova that was so bright that it could be seen during the day. That supernova formed what is now known as the Crab Nebula.

See the bright star to the lower left of the "spiral galaxy"? That's a supernova—brighter than other stars, because it's in the process of exploding!

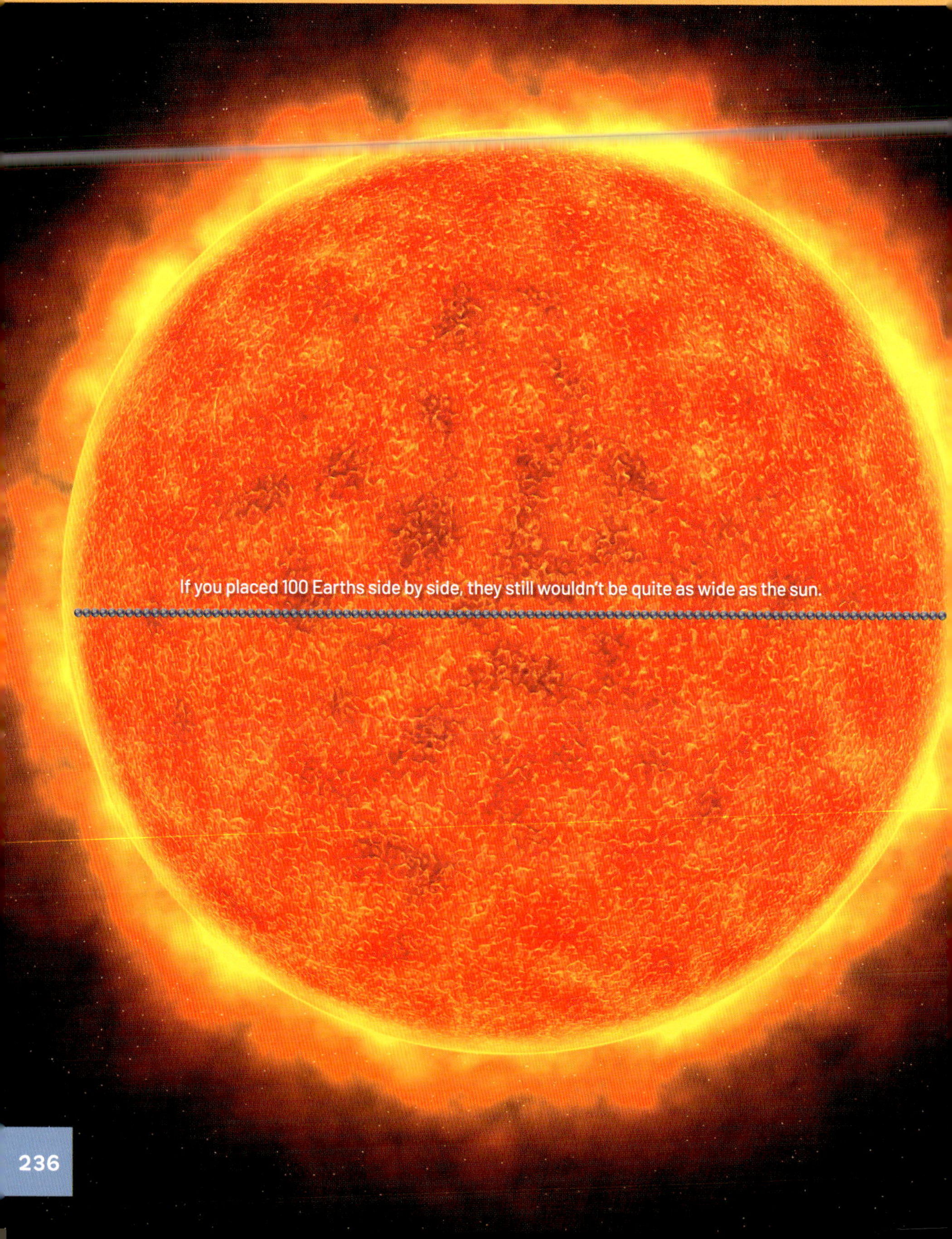
If you placed 100 Earths side by side, they still wouldn't be quite as wide as the sun.

Earth's Own Star: The Sun

When you see the sun, you're actually seeing a medium-sized star. The sun is made up of about three-quarters hydrogen and one-quarter helium. The sun's gravity holds planets and other objects in our solar system and keeps them orbiting around it.

The earth gets all its heat and light from the sun. Without that heat and light, plants and animals and people couldn't live on Earth. Our planet can support the different forms of life that live here because it is the perfect distance—about 93 millions miles—from the sun. If it were too much closer, the earth would be too hot to live on. If it were any farther away, it would be too cold to live here.

Maybe you haven't given much thought to the sun. . .other than how much you like it when it shines when you're outside. But here are some facts about the sun that just might amaze you. The temperature on the sun's surface is about 10,000 degrees Fahrenheit. Think that's hot? Try this: The temperature deep *inside* the sun is about 27 *million* degrees. The sun is about 870,000 miles wide—about 109 times wider than the earth.

Why We Have Seasons

Have you ever wondered why it's cold in the winter and hot in the summer? Or why the days get longer in the spring, then start getting shorter in the fall? The sun always gives off about the same amount of heat and light, so it can't be that someone just turns down the heat every winter.

Here's how it *really* works.

The earth travels all the way around the sun about once every 365 days. But it doesn't orbit the sun with the same spots on the planet pointing directly at the sun all the time. Earth leans to one side as it orbits the sun, so different parts of the earth point more directly at the sun than others during different times of the year. This means that different amounts of sunlight reach different points on the earth during different times of the year. The different amounts of sunlight cause different kinds of weather during those different times. In other words, it's colder when where you live on Earth is farthest from the sun and hotter when it's the closest.

During the summer in the Northern Hemisphere, that part of the earth is pointed more directly at the sun, so it receives more heat and light from the sun than it does in the winter. At that same time, the Southern Hemisphere is farthest away from the sun, so it receives less of the sun's heat and light. That means that when it's summer in the Northern Hemisphere, it's winter in the Southern Hemisphere.

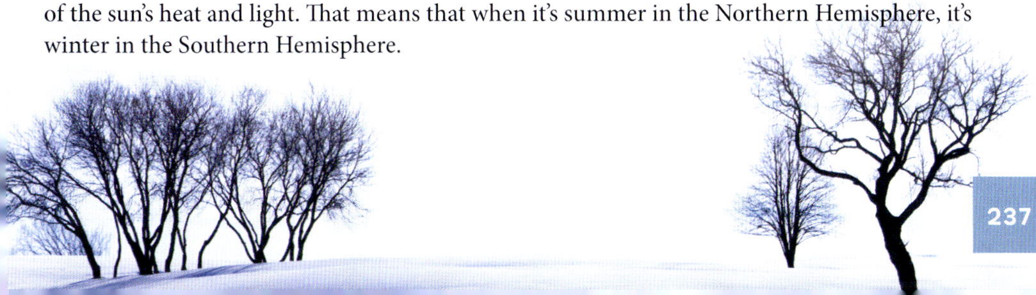

Astronomers Call It a Satellite. . . We Call It the Moon

The earth is one of eight planets that orbit the sun. Most of those planets have what scientists call *satellites* orbiting them. Our earth has a satellite of its own—one you can see in the sky most nights. You know this satellite better as the *moon*.

Even though the moon looks small from the earth, it is actually very large. The moon is about 2,160 miles across, which is about one-fourth the size of Earth. It only looks small because it is about 238,900 miles from Earth. Just as the sun's gravity holds the earth and other planets orbiting in place, Earth's gravity keeps the moon in place and orbiting the earth.

A few people have walked on the moon, but the moon can't support the kinds of plants and animals—or people—that live on Earth. That's because the moon has no air on it. The moon has no air on it because the gravity there is about one-sixth what it is on Earth. That's not even enough gravity for the moon to hold an atmosphere! Also, because the moon has no atmosphere to block out the sun's light or to help it trap heat, temperatures on the moon's surface range from up to 253 degrees Fahrenheit during the day, all the way down to minus 387 degrees Fahrenheit at night.

Even though the moon is the brightest object in the nighttime sky, it doesn't give off its own light. When you see the moon shining brightly, it's because the moon is reflecting light from the sun back to Earth. The moon orbits the earth, and it spins on its axis in about the same time it takes to orbit the earth. That's why we always see the same half of the moon's surface from Earth. The other half of the moon is called the "far side" of the moon. Some people have called that side of the moon the "dark side," but that isn't correct because the sun does shine on the side that is facing away from Earth.

Only 12 humans have ever visited the moon, all of them from the United States: Neil Armstrong (the first to step onto the moon's surface), Buzz Aldrin, Charles "Pete" Conrad Jr., Alan Bean, Alan Shepard Jr., Edgar Mitchell, David Scott, James Irwin, John Young, Charles Duke Jr., Eugene Cernan, and Harrison Schmitt.

Sometimes the moon looks like a big, shiny circle in the sky. But sometimes it is shaped like a crescent. At other times it looks like a sliver of light in the sky. That is because the moon shines on Earth in what are called *lunar phases*. It takes the moon about 29.5 days to complete the cycle of lunar phases and 27.3 days to orbit the earth. The moon looks different during its lunar phases because light from the sun is shining on it at different angles—at least as we see it from Earth. When the moon is full, it's because the sun is shining on the entire surface that we on Earth can see.

Our solar system. From right to left: the sun, Mercury, Venus, Earth, Mars, Jupiter, Saturn, Uranus, Neptune, and Pluto. This picture only shows the order of the planets—it's not to scale. The planets are much farther away from each other, and the sun is much, much larger than shown here.

Our Solar System: The Place Our Sun Calls Home

Our earth is part of a *solar system*. A solar system is made up of a star that has planets and other things orbiting around it. Our solar system includes the sun, a total of eight planets, some *dwarf planets* (more about them later), and other objects such as *comets* and *asteroids*.

Many astronomers believe that our solar system may be only one of many billions placed in the Milky Way Galaxy, the galaxy our solar system is located in, alone. There are more stars in the universe than we can actually count, and astronomers believe that if even a small fraction of those stars are centers of solar systems, then there could be countless hundreds of billions of solar systems in the entire universe.

Our sun is the center of our solar system. But it's a lot more than that. The sun is far bigger and heavier than the rest of the bodies in our solar system combined. The sun actually accounts for 99.9 percent of all the mass in our solar system. That means that if you put a value of $1,000 on all the material in our solar system, the sun would be worth $999, with all the rest of the material worth one buck!

THE WAY IT USED TO BE

Galileo Galilei (1564–1642)

Hundreds of years ago, people really believed that the earth was the center of the universe. That means they believed that the sun, the moon, the stars, and the other planets revolved around the planet we live on. That began to change when astronomers like Galileo and Nicolaus Copernicus began watching the rotations of the movement of the planets. It took awhile, but in time people came to accept the fact that the earth revolved around the sun, not the other way around.

Nicolaus Copernicus (1473–1543)

Our Neighbors in the Solar System

The eight planets in our solar system are the biggest objects orbiting our sun. Those eight planets—from the closest to the sun to the farthest away—are Mercury, Venus, Earth, Mars, Jupiter, Saturn, Uranus, and Neptune.

Up until 2006, scientists believed there were nine planets in our solar system, because they had classified Pluto as a planet. Pluto is still out there just like it always has been, but scientists have now placed it in a new class of objects in the solar system called *dwarf planets*. Dwarf planets are a lot like planets. They are sphere-shaped (like a basketball) and they orbit the sun. Some astronomers hold that dwarf planets are different from planets in that they orbit in areas of the solar system where there are many other objects also orbiting.

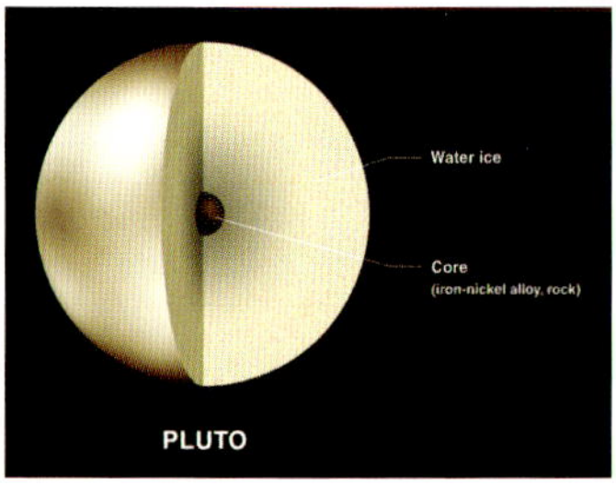

Scientists believe Pluto is mainly frozen methane, with a small center of metal and rock. Far from the sun, Pluto is very, very cold—hundreds of degrees below zero.

Mercury is the smallest planet in our solar system. It is only a little bigger than our moon. Venus is sometimes called Earth's Twin Sister because it is almost the same size as Earth. Mars is a little over half the size of Earth. Uranus is about four times bigger than Earth. Saturn is the second biggest planet in the solar system. At about 75,000 miles in diameter, it is about ten times wider than Earth. Jupiter is the largest planet in our solar system. Jupiter's diameter is about eleven times the diameter of Earth. Scientists estimate that Jupiter is so big that about 1,000 planets the size of Earth could fit inside a hollowed-out Jupiter.

Listed from the smallest to the largest, our solar system's planets are Mercury, Mars, Venus, Earth, Neptune, Uranus, Saturn, and Jupiter.

Earth is the only planet that can support life as we know it. First of all, other planets are either too hot (like Mercury and Venus) or too cold (like Mars) for humans or other forms of life on Earth to live on. Secondly, there's no air—at least the kind we have here on Earth—or liquid water on the other planets. And never mind the fact that Jupiter and Saturn are made mostly of gases we can't breathe!

THAT'S WEIRD!

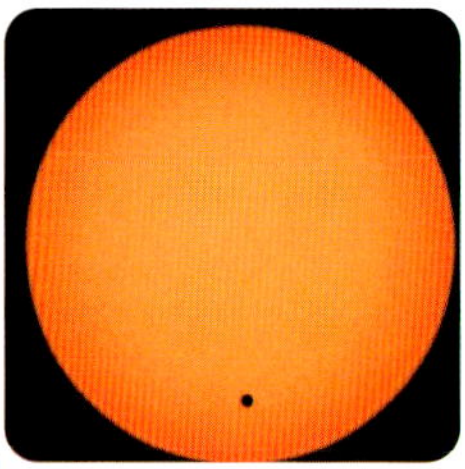

Venus, the second closest planet to the sun in our solar system, spins in the opposite direction compared to the earth and most other planets. Because of that, the sun rises in the west and sets in the east on Venus. But even if you could live on Venus, you wouldn't see the sunrise or sunset very often. That's because one day on Venus is equal to about 243 Earth days.

What's that black spot on the sun? It's the planet Venus passing between the sun and the earth. This rare event, called a "Venus transit," was photographed in 2004.

More Cool Stuff in Our Solar System

Planets and dwarf planets are not the only objects that orbit our sun. There are also some really amazing objects out there that fit into their own classifications. That includes asteroids and comets.

Asteroids are a lot like planets, only smaller. Asteroids orbit the sun like planets do, and they can't make their own light. Most asteroids are made out of rock, but some are made out of metal.

There are tens of thousands of known asteroids in our solar system, with thousands of new ones being discovered every month. Most of the known asteroids orbit the sun between the orbits of Mars and Jupiter in what is called the *main asteroid belt*.

Astronomers believe there are between one million and two million asteroids bigger than half a mile across in the main asteroid belt and millions of smaller ones. A few asteroids are more than 300 miles wide! At 605 miles wide, Ceres (which was also classified as a dwarf planet in 2006) is the biggest object in the asteroid belt.

Halley's Comet streaks through space at 103,000 miles an hour in this photograph from 1986. The "tail" you can see behind the comet is about 450,000 miles long.

While asteroids are made of rock and metal, comets are dirty, dusty balls of ice. That is why they are often called *dirty snowballs*. Many comets orbit the sun differently than the planets and asteroids. Some comets orbit from outside the solar system, then into the solar system, and then back out into outer space.

The word *comet* comes from a Greek word meaning "long-haired." Comets got that name because when they have long tails they are visible from Earth. Comets grow tails when they move close to the sun, where solar heat causes the frozen gases and dust to partially melt and form a long trail of vaporized gas, dust, and rocks.

The most famous comet is Halley's Comet, which can be seen from Earth once every 76 years as it passes close to the sun. But a comet called Shoemaker-Levy 9 became famous in July of 1994 when 20 fragments of the comet crashed into the planet Jupiter.

THE WAY IT USED TO BE

People throughout history have seen bright comets in the night sky, and they believed that when they saw them it meant bad things were going to happen. They believed comets actually entered the earth's atmosphere, and they blamed wars, famines, and death on them. Some people wouldn't even leave their homes when there was a comet overhead! We now know that comets aren't signs of anything good or bad—just another part of God's creation.

In an ancient tapestry, astrologers (left) predict trouble for England's King Harold II (far right) because of the appearance of a comet (top center) during his reign. Harold ruled for nine months in 1066.

The Milky Way Galaxy: A Good Home for a Solar System

This galaxy—called NGC 7331—probably looks very much like our own Milky Way galaxy. The photo was taken by the Spitzer Space Telescope.

The sun at the center of our solar system is just one of literally billions of stars God placed in what is called the *Milky Way Galaxy*. The Milky Way Galaxy is more than 100,000 light-years across and is home to between 100 and 400 billion stars.

A *galaxy* is a huge gathering of stars and other objects organized into a certain shape. Up until the 1920s, the Milky Way was the only known galaxy in the universe. But in 1924 an American astronomer named Edwin Hubble proved that there were several other distant galaxies in space. Since then, we have learned that there are hundreds of billions of galaxies in the universe. Most galaxies are tens of thousands of light-years across and contain billions of stars.

Galaxies come in many different shapes and sizes. The Milky Way Galaxy is what is called a *spiral galaxy*. Spiral galaxies are shaped like giant, spinning wheels with a *hub* (a center that all the stars spin around) and curved *arms* sticking out from the center. The arms of the spiral galaxy are actually tight groups of stars. There are several types of spiral galaxies, and they are classified by the tightness of their arms.

Elliptical galaxies are egg-shaped collections of stars. These are the biggest galaxies—as large as 18 million light-years across. The third kind of galaxy, an *irregular galaxy*, has an unusual shape, so it can't be put in other groups.

Galaxies spin on their hubs at amazing speeds. That includes the Milky Way. In fact, the sun and all the planets and other objects in our solar system are zipping around the center of the Milky Way at around 150 miles per second. And if that seems fast, think about this: Our entire galaxy is traveling through space at about one million miles per hour!

EXPLORING THE HEAVENS

Even if you don't own a telescope or live near a planetarium, you can still learn about some of the wonders of God's creation as they appear in space. It's as easy as stepping outside, looking up, and writing down what you see! Try this: Check out a book on astronomy from the library and look up the names of the constellations (there are eighty-eight of them), and see what they look like and which stars are in them. After you've done that, step out your front door, look up, and see how many of them you can find in the night sky.

CHAPTER 6

Day 5

Things with Fins, Things with Feathers

Then God said, "Let the waters swarm with fish and other life. Let the skies be filled with birds of every kind." So God created great sea creatures and every living thing that scurries and swarms in the water, and every sort of bird—each producing offspring of the same kind. And God saw that it was good. Then God blessed them, saying, "Be fruitful and multiply. Let the fish fill the seas, and let the birds multiply on the earth."

And evening passed and morning came, marking the fifth day.

GENESIS 1:20–23

By the end of the fourth creation day, God had already made everything He knew would be needed for all the different kinds of animals to live on Earth. He made the earth itself and had separated dry land from the water, and He had stocked the earth with plenty of water for the animals to live in and to drink. He had provided the sunlight that is so vital to the growth of plants that would feed the animals and that would supply them with oxygen to breathe.

God had prepared everything perfectly for the animals He was about to create on the fifth and sixth days of creation. It was now time for Him to create what we now call the animal kingdom. He started His work of populating the world with animals by creating fish and birds.

Natural Kingdoms

The Bible doesn't list every type of living thing God created. It doesn't even list what humans would later call *kingdoms*. Maybe that's because He just wanted us to know the basics of creation. Whatever the reason, we can know that He created everything that lives on Earth today.

Not everything that lives on Earth is considered an animal. Over the years, scientists have broken down the world of all living things into what they call *kingdoms*. All living things are divided into five kingdoms: the *Monera kingdom* (includes single-celled creatures called *bacteria*), the *Protista kingdom* (some kinds of algae and single-celled creatures called *protozoa*), the *Fungi kingdom* (molds, spores, and mushrooms), the *Plant kingdom*, and the *Animal kingdom*.

On the fifth day of creation, God began making the animal kingdom. The animal kingdom includes worms, insects, arachnids (animals with eight legs, like spiders and scorpions), mollusks (such as clams, oysters, and octopuses), crustaceans, fish, reptiles, amphibians, birds, and mammals. It also includes creatures you might not have known are animals—creatures such as sponges and corals.

All these living creatures have some special traits in common that make them animals. All of them are made up of many individual cells, and all of them rely in some way or another on other living things for their nourishment. Also, most animals eat their food and digest it inside themselves.

A red-billed tropicbird photographed over the Caribbean Sea

Moving Down the Family Tree

Scientists not only break down all living things into the five kingdoms, but they also break down the animal kingdom into smaller groups called *phyla* (the plural of *phylum*). Most scientists believe there are 38 animal phyla and that most animal species belong to the nine biggest of them.

Each phylum includes smaller groups of animals called *classes*. Classes of animals are then divided into smaller groups called *orders*. Orders are divided into *families* (and sometimes subfamilies), and each family includes a number of different *genera* (the plural of *genus*). Finally, each genus is broken down into one or more *species* of animal.

Fish and birds—the animals God made on the fifth day of creation—are part of the phylum Chordata, which includes all animals that are considered vertebrates. *Vertebrates* are animals that have backbones. *Invertebrates*, on the other hand, are animals that don't have backbones—like crabs, spiders, and insects. Those three animals are called *arthropods,* and they belong to the phylum *Arthropoda*.

Birds all belong to one class of animals called *Aves*. But there are several classes of fish living in the world today.

A blue-spotted stingray photographed off Thailand

Fish's Big Place in the Animal Kingdom

Altogether, there are about 28,000 different species of fish populating the world's waters—with new species still being discovered every year. Some *ichthyologists* (scientists who study fish) say there may be many thousands more fish species yet to be discovered and named.

If you were to look at a chart of different kinds of fish, you would see at the top of their family tree the *superclasses* and *classes*, then what are called *subclasses*. The subclasses are followed by *infraclasses*. If you kept moving down the chart, you'd see the *superorders* of fish, followed by the *orders*, then the *superfamilies* and then the *families*.

There are three superclasses of fish living today, and each of them includes several classes. The biggest superclass of fish is *Osteichthyes* (fish with skeletons made of bone). This class of fish includes the subclass *Achtinopterygii*, which scientists call "ray-finned" fish. If you can't pronounce the word Achtinopterygii, don't worry. You can just think of them as typical fish, because for the most part they look like you'd expect a fish to look. This class of fish includes around 27,000 species, making it not only the largest class of fish but the largest class of vertebrates.

The *Agnatha* superclass of fish is known for having skeletons made of cartilage and not out of bone, like most fish. They also don't have jaws. This class includes lampreys and hagfish. And here's something really strange about this class of fish: They have digestive systems, just like any other fish, but they don't have stomachs!

The *Chondrichthyes* superclass of fish, which also has skeletons made of cartilage, includes sharks and rays. This class of fish includes some species you have no doubt heard about, including the whale shark, the largest fish alive on Earth today, and the great white shark.

There are literally hundreds of families of fish, but one-third of all species belong to the nine largest families. The family with the most species (at about 2,400) is called the *Cyprinidae* family, which includes carps and minnows. Since goldfish are carps, they belong to this family of fish.

To help you better understand the basics of how scientists classify fish, take a look at the chart below, which shows you where a common goldfish fits in the animal kingdom:

- Kingdom: *Animalia* (all animals)
- Phylum: *Chordata* (animals with backbones)
- Class: *Actinopterygii* (all ray-finned fish)
- Order: *Cypriniformes* (carps, minnows, roaches, and their relatives)
- Family: *Cyprinidae* (carps, minnows, and barbs)
- Genus: *Carassius* (Crucian carps)
- Species: *Carassius auratus* (the goldfish)

RECORD BREAKING

At up to 40 feet long and weighing up to 15 tons, the whale shark is the world's biggest fish. If you ever saw a whale shark, you wouldn't need to worry about being attacked, even if you were in the water with it. A whale shark eats only plankton—tiny plants and animals that live in the sea—and other small organisms, which it catches by taking water into its huge mouth and then straining out the food through its gills. In fact, it has been reported that whale sharks are gentle creatures that sometimes seem to enjoy playing with divers.

A diver swims with a whale shark in the Indian Ocean.

What Makes a Fish a Fish?

Fish are some of the most amazing members of the animal kingdom. All fish are vertebrates, which means they have backbones. All birds and mammals, including human beings, are also vertebrates, but more than half of all known species of vertebrates living in the world today are fish.

On the fifth day of creation, God made fish and many other forms of life that live in the water. That included many types of life that are not fish, even though they may have some of the same characteristics as fish. Different species of jellyfish, starfish, shellfish, sea anemones, coral, crustaceans (crabs, shrimps, lobsters, and others), and thousands of other animals also live in the earth's water, but they aren't fish.

So what makes a fish a fish? Fish come in every size, color, and shape you can imagine—and some you probably can't—but they all have certain things in common. . .other than having a backbone, that is. All fish are *cold-blooded*, meaning that their body temperature adjusts to the temperature of the water they live in. All fish have gills that absorb oxygen from the water into their bloodstreams. All fish have fins, though some species have more than others. And most fish have scales that protect their bodies.

THAT'S AMAZING!

Even though there's a lot of mystery around what kinds of fish and other sea creatures live in the deepest part of the world's oceans, scientists know that the record for fish living in the deepest waters goes to a type of fish in the brotulid family. These fish live in the ocean at depths of 23,000 feet or more. One species of fish—with the tongue-twisting scientific name of Abyssobrotula galatheae—was captured in the Puerto Rican Trench from an amazing depth of almost 27,500 feet—or more than five miles down. Most fish living at these depths have lost the use of their eyes—if they have eyes at all—simply because sunlight can't penetrate that deep into the ocean.

Where Fish Live

Fish live in just about any area of the world where you can find bodies of water. Some live in the saltwater of the world's oceans and seas. But many also live in freshwater lakes, rivers, streams, and other bodies of water. Some freshwater fish live in slow-moving or still water (in lakes and ponds), but others tend to live in fast-moving streams and rivers. Still other species of fish live in what is called *brackish* water, which is a mixture of saltwater and freshwater found in some coastal areas. One place you'll never find a fish living is in very salty bodies of water, like the Great Salt Lake in Utah.

Some types of fish live in places where the conditions would kill most other forms of life. There are fish that live in streams and pools in caves where no sunlight reaches them. Some fish live in the deepest parts of the ocean, several miles down. Some fish live in desert ponds and streams that dry up every year. These fish have the amazing ability to bury themselves in the mud, hibernate for up to two years, then swim free when the water returns. Some fish even live under the polar ice caps!

THAT'S WEIRD!

Can you imagine walking down the street and seeing a fish crawling along in front of you? That's exactly what happens sometimes in some neighborhoods in Florida, where a really strange fish called the walking catfish is sometimes seen crawling on dry land from one body of water to another. This weird species of fish has the ability to "walk" (actually, they crawl using their pectoral fins as legs) on dry land for a short time and breathe air as it moves from one body of water to another. The walking catfish first came to the United States in the 1960s, when they were imported from Asia for home aquariums.

How Fish Breathe

A fish's gills are amazingly designed organs. The gills are made up of tiny threadlike strands filled with tiny blood vessels. The fish breathes by taking water in through its open mouth and then forcing the water over the filaments when it closes its mouth. The filaments absorb the oxygen and move it into the fish's bloodstream.

Even though all fish have gills to collect oxygen from the water, some fish also take oxygen out of the air, using specially designed organs that do the same work your lungs do. Some species of lungfish can bury themselves in the mud when the body of water they live in dries up. These fish can survive on oxygen from the air for up to two years, or until the water returns.

Some kinds of fish have labyrinth organs that they use to breathe air from the atmosphere so that they can survive in oxygen-poor water. They still have gills just like any other fish, and they get most of their oxygen from the water. These fish are called *labyrinth fish*, and they include the betta (or Siamese fighting fish), a fish you can find in just about any pet store or aquarium shop.

How Fish Reproduce "After Their Own Kind"

When God created the different species of fish, He designed them to reproduce in a variety of ways. Most fish reproduce by laying or scattering their eggs in the water. This process is called *spawning*, and it happens when the female fish releases her eggs into the water and the male fertilizes them with his sperm. Some fish give birth to live babies. That means that the male fish must deposit his sperm inside the female fish, where her eggs are fertilized and later grow into baby fish that are born alive. Most fish leave their eggs or young to fend for themselves, but some are very good parents that protect their nests and babies until their offspring are able to take care of themselves.

Most fish reproduce in the same water they live in their whole lives. But some fish begin their lives in freshwater, migrate to saltwater, where they spend most of their lives, then return to freshwater to spawn. These are called *anadromous* fish, and they include salmon, smelt, shad, striped bass, sturgeon, and others. On the other hand, there are fish that are born in saltwater but live most of their lives in freshwater, only to return to saltwater to spawn. These are called *catadomous* fish, and they include most kinds of eels.

DID YOU KNOW. . . ?

While most fish lay their eggs or give live birth to their young and then pay no attention to them (other than to eat them, in some cases!), some species of fish are very good parents. For example, many species from the cichlid (pronounced "sick-lid") family—some of which are kept in freshwater aquariums as pets—are some of the most devoted, protective parents in all creation. Some species of cichlids fiercely guard their eggs and young from any and all predators—even those that are far bigger than they are! Probably the best examples are the mouthbreeders, which care for their eggs and young by carrying them in their mouths.

EXPLORING THE WORLD OF FISH

If you're interested in exploring the world of fish, you don't need to go any further than your local pet store or aquarium shop. When you go, take a pencil and notepad, and as you look at the different kinds of fish, write down what you see, including the name of the species. Then go to your library—or log on to the internet—and see what you can learn about the fish you've just seen: what they eat, how they reproduce, where they live in the wild. As you do these things, you'll learn to understand and appreciate God's creativity in making these fish you've just seen.

Birds, Birds Everywhere!

Birds live all over the world. They are found on every continent and in almost every kind of climate. Leading the world with the most species of birds—3,200—is South America. That includes the nations of Colombia, Bolivia, and Peru, each of which is home to around 1,700 species. About 2,900 species of birds live in Asia, and Africa is home to about 2,300. North America—which includes the United States and Canada—accounts for about 2,000 species, with another 1,000 living in Europe. There are even 65 kinds of birds living in Antarctica!

Doesn't he look cold? This "chin-strap penguin" of Antarctica is named for the black line that runs under its beak.

Of course, there are far more kinds of birds living in more ordinary climates where there are no extremely hot or extremely cold temperatures. But God also has designed and equipped certain birds to live in places where it's hard to imagine any living thing surviving for very long.

Tiny hummingbirds have long, thin beaks they use to suck nectar from delicate flowers.

Birds are found in the hottest, driest deserts. Others are found in the coldest parts of the Arctic and Antarctic. Different kinds of birds live in open grasslands, in forests and jungles, on cliff faces and mountaintops, and on river banks and seashores. Some birds like to make their homes in manmade structures like barns, mineshafts, and the roofs of houses.

Some birds live only near or in water. These kinds of birds, which are called *aquatic birds*, also get most or all of their food from the water. Some species of aquatic birds, such as loons, tend to live near freshwater lakes, and some tend to live near saltwater. Some aquatic birds live near both saltwater and freshwater. Birds like ducks, geese, and swans—birds called *waterfowl*—live near freshwater lakes, ponds, and marshes.

Large macaws have short, tough beaks they use to crack nuts.

Birds that live in different kinds of environments look and behave very differently from one another. The easiest differences for you to see are the bird's size, body shape, color, beak or bill shape, and the length of the legs and neck. None of these differences happened by accident. They happened because the same God who created the environment where the bird lives also designed each bird to live in the environment He placed it in.

Sparrows are common birds, and a good example of passerines, birds that perch.

The common loon is a duck-like bird of North America.

Some turkeys are raised on farms. This is a "wild turkey" showing off his plumage (tail feathers).

The budgie, a type of parakeet, is a common pet bird.

The Bird Family Tree

Earlier, you read about the long and complicated "family tree" of the world's fish. Birds have their own family tree too, but it isn't nearly as large or complicated as that of fish.

Like all fish, all birds are part of the phylum *Chordata*, which means they are all animals with backbones. But unlike fish, all birds belong to just one class of animals. That class is called *Aves*. *Ornithologists*—scientists who study birds—have placed birds into about two dozen groups called *orders*. Those orders are divided into about 160 families, which are then grouped into birds of the same genus. Finally, the genus is divided into the different species of birds.

There are about 10,000 known species of birds living all over the world today, and more than half of them are from the order *Passeriformes*. They are more often called *passerines*, and they are from the order scientists have listed as *perching birds*. These birds' toes and legs are designed so that they can balance themselves on tree limbs, twigs, and telephone wires. Common birds like sparrows, finches, warblers, crows, blackbirds, thrushes, and swallows are all considered perching birds.

There are other orders of birds that include kinds of birds you have probably either seen or heard of. That includes the order *Anseriformes*, which includes ducks, geese, swans, and other kinds of waterfowl. The bald eagle, as well as other kinds of birds of prey like hawks and falcons, belongs to the order *Falconiformes*. Turkeys and chickens, both important birds for food, are from the order *Galliformes*. And the parrots, macaws, parakeets, and several other kinds of birds you see at your local pet store? They are from the order *Psittaciformes*.

When you get down the family tree for birds to the branch scientists call the *genus*, then you'll start to see how much certain kinds of birds are very much like other kinds in that genus. For example, the white stork and the black stork are from the same genus (called *Ciconia*) and look very much alike (except for the color), but they are two different kinds of birds.

To help you better understand how scientists have put together the family tree for birds, take a look at the following chart. It will show you where the American robin, a bird you have probably seen many times, fits in:

The American robin

- Kingdom: *Animalia* (all animals)
- Phylum: *Chordata* (animals with backbones)
- Class: *Aves* (all birds)
- Order: *Passeriformes* (perching birds)
- Family: *Turdidae* (all thrushes)
- Genus: *Turdus* (similar thrushes)
- Species: *Turdus migratorius* (the American robin)

What Makes a Bird a Bird?

God created birds in many different sizes, shapes, and colors. The tiny bee hummingbird is the smallest bird known. It measures less than 2.5 inches long when fully grown and weighs less than .10 ounces. Ostriches, on the other hand, are the world's largest bird. Ostriches can grow to 8 feet tall and can weigh more than 300 pounds.

But no matter how big or small a certain kind of bird is, no matter what color its feathers are, and no matter where it lives or how it eats or nests, it has certain things in common with all other birds.

Like fish, birds are vertebrates, and that means they have backbones. But instead of fins and scales, birds have wings, feathers, and a beak (or bill) with no teeth. Birds are also *warm-blooded*, which means that their body temperature stays pretty much the same all the time. All birds reproduce by laying eggs.

Most species of birds can fly, and they use that ability to hunt for food, to escape predators (including other birds sometimes), and to migrate from one place to another so they can get away from weather that is too cold or too hot. Birds that can fly are designed to be some of the world's greatest athletes. They have strong, hollow bones, powerful muscles, and strong hearts and lungs. They also have amazingly designed wings and powerful flight muscles that give them the ability to take off, to stay in the air, and to reach sometimes amazing speeds in midair.

But do you know what one characteristic sets birds apart

The bee hummingbird—the smallest known bird—lives in Cuba. This is a female, which is slightly larger than the male.

from all other animals? It's not the fact that they all reproduce by laying eggs. Most species of fish, reptiles, and amphibians—as well as a few mammals—lay eggs. So do insects and many other living creatures. It's not the fact that they all have wings and that most of them can fly. Bats are mammals, but they have wings and can fly. So can most insects. It's not even the fact that they all have beaks or bills.

RECORD BREAKING

A peregrine falcon snatches a smaller bird in flight.

The peregrine falcon, which lives almost everywhere on Earth, is not only the world's fastest-flying bird but also the fastest creature of any kind on Earth today. Peregrines can fly at speeds of well over 200 miles per hour. They use their speed to hunt for food. They swoop from great heights to catch prey on the ground and other birds in midair. Peregrines eat mostly medium-sized birds, but they also sometimes eat small mammals and reptiles and insects.

If you want to know for certain if an animal is a bird, remember this: *If it has feathers, it's a bird!* In all the animal kingdom, only birds have feathers. Not only that, *all* birds have feathers!

God didn't put feathers on birds just to make them look pretty. Different types of feathers on a bird's body serve different purposes. The long, wide feathers on the bird's wings and tail allow the bird to fly (the tail feathers help the bird to steer itself while in flight), and the softer feathers that grow close to the skin help insulate the bird from heat or cold. Some male birds have big, colorful feathers they use to attract their mates, while the females usually have duller-colored feathers that help them to blend into their surroundings while they nest. That way they can escape the notice of predators that like to eat eggs. . .or the mother bird herself.

DID YOU KNOW. . . ?

You probably know that ostriches can't fly. Their bodies are too heavy and their wings are too small for them to even attempt flying. But did you know there are actually 40 species of birds living on Earth today that can't fly? The list also includes several different species of kiwis, which live in New Zealand, as well as the emu, which is a native of Australia. Penguins, which live in the earth's Southern Hemisphere, are also flightless birds, but they use their wings for swimming. In case you're wondering, chickens don't fit on the list of flightless birds because they can actually fly.

Drivers in New Zealand see this sign to warn them of kiwis ahead!

How Birds Reproduce

All birds reproduce by laying eggs with hard shells. The number of eggs the female bird lays at one time depends on the species. Some birds lay one egg per nesting, while others lay more than a dozen at a time. All birds' eggs are fertilized during mating while they are still inside the female bird's body.

The southern masked-weaver is an African bird that "weaves" its nest from grass, reeds, and other natural materials.

Most birds build nests to protect their eggs from weather and predators. What the nest looks like and where the bird builds it depends on the species of bird. Many birds nest in trees, but others nest on the ground or underground. Some birds like to nest in man-made structures like housetops, gutters, barns and sheds, and other places. Some birds weave beautiful nests of grass, twigs, feathers, and other materials, but some nest in hollowed-out trees. Other kinds of birds, like eagles, nest in high treetops, while others just dig out a hole in the sand or dirt to nest. Some birds even nest in underground burrows.

Almost all birds sit on their eggs to keep them warm until they hatch. Most bird "couples" stay together during the nesting time and take turns sitting on the eggs so both the male and the female have a chance to feed. That is not true for all birds, though. Male emus do all the sitting and also care for the babies once they hatch. The male emperor penguin cares for his mate's egg during its incubation period.

Once the egg has hatched and the female penguin returns from the sea where she has been feeding, she begins helping care for the newly hatched chick.

When most baby birds first hatch, they are completely dependent on their parents for food. Both parents feed the young, whose mouths are always open waiting for Mom and Dad to feed them. Some birds feed their young by eating and partly digesting the food, then vomiting it into their chicks' mouths. That's called *regurgitation*, and although it might sound kinda gross, for the baby birds it's as tasty and nutritious as a big pancake breakfast is to you!

Some baby birds are able to eat on their own almost as soon as they hatch. Baby ducks, geese, chickens, quails, and other types of birds get up and walk soon after they hatch, but they stay close to their mothers, who protect them and take them to places where they can find food.

THAT'S WEIRD!

The killdeer is an amazing—and really noisy—bird that uses a really strange method for protecting its nest. When a predator, looking for a quick egg breakfast, gets too close to the killdeer's nest, the mother will use a broken-wing act to distract the predator. The bird will walk away from the nest, then start flopping around on the ground and squawking as if it is injured and can't fly. Once the mother has distracted the predator into thinking it has found an easy meal, she suddenly seems to get better. She then flies away and circles the area before she returns to her nest.

THAT'S AMAZING!

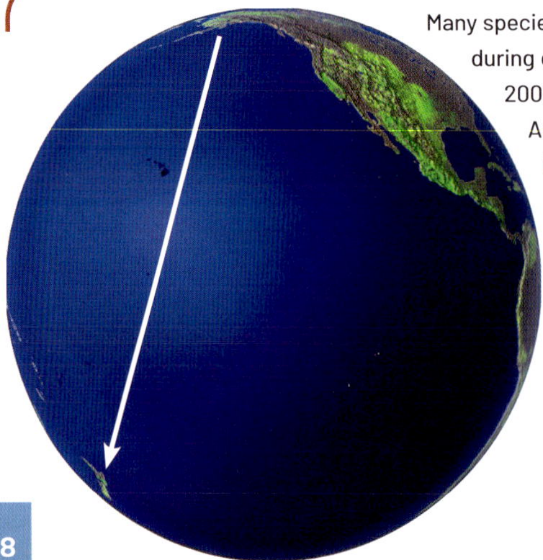

Many species of birds are migratory, which means that they travel during certain seasons to find warmer weather or to mate. In 2007 a bar-tailed godwit—a wading bird that mates in the Arctic coasts and tundra—made an amazing journey. . . in an amazingly short period of time. Scientists tracked the bird as it flew south from Alaska to New Zealand—a distance of 7,145 miles—in just nine days. This amazing bird never stopped to eat, drink, or rest, and it lost more than half its body weight by the time it touched down in New Zealand.

Eating Like a Bird

Eww, gross! The deader the better for scavenging birds like vultures.

Ever hear the phrase "eats like a bird"? That is usually what people say about someone who doesn't eat very much. But the truth about birds is that most of them consume a lot of food for their size. They have to eat a lot because they use up so much energy flying.

What a bird eats depends on the kind of bird it is. Many birds eat almost nothing but fruit and seeds, while others eat green plants. Birds such as hummingbirds eat nectar they find in flowers. Many species of birds eat insects and other bugs. Some birds of prey eat fish, small reptiles, and rodents, while others eat mammals and other birds they catch. Some birds, like vultures, are scavengers that eat only the bodies of dead animals.

The size and shape of a bird can tell you a lot about how it finds food and how it eats it. Every bird is equipped with everything it needs to gather or catch the kind of food it eats. For example, if a bird has long legs and a long neck—like a crane or flamingo—it probably spends most of its time walking on land or wading in water. Birds with long legs need long necks so they can reach food on the ground or in the water.

Hummingbirds have long, thin beaks and slender tongues they use to dip into flowers to gather nectar. Swallows, swifts, and other birds that eat insects have short beaks and wide mouths that are perfect for catching flying insects. Parrots and other seed-eating birds have powerful, curved beaks that help them in cracking open nuts to eat.

These ducks aren't shy—they're looking for food underwater!

Birds of prey, such as eagles, hawks, ospreys, and owls, use their sharp eyesight and hearing to find food. They also use their strong claws (or *talons*) and hooked beaks to kill and eat their prey once they catch it. Some species of owls swallow their prey whole once they catch it, then vomit up the bones, fur, and other parts of the animal they can't digest.

Pelicans, geese, and swans all swim well and also have short legs and long necks that allow them to submerge their heads in the water to find food. Other water birds—such as cormorants—are considered diving birds. Their bodies are shaped a lot like torpedoes, and that allows them to dive deep and fast into the water to catch fish.

EXPLORING THE WORLD OF BIRDS

Whether you live in a big city or out in the country, you live in a place where you can see many types of birds. One good way to get a good look at the species of birds in your area is to set out a bird feeder. . .then just watch who comes to have a free meal! When birds come to eat at your feeder, take a good look at them—and take pictures of them if you can—then see if you can identify which species of birds live near you.

Why Fish and Birds Are Important to You

The Bible tells us that the very first animals God created were fish (and other creatures that live in the water) and birds. When you look at the variety of fish living in the earth's bodies of water and at the different kinds of birds that live on Earth, you can see that God really likes variety.

Many of the eggs we eat come from large farms. These eggs are being processed on a conveyor belt.

But there's something else we can learn about God as we look at the living things He placed on Earth. As you will read later on in this book, God didn't create all the animals that live on Earth just so that He could have a huge zoo and aquarium to enjoy for Himself. God created all these things for the benefit of the most valuable and important part of His creation—us!

The fish and birds God created are important gifts to us humans for a lot of reasons. First of all, fish and birds are an important source of food for people in nearly all cultures. Fish are plentiful in many parts of the world and serve as a source of protein as well as useful fatty acids that help keep people's hearts healthy and operating properly.

Some kinds of birds are important sources of food. Can you remember the last time you had a chicken dinner with your family? Or when you had scrambled eggs or an omelet for breakfast? And you know that every Thanksgiving holiday many Americans cook a big turkey dinner to celebrate with their friends and families. People also often eat geese, pheasants, ducks, grouse, quail, and other game birds. In some parts of the world, people even eat the meat of emus and ostriches.

People also enjoy fish and birds for recreation and as pets. Both saltwater and freshwater sport fishing are popular in many parts of the world. So is hunting for birds. Many people in different parts of the world enjoy keeping aquariums in their homes so that they can enjoy caring for and breeding different types of fish.

Colorful birds like parrots, cockatiels, parakeets, and other species are kept as pets because they are pretty to look at. Some birds are also popular because they can be taught to copy human speech.

Some birds are intelligent pets that enjoy bright, noisy toys.

Some people also enjoy just going out and watching birds in the wild. These people call their activity *birding*—even though you probably know it better as *bird-watching*. Some bird-watchers just go out with a pair of binoculars to enjoy seeing birds in their natural habitat, but some enjoy taking cameras along so they can "collect" pictures of wild birds.

So the next time you enjoy a nice fish or chicken or turkey dinner, or the next time you have eggs with your breakfast, don't forget to thank God for both His creativity and for providing you with the foods you eat. And the next time you go out fishing with your family, watch fish in an aquarium (at home or anywhere else), or watch birds enjoying life in the wild, remember that it was God who made these creatures for you to enjoy.

A bird book, binoculars, and a camera are nice for bird-watching—but not necessary. You can observe birds anywhere at any time!

CHAPTER 7

Day 6, Part I

All the Land Animals

Then God said, "Let the earth produce every sort of animal, each producing offspring of the same kind—livestock, small animals that scurry along the ground, and wild animals." And that is what happened. God made all sorts of wild animals, livestock, and small animals, each able to produce offspring of the same kind. And God saw that it was good.

Genesis 1:24–25

When the sixth day of creation started, the earth had already been completely formed and filled with all kinds of plants, fish, and birds. God's next step in preparing our planet for us humans to live on was to create the different kinds of animals that live on land.

When you think of the animals that live on land, your mind probably goes to the animals that people are closest to—like dogs, cats, and horses. Some animals just seem to be designed for people to enjoy in special ways. Many people keep dogs and cats in their homes and treat them like members of the family. Other people like horses because they can train them and ride them and enjoy spending time with them.

But many of the land animals God created are important to humans for other reasons. Many land animals are sources of food. Other animals help people do their work. Amazingly enough, God had a purpose for *all* the land animals He created—from the biggest mammals (like elephants) to the tiniest insects (like ants).

Land Mammals. . .Including You!

This picture is about the same size as a real mouse.

Did you know that you are a mammal? It's true! People are mammals because they share some of the same features as animals like horses, cats, dogs, cattle, and all the rest of the 4,000 to 5,000 kinds of mammals living in the world today.

Land mammals come in a large variety of sizes, shapes, and colors. The smallest mammals are so tiny that it's likely you wouldn't see them if you were standing right next to them. The largest land mammals—the elephants—would be hard for anyone to miss! (The blue whale is actually the world's largest mammal, but it lives in the ocean and was probably created on the fifth day of creation.)

Some of the land mammals God created are known for their physical beauty. Who can't look at a Bengal tiger or a leopard and appreciate how beautiful and majestic God made those big cats? But some animals will never win any beauty contest. In fact, some land mammals are among the funniest-looking creatures in the entire animal kingdom. One example is the star-nosed mole, a species commonly found living near swamps and ponds in the eastern part of the United States. The star-nosed mole has a snout made up of 22 fleshy tentacles that make its nose look like a starfish with too many arms.

The aye-aye is related to monkeys but looks kind of like a cat—until you see those long, skinny fingers.

One of the weirdest-looking—and most misunderstood—land mammals is a small primate (the same family of animals as apes and monkeys) called the aye-aye. The aye-aye, which uses its long, slender middle finger to find and scoop insects to eat out of trees, is far from the most handsome animal in the world (go ahead and look it up!). It has large, yellowish-colored eyes and long, slender fingers. The residents of Madagascar, where it lives, often kill it because they think it is an evil spirit or a sign of bad luck. That is one reason the aye-aye is an endangered species.

Not only does the star-nosed mole have a strange face, look at the size of those paws! They're extra big to help him dig through the soil.

RECORD BREAKING

You probably already know that the elephant is the biggest land animal on Earth today. But there are actually several species of elephants, including the biggest one of all: the African bush elephant. This species of elephant can weigh 225 pounds when it is born, and most of them grow to around 20 to 24 feet long and 10 to 12 feet tall at the shoulder, and weigh between 13,000 and 20,000 pounds. The biggest African bush elephant on record weighed 27,060 pounds and stood almost 14 feet tall.

DID YOU KNOW. . . ?

You have probably heard that no two people have exactly the same fingerprints. (Yes, that means your fingerprints are yours and yours alone.) But did you know that each giraffe and each zebra also has its own one-of-a-kind identifiers? It's true! No two giraffes have the exact same pattern of spots, and no two zebras have the same pattern of stripes. That means that each giraffe and each zebra is a one-of-a-kind creation with its own identity—just like you!

Where Land Mammals Live

Land mammals live in almost all kinds of environments. Polar bears and some kinds of seals live in the coldest parts of the world, while camels and other animals live in some of the hottest. Moles and other burrowing animals live underground, and bats live in caves and other places where they can keep out of the sunlight during the day. Other animals live in forests and jungles, in deserts and open fields, and in mountains and valleys.

Like the other kinds of life God created, the way different mammals look and behave can tell you a lot about the kind of surroundings they live in. God equipped the cold-weather specialists like polar bears with thick fur and layers of fat to help keep them warm. He also equipped animals that live in hotter areas with thick fur and skin that help insulate them from the heat. And He gave the animals that live in warmer areas of the world the ability to pant or sweat in order to release extra heat from their bodies.

God also designed different animals to eat different kinds of food. He gave animals that eat only plants the kind of teeth and digestive systems that work best for eating grass, grains, fruits, and vegetables. These mammals are called *herbivores*. He also gave animals that eat meat—they are called *carnivores*—strong jaws and sharp teeth that work best for eating the meat from other animals. God also equipped some carnivores with the speed and strength they need to hunt their prey.

THAT'S AMAZING!

A female cheetah chases a young gazelle in Kenya.

Without a doubt, the cheetah is the top track star out of all the land mammals. Cheetahs, which are found in Saharan Africa, can go from 0 to 45 miles an hour in less than two seconds and can reach top speeds of up to 70 miles per hour. Cheetahs are built for speed. They have long, slender legs and a tail they use for balance when they make quick cuts. They use their amazing speed and agility to catch their prey, which includes impalas, gazelles, rabbits, birds, and other small animals. Even though cheetahs are fast, they can only reach their top speeds in short bursts.

The Land Mammal Family Tree

Scientists have classified and named mammals the same way they have classified and named the fish and birds that live on Earth. The different kinds of mammals are broken down into one class—called *Mammalia*—that includes about twenty different orders of animals—give or take an order or two, depending on who you talk to. Each order of mammals is broken down into families and sometimes subfamilies, and each of the families is broken down into one or more genera (remember, that's the plural of *genus*). Each genus includes a certain number of kinds of animals that are all very much alike in many ways.

DID YOU KNOW. . . ?

The "Indiana bat" is a tiny mammal!

This will probably surprise you, but nearly one-fourth of all species of mammals have the ability to fly. Strange but true! There are about 985 species of bats, which accounts for just over 23 percent of all known kinds of mammals. Though there are a few mammals that can glide through the air—such as flying squirrels and flying possums—bats are the only mammals that can really fly. Most bats are insectivores, meaning they eat bugs, but some eat nectar and pollen, while others eat fish, frogs, lizards, small rodents, birds, or other bats. A few species of bats drink fresh blood.

A chimp gets a piggyback ride from her human handler, who is preparing the animal to return to the wild.

Scientists have placed us humans in the same order of mammals as apes and monkeys. This order of mammals is called *Primates*. That means that out of the entire animal kingdom, the mammals that are most like us are the apes—including gorillas, chimpanzees, and orangutans—and monkeys, as well as other members of that order. While these kinds of animals lack some of the special traits God gave only humans (you'll read more about that in chapter 8), they are like us in many ways. For one thing, they are among the most intelligent animals in all creation.

It might surprise you to know that the order of mammals with the most species is *Rodentia*, or rodents. There are as many as 2,277 different kinds of rodents living in the world today. Mice

and rats are rodents, and so are squirrels, chipmunks, gophers, hamsters, gerbils, guinea pigs, prairie dogs, and groundhogs. It may surprise you to know that porcupines and beavers are also rodents.

Land mammals like cattle, deer, pigs, and camels are placed in the order *Artiodactyla*. All the mammals in this order have hooves with an even number of toes. Hooved mammals like horses, donkeys, and zebras are placed in the order *Perissodactyla*. All animals in this order have hooves with an odd number of toes. The order *Carnivora* includes meat-eating mammals like cats (the ones that live in the wild, like lions, tigers, and cougars, as well as cats people keep as pets), dogs (including wolves, foxes, and coyotes), bears, raccoons, and many others.

These prairie dogs were photographed in Wyoming. They generally live west of the Mississippi River.

Did you know that male donkeys are called "Jacks" and female donkeys "Jennies"?

Some kinds of animals are placed in smaller orders because they have some very unusual traits. For example, the order *Marsupialia* includes only animals that carry their babies in a pouch—like the kangaroo. And the order *Proboscidea* is made up of only one family of mammals: elephants! It might make you laugh to read this, but the name *Proboscidea* means "eats with the nose." That name comes from the fact that elephants use their noses—which are really called *trunks*—to gather food and put it in their mouths.

The opossum is a marsupial, because—like the kangaroo—it carries its babies in a pouch. But these babies are big enough to ride on mom's back!

What Makes a Mammal a Mammal?

Like fish and birds, mammals are all part of the phylum *Chordata*. Remember, most animals from that phylum are considered vertebrates, which means they have backbones. All mammals are also warm-blooded. Remember, *warm-blooded* means that an animal's body is designed to stay at a certain temperature, no matter how warm or cold it is where it lives.

But there are a lot of animals living today that have spinal columns and are warm-blooded. Fish and birds—the first animals God created—all have backbones. So do all reptiles and amphibians. And birds are warm-blooded, just like mammals. So in order to know what makes a mammal a mammal, we're going to have to narrow things down a bit.

So, what else do you think all mammals have in common?

First of all, every mammal has hair or fur. It's pretty easy to see hair on most mammals. Most dogs and cats have thick hair and fur all over their bodies. So do bears, cattle, horses, and many other mammals. Even mammals whose hair is hard to see have hair. That includes mammals that live in water, like dolphins and whales. Even though you can't easily see hair on these animals, it's there—it's just really small.

Not only do all mammals have hair or fur, but they are the only animals on Earth that do. "Wait a minute!" you might be saying. "I've seen pictures of tarantulas, and they are covered in hair!"

RECORD BREAKING

The smallest mammal in the world is the Kitti's hog-nosed bat, which lives in Thailand and feeds on small insects. This tiny bat grows to only 1.14 to 1.3 inches long and weighs just .07 ounces when it is fully grown. At that size, it is a lot smaller than a lot of insects. The Kitti's hog-nosed bat barely beats out Savi's pygmy shrew—also known as the white-toothed pygmy shrew—as the world's smallest mammal. These tiny creatures, which are found in southern Europe, grow to less than 1.75 inches long and weigh less than .10 ounces as adults.

Hair on a dolphin? You'll have to look very closely. . .

Breakfast time for a kid—of the goat variety

It's true that tarantulas and other creatures that aren't mammals *look* like they are covered in hair. But what seems like hair on a tarantula isn't really hair at all. Real hair is made up of dead strands of a substance called *keratin*. It's the same stuff your hair and fingernails and the hooves and horns of animals are made of. The difference is that what looks like hair on a tarantula actually contains living parts of the spider.

Another way that all mammals are alike is that they feed their babies with milk that comes from the mother's body. From the biggest elephant in the world to the tiniest mouse or bat, every mammal mother gives her baby the nourishment it needs to grow in the form of milk. Because mammal babies rely on their mother's milk to live and grow, mammal mothers all care for their young.

So there you have it! If an animal is a warm-blooded creature with a backbone and has hair on its body and feeds its young with milk, then it's a mammal! If an animal lacks any of those things, then it's something else.

THAT'S WEIRD!

Ever seen a duck-billed platypus? Other than having a strange name and also looking really funny, the platypus, which lives in eastern Australia, is one of only a few mammals that lays eggs instead of giving birth to its young. When scientists from Europe first saw the platypus—which has a mouth like a duck, a tail like a beaver, and feet like an otter—they thought someone was playing a joke on them. But it was real! And it's one of the weirdest-looking mammals God created!

The platypus is not only strange looking, it can be dangerous. Male platypuses can sting other creatures with a venom that comes through a sharp "spur" on their ankles.

Mammal Moms

Nearly all mammal mothers carry their babies inside them before giving birth. The amount of time the baby spends in its mother's body before it is born is called the *gestation period*. The amount of time it takes for the mammal baby to develop before it is born depends on the kind of mammal. Baby opossums are inside their mother's body just 12 days before they are born. And baby hamsters take 16 days to develop. Human babies are born about 266 days after the mother's egg is fertilized. The longest gestation period in the mammal world? The Indian elephant, at an amazing 624 days!

As a group, mammal mothers are just about the best in all creation. They care for their young, protect them from predators and other dangers, and, of course, they feed them every day. Because all baby mammals rely on their mother's milk to live and grow, the mother must care for the young at least until they are able to feed themselves and survive on their own. That means that mammal moms spend all of their time caring for their babies. The length of time a mammal mother cares for its young depends on the kind of animal. Some mammals—like certain kinds of rodents—care for their young for just a few weeks.

Nearly all mammal babies, including humans, have baby teeth or *milk teeth*. That makes it easier for the mother to feed its young the milk they need to live and grow. The exception to this rule in the mammal world is anteaters and a few other species of mammals that never grow teeth.

Reptiles: Land Animals with Scales

Out of all the animals that live on Earth, reptiles probably have the hardest time being accepted by humans. Some people are afraid of reptiles. Maybe it has something to do with the fact that all reptiles are covered with scales. Or maybe people just don't like animals that crawl or slither on the ground.

Even though there are some kinds of reptiles that are poisonous—like some snakes and lizards such as Gila monsters—they are still important members of

the animal kingdom. Reptiles are helpful to humans in several ways. Many reptiles eat rodents and other "pests," which helps farmers and other people who grow food for humans. In some cultures people eat certain reptiles, and some people enjoy keeping them as pets.

There are about 8,200 to 9,000 different species of reptiles living on Earth today. That includes many species each of turtles, snakes, crocodiles, lizards, and others. Reptiles live on every continent on Earth except Antarctica. Reptiles come as small as the dwarf gecko, which grows to less than an inch long, and as big as the saltwater crocodile, which can grow to more than 17 feet in length and weigh more than 3,000 pounds.

Is It Just the Scales?

This close-up of a python shows the many small scales that cover a snake's body. This snake is from the Pacific island nation of New Guinea.

Like other members of the animal kingdom, all reptiles have certain special traits that make them a part of their own family of animals. In reptiles, the two most important traits are that they are all cold-blooded and that they are all covered in scales.

Since a reptile is cold-blooded, its body temperature adjusts to its surroundings. That means that when a reptile gets too hot, it must move to water or shade to cool itself off. And if it gets too cold, it has to move to a sunny place to warm itself up.

One of the myths about reptiles, especially snakes, is that they are slimy to the touch. Actually, since all reptiles have scales, they are anything but slimy. The skins of some reptiles are very smooth because they are covered with very small scales. Some reptile skins are used to make people's clothing and shoes.

Most reptiles reproduce by laying eggs, but a few kinds give birth to live young. All turtles, tortoises, crocodiles, and alligators lay eggs. So do most lizards. All boas, vipers, and garter snakes give birth to live babies. So do a few species of lizards called *skinks*.

Most reptiles lay their eggs or give birth to their young, then leave them on their own. A few kinds of reptiles protect their eggs until they hatch. Alligators and crocodiles are known for guarding their nests and for helping their babies emerge from their eggs. Female pythons are known for coiling their bodies around their eggs to give them protection from predators and to keep them at the right temperature.

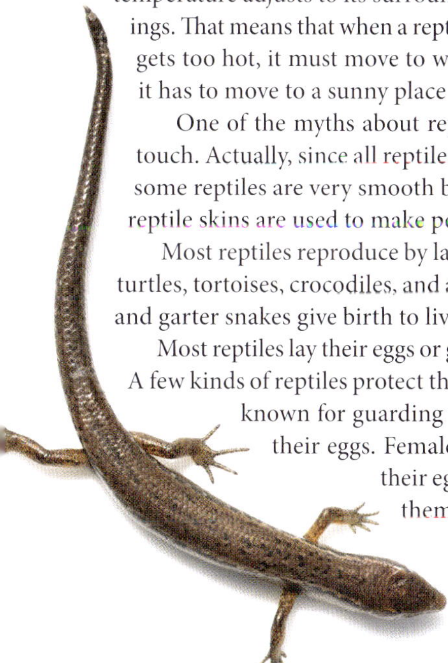

The skink (not skunk) eats mainly bugs—like crickets, grasshoppers, and beetles.

THE WAY IT USED TO BE

The eastern milk snake is a colorful species found in North America and South America. It got its name because in the past people believed they often went into barns and sucked milk from dairy cows. Of course, this story wasn't true. Actually, snakes don't drink milk at all! Milk snakes are actually beneficial to farmers because they help keep the population of rodents, which they eat, in check. Although milk snakes look a lot like the poisonous coral snake, they aren't venomous.

The Reptile Family Tree

All reptiles have backbones, and that means that they are all vertebrates from the phylum *Chordata*. There is only one class of reptiles, which scientists refer to as *Reptilia*.

Why are they called "snapping turtles"? Because they can snap at you with those sharp beaks!

Scientists have placed reptiles that live on Earth today in four orders and a few suborders. The largest order of reptiles (about 7,900 species) is *Squamata*. This order includes lizards, snakes, and creatures in the family *Amphisbaenids* (better known as worm-lizards). The second biggest order of reptiles (300 species) is *Testudines*. It includes the shelled reptiles—turtles, tortoises, and terrapins. The order *Crocodilia* includes 23 species of crocodiles, alligators, gavials, and caimans. The order *Sphenodontia* includes just two lizardlike species that live in New Zealand.

The orders of reptiles are broken into families and subfamilies. The order Squamata, for example, includes about 20 different families of lizards and about 18 different families of snakes. Each of these families is broken down into different genera, and each genera includes a certain number of species.

There are almost 5,000 species of lizards living in the world today, making them the most common of reptile species. Second among the reptiles as far as the number of species is concerned is snakes. There are about 2,700 different kinds of snakes; only 375 of them are poisonous.

The Mystery of the Dinosaurs

The biggest reptiles ever to live on Earth were the dinosaurs. All dinosaurs are extinct now. That means that they no longer live on Earth. No one knows for sure why all the dinosaurs became extinct. What scientists *do* know is that there were many kinds of dinosaurs in many shapes and sizes.

This tiny worm lizard is found in the Virgin Islands.

They know that because they have found many dinosaur bones that were left behind when the dinosaurs died out.

Did you know that the name *dinosaur* came from an old Greek word that means "terrible lizard"? Actually, dinosaurs weren't really lizards, even though they were reptiles. Most of them weren't so terrible, either. Most dinosaurs were really big reptiles that ate plants. But some of the dinosaurs, like the tyrannosaurs, ate meat.

For a long time, the brachiosaur was thought to be the largest dinosaur. Many scientists believe the brachiosaur grew up to 82 feet long, but some believe they could have been even bigger. The brachiosaur had a long neck like a giraffe, and scientists believe it could raise its head more than 40 feet above the ground. But scientists believe there were dinosaurs even bigger than the brachiosaur. Bones from an enormous dinosaur called *Argentinosaurus* were recently discovered in South America. Scientists believe this dinosaur could have grown to over 100 feet long and weighed over 100 tons. Another dinosaur, called *Sauroposeidon*, was recently discovered that may have been heavier than the brachiosaur.

Different people believe different things about where dinosaurs fit in with the creation story in Genesis 1. Some believe that God created everything in six actual 24-hour days and that the earth is between 6,000 and 10,000 years old. That would mean that dinosaurs and people lived at the same time. Other people believe that the six days God used to create the world and all life on it weren't really actual days. Instead they believed that these "days" were really long periods of time with gaps in between them. They believe that the earth is millions or billions of years old and that dinosaurs had become extinct a long time before God created humans.

Some people even believe that dinosaurs are mentioned in the Bible. They point to names in scripture like *leviathan*, *behemoth, sea serpent*, and *dragon*. But the Bible doesn't say anything at all about what happened to the dinosaurs—or any other of the many creatures that at one time lived on Earth but are now extinct.

Amphibians: Animals that Live Two Lives

There are more than 6,000 species of amphibians living on Earth today. That includes frogs, toads, salamanders, newts, and strange creatures called *caecilians* (tropical amphibians that look like snakes or worms at a glance because they have no legs and a very short tail).

Some amphibians are among the strangest animals on Earth. For example, the Chinese giant (and we mean *giant*!) salamander is the world's biggest amphibian, growing up to almost six feet long. Then there's the olm, a blind salamander with transparent skin that lives in water that flows underground and can survive without food for ten years. And there is also the lungless salamander of Mexico, a species that doesn't have lungs but takes in oxygen through its skin and mouth lining.

All amphibians are vertebrates that belong to the class of animals called *Amphibia*. *Amphibia* is a Greek word that means "two lives." That's because amphibians spend their lives in two places: in water and on land.

Amphibians that live on Earth today all belong to the subclass of animals called *Lissamphibia*. This subclass includes the orders *Anura* (frogs and toads), *Caudata* (salamanders and newts), and *Apoda* (caecilians). These orders are broken down into families, with the families broken down into genera. Each genus includes one or more individual species.

Amphibians: Kind of Like Reptiles . . . but Different

Amphibians are a lot like reptiles in some ways. Both are cold-blooded vertebrates that can be found all over the world. And most kinds of reptiles and amphibians reproduce by laying eggs.

But amphibians are also a lot different from reptiles in some very important areas.

The most important way amphibians are different from reptiles is in how they reproduce. Reptile eggs have hard, leathery shells that are designed to protect the developing babies living inside. Many reptiles lay their eggs in well-hidden nests that are protected from hot or cold weather. Amphibians, on the other hand, lay soft eggs that don't have a protective shell. They usually attach the eggs to the stems of plants growing in the water. If you were to look around pond plants during the mating season of amphibians, you would likely find clear blobs of goo with tiny frog or salamander eggs inside them.

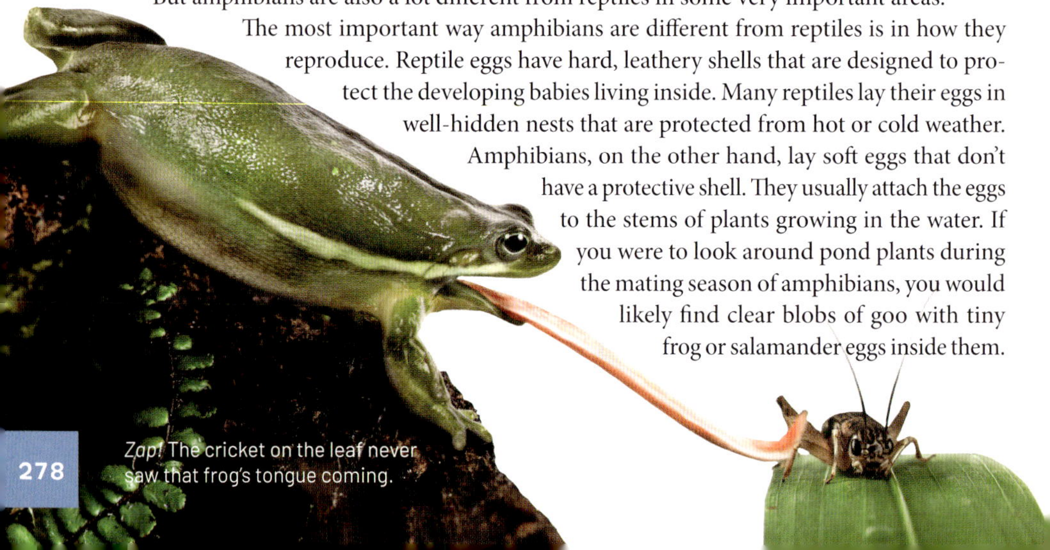

Zap! The cricket on the leaf never saw that frog's tongue coming.

Most newly hatched reptiles look pretty much like the adults of the species. But most amphibians begin their lives in water and look nothing like their parents. This is called the *tadpole stage* of the amphibian's life. During that stage, the amphibian looks and acts more like a fish than an amphibian. It has fins and a tail and breathes using gills. Most of the time, it doesn't have legs. Most tadpoles feed on plants and algae they find in the water, but some feed on smaller tadpoles and other animals that live in water.

As the tadpole begins growing into an adult amphibian, it loses its gills as it develops lungs and forms legs so that it can begin its life on land. During that time, its mouth will also grow into the same width as its head, preparing it for feeding on what full-grown amphibians eat.

THAT'S WEIRD!

A Betic midwife toad is actually a species of frog that lives in Spain. These frogs are known for two weird things. First, they have warts on their backs that give off a strong-smelling poison when they are attacked or scared. Second, after mating, the female lays strings of fertilized eggs, which the male carries around his hind legs until they are ready to hatch. When it is time for the tadpoles to emerge from the eggs, the male deposits them in the water, where they begin the process of maturing into baby Betic midwife toads.

A frog sits in the water, surrounded by its eggs (also called "spawn").

Arthropods: Creation's Creepy Crawlers and Flyers

Can you remember the last time you came face-to-face with a kind of animal called an *arthropod*? If you're not so sure when you have, then there are a few things about arthropods you need to know.

First of all, there are millions of species of arthropods. Second, arthropods live all over the world—in saltwater, in freshwater, on land, in the air, and in the soil. Between 80 and 85 percent of animal species alive on Earth today are arthropods.

If you're still not so sure when the last time was that you saw an arthropod, then consider this: All insects are arthropods. So if you've seen an ant, a housefly, a bee, or a butterfly today, you've seen an arthropod.

Insects aren't the only animals scientists classify as arthropods. Spiders, centipedes, mites, ticks, lobsters, crabs, crayfish, scorpions, and many other animals are also arthropods—and they are all important parts in God's perfect plan of creation.

Spiders weave a web of silk to catch other spiders and bugs as food. Some large spiders can catch and eat small birds and lizards!

What Is an Arthropod?

Most millipedes eat dead leaves and live between one and ten years.

Arthropods all share certain traits that make them arthropods. First of all, arthropods are all invertebrates. Other animals you have already read about in this book—fish, birds, mammals, reptiles, and amphibians—are vertebrates, which means they have backbones. An invertebrate, on the other hand, is an animal that has no backbone.

Instead of a backbone, or any other bones, arthropods have what *entomologists*—scientists who study insects—call an *exoskeleton*. An exoskeleton is basically a hard shell on the outside of the body that acts like a coat of armor. The exoskeleton protects the arthropod from predators and other outside dangers. An arthropod's exoskeleton is soft when it is first born, but it hardens as the animal matures. Many young arthropods shed their exoskeletons and grow new ones as they get bigger.

Arthropod is a Greek word that mixes the words *joint* and *foot*. This means that any animal that has more than four jointed legs is an arthropod. That includes all insects, spiders, centipedes, crustaceans (like crabs and lobsters), and a long, long list of other animals. Spiders, crabs, and other species of arthropods have eight legs. Centipedes and millipedes can have anywhere from 30 to hundreds of legs.

Arthropods are also known for their *segmented bodies*. That means that their bodies are made up of more than one part. Flies and other insects have three body segments, while spiders have two. Most millipedes have 30 to 40 body segments.

Like fish, reptiles, and amphibians, arthropods are cold-blooded animals. Remember, the body temperature of all cold-blooded animals depends on the temperature of the water or air that surrounds them.

The Arthropod Family Tree

Flies—like this common house fly—have large "compound eyes" made up of thousands of round lenses.

Scientists believe there are between four and six million species of arthropods living in the world today. That is more species than the rest of the animal kingdom combined! All arthropods belong to the phylum of animals called *Arthropoda*.

Scientists have placed all known arthropods into eleven different classes of animals. The class with the most known kinds of animals is called *Insecta*—you guessed it. . .insects! Even though scientists have identified and named just over one million species of insects, they believe there could be between six and ten million species living in the world today.

Insects all have the hard outer skeletons all arthropods have. They also have a three-part body (head, thorax, and abdomen) and three pairs of jointed legs. Insects also have what are called *compound eyes*. Compound eyes have many different lenses to see out of, instead of just one like human eyes have. Insects also have two antennae. Ants, bees, beetles, butterflies, moths, grasshoppers, and dragonflies are all insects, and there are thousands to hundreds of thousands of species of each of them.

A ruby tiger moth shows off its antennae (in white).

Another large class of arthropods that live on land is called *Arachnida*. These animals are more commonly called *arachnids*. Spiders, ticks, mites, and scorpions are all arachnids. All arachnids have eight legs—even though some arachnids' front legs are designed as claws. The best-known arachnids are spiders. There are about 38,000 known species of spiders living in the world today.

The Importance of Arthropods

Many arthropods are creepy, crawly creatures, and some of them are kind of scary looking. Most people consider some arthropods—like houseflies or grasshoppers—pests.

But hey, even if they are a little on the scary or ugly side, and even if they are capable of causing people trouble, they're also creations of God—and they are important to humans and other animals for many different reasons.

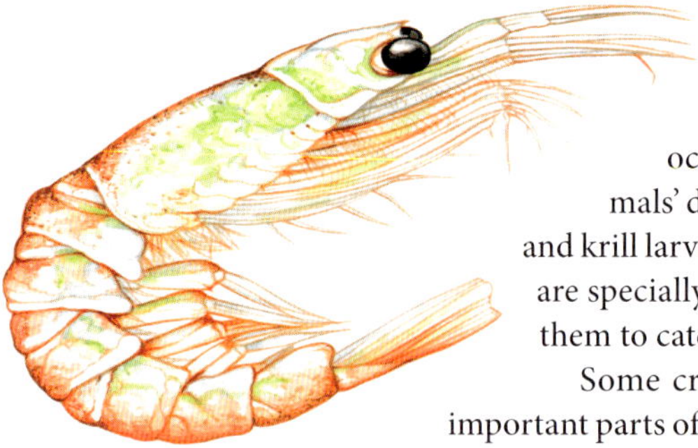

This krill looks something like the shrimp you might eat at a seafood restaurant.

Many species of fish, birds, and mammals often eat arthropods, and some of them eat *only* arthropods. Krill, which are shrimplike arthropods that live in the ocean, are an important part of many sea animals' diets. Many freshwater fish eat mostly insects and krill larvae. And as you read in chapter 6, some birds are specially equipped with beaks that make it easy for them to catch insects to eat.

Some crustaceans, which are all arthropods, are important parts of the human diet in many parts of the world. Crabs, lobsters, crayfish, shrimps, and prawns are all popular for food all over the world. In some cultures, insects and their *grubs* (larvae) are eaten raw or cooked. Believe it or not, tarantulas are considered a delicacy in some parts of the world!

Yes, that's a bowl full of cooked tarantulas. They're a snack in the Asian nation of Cambodia.

The arthropod that plays the most important part in supplying food to humans around the world is the bee. That's not just because many people like to eat honey. Bees help in pollination, which is a process absolutely necessary in the production of many fruits and vegetables. *Pollination* happens when pollen is transferred from one plant to another plant of the same species. That process allows plants to reproduce and bear fruit.

Many arthropods are important to humans because they help control populations of pests that destroy crops. Spiders and scorpions eat insects that eat plant life, including plants that produce food for humans. Ladybugs are even important this way because they eat aphids, tiny plant-eating insects that can make short work of a vegetable garden if they aren't controlled.

EXPLORING THE WORLD OF LAND ANIMALS

What kind of land animals do you find most interesting? Mammals? Reptiles? Amphibians? Arthropods? Take the time to learn about the kind of animal that is most interesting to you. Read about these kinds of animals, or visit a city zoo, wildlife center, or other place where you can see the animals in person. As you read and observe, ask yourself these questions: How are these animals different from other types of land animals? How are they like other land animals? What do they eat? Where do they live in the wild? How do they benefit humans? Maybe you can use what you learn in a school report, but maybe you'll just have fun learning about the animals you think are most interesting!

One Final Step to Go!

God spent most of two days creating the millions of animals that live in the water and on dry ground—and some that split their time in both places. He made the animals that swim, animals that fly, animals that walk, animals that crawl, animals that burrow, and animals that just stay in one place most of their lives.

You probably wonder why God made many of the animals He did. Some of them don't seem to have any real purpose other than just being what they are. But every animal God made had its own special place in His wonderful plan of creation. Every animal would become part of a kingdom that would feed itself and reproduce itself until the end of time.

But God wasn't finished. Now that He had created everything you can see—and some things you can't—it was time for Him to finish His work of creation by making the one being He did it all for in the first place. That means you!

CHAPTER 8

Day 6, Part II

Humans: Made in God's Image

Then God said, "Let us make human beings in our image, to be like us. They will reign over the fish in the sea, the birds in the sky, the livestock, all the wild animals on the earth, and the small animals that scurry along the ground."

So God created human beings in his own image. In the image of God he created them; male and female he created them.

Then God blessed them and said, "Be fruitful and multiply. Fill the earth and govern it. Reign over the fish in the sea, the birds in the sky, and all the animals that scurry along the ground."

GENESIS 1:26–28

After working more than five days to create the universe, the earth, and everything that lives on Earth, God did something very different from what He had been doing. The Bible tells us that when He created us humans, it was the first time He made something "in his own image" (Genesis 1:27).

You can see a lot of what God is like in everything He created. When you look outside of Earth and see the stars, planets, galaxies, and other things He placed in outer space, you can see just how big and powerful He is. When you look at the earth and how it is put together, you can see that God pays close attention to the details and that He made sure that every living thing He later created would be cared for. And when you look at the amazing number of plants and animals and other living things on Earth now, you can see that God is very creative and really likes variety.

But none of those things—as amazing and wonderful as they are—are made in God's own image like we humans are.

What Sets You Apart from Animals

What do you think it means that we humans are created in God's own image? Actually, it means a lot of things.

It doesn't mean that God has a physical body like you do. It also doesn't mean that you have the power God has, to create something out of nothing. But God created us humans to rule over the world and over all the animals that live here with us.

Dolphins raise their tails at a trainer's command—and receive a treat in return.

God made some animals to be a lot like us humans in some ways. For example, some of the world's most intelligent animals—such as primates, some water mammals (like dolphins, which are known for their amazing intelligence), and others—seem to have the ability to use their brains in ways very much like you use yours. In other words, they're just plain smarter than most animals. And some animals are very sociable, which means they live and travel in tightly knit families.

But God made people different from animals—and like Himself—in many important ways. First of all, we're made different from animals in how we think and reason. Even the most intelligent animals on Earth aren't able to use their brains the way we humans can. For example, only humans are able to read and understand the Bible and other written materials. And no animal is able to solve a complicated math equation or to figure out how to take apart and reassemble things like puzzles or car engines.

You can dress up a chimpanzee—but you can't make him human!

God also gave us humans the gift of creativity. Even though humans can't create on the same scale as God has, we all have the ability to use our minds and hands to create all sorts of new things—like art, music, technology, and other important human creations.

God also made us like Him in the way we communicate—both with God and with one another. While some animals have the ability to communicate using different sounds, none of them has the ability to use words like we can. God began creation with the simple words "*Let there be...*" and it was so.

From tiny computer chips to massive skyscrapers, the creativity of human beings is unmatched in the animal world.

God made us humans different from animals in that we can know the difference between good and evil and right and wrong. He also gave us the free will to choose right and wrong. Adam and Eve, the very first humans in all creation, were given the choice between right and wrong. Sadly, they chose to do the wrong thing—the one and only thing God told them *not* to do. But even though Adam and Eve messed up, we humans still reflect the image of God because we can choose to do what is right in His eyes.

The most important way God made us humans different from animals is that we have an awareness of our Creator. Not only that, we also have the ability to communicate and fellowship with Him. God also gave each of us an eternal soul, the part of us that lives on after our bodies die. And God has lovingly given us the opportunity to be with Him forever after we die.

Satan, in the form of a snake, tempts Eve to disobey God by eating the "forbidden fruit."

Your Body—God's Most Amazing Creation

Before God created us humans, He put together an amazing universe and planet Earth. He created billions of galaxies, each of which contains billions of stars. He created our solar system and designed it perfectly so that our earth could support us and millions of other living things that make their home here.

But as awesome as all these creations are, they've got nothing on the human body. Your body is the most incredible, complicated living thing in the whole world. God designed your body with many different *systems* that all work together perfectly to keep you moving, thinking, talking, and growing.

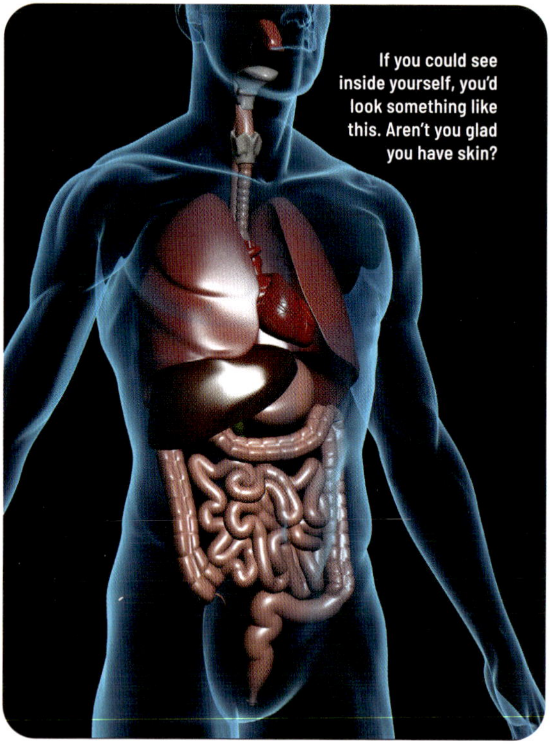

If you could see inside yourself, you'd look something like this. Aren't you glad you have skin?

These different systems include your

- nervous system (your brain, spinal cord, and nerves);
- cardiovascular system (your heart, blood, and vessels);
- lymphatic/immune system (your lymph and lymph nodes and white blood cells);
- respiratory system (your nose, trachea, and lungs);
- digestive system (your mouth, esophagus, stomach, and intestines);
- muscular system (your muscles and tendons);
- skeletal system (your bones);
- dermal system (your hair, skin, and nails);
- excretory system (your lungs, large intestine, kidneys, and skin);
- endocrine system (your glands); and
- reproductive system (your reproductive organs);

All these systems—and a few others—together make up your entire body. And by the time you are fully grown, they will account for about 100 trillion individual cells, 206 bones, 600 muscles, and 22 internal organs.

DID YOU KNOW. . . ?

There are a total of 206 bones in the bodies of adult human beings (more than half of which are in the hands and feet), but between 300 and 350 bones in the body of a baby. That's because some of the bones of babies fuse together as they grow. There are four classes of bones in the human body. There are the *long bones*, which make up the limbs. There are the *short bones*, which are grouped together to strengthen your skeleton. There are the *flat bones*, which protect your body and provide a place for the muscles to attach. Finally, there are the *irregular bones*, oddly shaped bones that don't fit into the other three classes.

No wonder that thousands of years ago, a man named David—the greatest king the nation of Israel ever had and the man who wrote many of the Old Testament psalms—declared his amazement at the design of his own body when he wrote, "You made all the delicate, inner parts of my body and knit me together in my mother's womb. Thank you for making me so wonderfully complex! Your workmanship is marvelous—how well I know it" (Psalm 139:13–14).

How We've Learned about the Human Body

One of the most important ways humans have used their God-given capacity for creativity and thought is in the study of the human body and medicine. We humans have always had a curiosity about how our bodies work, as well as a need to understand how to diagnose and treat people who are sick or injured. Over the past century, what we know about the human body has grown incredibly. So have the technology and knowledge doctors use to help people who are sick or injured.

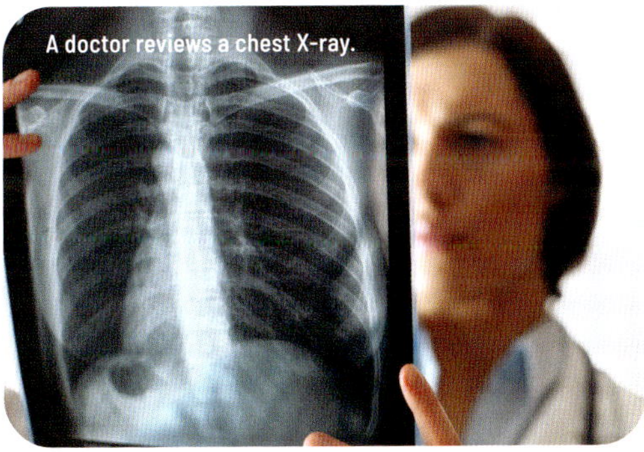

A doctor reviews a chest X-ray.

The technology scientists and doctors use on the human body is nothing more than the harnessing of what God has already created and using it in medicine. For example, the sun and other stars give off X-rays, which are used in medicine today. X-rays have also been called

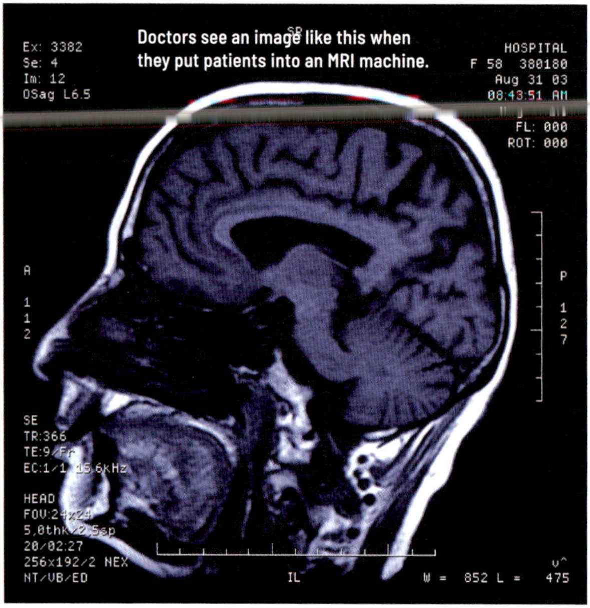

Doctors see an image like this when they put patients into an MRI machine.

Roentgen rays, after Wilhelm Konrad Roentgen, the German scientist who discovered them and developed ways to use them in medicine. Doctors use X-rays to see images from inside the body, such as the skeleton, and also in *angiograms* (picture images of the blood vessels).

While an X-ray gives doctors a *two-dimensional* (flat, like the pages of a book) look at some parts of the human body, a Computed Axial Tomography scan (or CAT scan) allows doctors to have a *three-dimensional* (height, width, and depth) look inside the human body. A CAT scan of the brain or other organs gives a lot more information than a regular X-ray. The CAT scan can allow a brain specialist to look at "slices" of the brain, which helps make finding tumors and other problems easier.

Magnetic Resonance Imaging (MRI) is a form of medical technology that gives detailed pictures of internal body parts. Unlike the X-ray or the CAT scan, the MRI doesn't use radiation or other radioactive substances of any kind. Instead, the patient is placed in a magnetic field while radio waves, which are completely harmless to the human body, are turned on and off. The body then emits its own weak radio signals, which are picked up by an antenna and fed to a computer. This produces detailed images of what is going on inside the body.

THE WAY IT USED TO BE

Today, if you were to get really sick, you would go to a doctor who would figure out what is wrong with you and then give you the medicine you need to get well. But there was a time when doctors used leeches—little creatures that look kinda like slugs and feed on blood—to treat their patients. Up until about the mid-1800s, it was believed that people got sick because of imbalances in their bodies and that one of the best ways to get rid of those imbalances was to allow leeches to take out the "bad blood" that caused those imbalances and made people sick. This procedure was called *bloodletting*.

A Perfectly Designed "Control Center"

You probably haven't given a lot of thought about just how your family's car works—other than it needs fuel in order to take you and your family where you need to go. But today's car engines are designed to operate best through a small computer inside the dashboard that acts as a control center that keeps everything in working order.

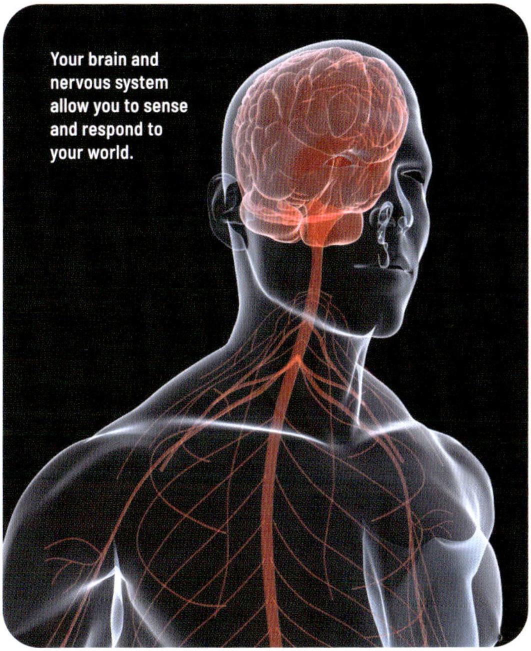

Your brain and nervous system allow you to sense and respond to your world.

God designed your body with a "control center" of its own that keeps every part of your body working the way He meant it to work. It's called your *brain*, and it is the key part of what is called your *nervous system*.

Your nervous system is made up of the brain, the spinal cord, and a huge arrangement of nerves that start at the top of your head and go all the way to the bottom of your feet. Your brain weighs about three pounds, and it sends messages to and receives messages from about 45 miles of nerves that run through your entire body.

Your brain is the most amazing organ in your whole body. You use your brain to store different kinds of information—like people and facts you know, things you need to remember, and what you need to do at certain times and in certain situations. You also use your brain to do things you choose to do—like eating, walking, reading, and playing ball. And of course, you use your brain for thinking!

DID YOU KNOW. . . ?

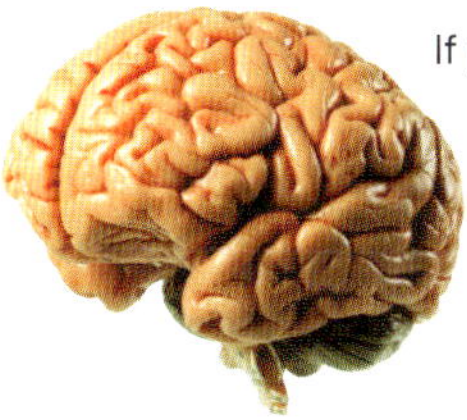

If you've ever been to a meat market and seen calves' brains—yes, believe it or not, some people like to eat calves' brains—then you have a general idea what your own brain looks like. Your brain will never take first place in a beauty contest. In fact, it looks kinda gross! But of all the things God created, there are few more amazing than that three-pound organ He put between your ears. Your brain is made up of more than 10 billion nerve cells and more than 50 billion other cells.

Your brain also controls every other function of your body, including the things you don't have to think about doing. You breathe because your brain tells your lungs to take in air. Your heart beats because your brain sends it signals telling it to pump blood throughout your body. And your digestive system does what it needs to do because your brain tells your mouth, your stomach, your intestines, and other parts of your digestive system what to do and when to do it.

Your brain is made up of five parts: the cerebrum, the cerebellum, the brain stem, the pituitary gland, and the hypothalamus. Each of these parts plays a vital role in how your mind and body function. The *cerebrum* is the largest part of your brain. It is the part you use for thinking, for memory, and for voluntary muscle movements. The *cerebellum* is the part of the brain that controls your balance, movement, and coordination. Without your cerebellum doing its work, you couldn't walk, stand, or move around.

Your Cardiovascular System

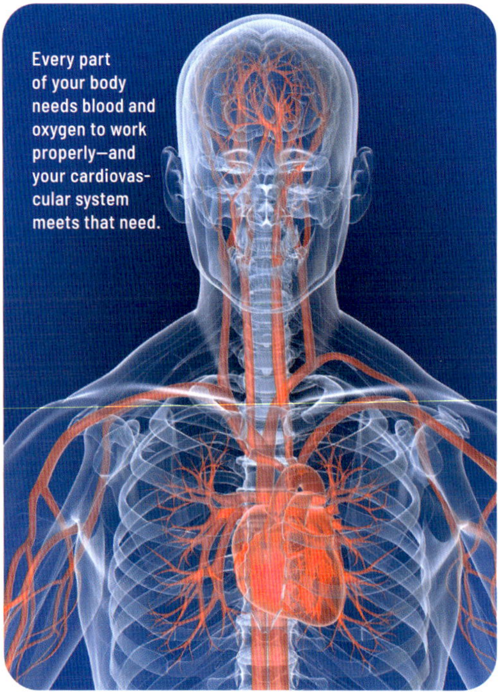

Every part of your body needs blood and oxygen to work properly—and your cardiovascular system meets that need.

If you think your nervous system is the most incredible part of your body, then you might find the *cardiovascular system*—which consists of your heart, blood, and blood vessels—a close second.

Your heart is the single largest part of your cardiovascular system. Your heart's job is to pump blood through your body. The heart of an average grown-up human beats just a little under 104,000 times a day, while a child's heart beats about 129,000 to 172,000 times a day. As the heart beats, it pumps blood through your body so that it can provide your body with the nutrients and oxygen it needs.

Your body contains an amazing 60,000 miles of *blood vessels*, which are tubes that carry blood from one part of the body to another. There are three kinds of blood vessels in your body. There are the *arteries*,

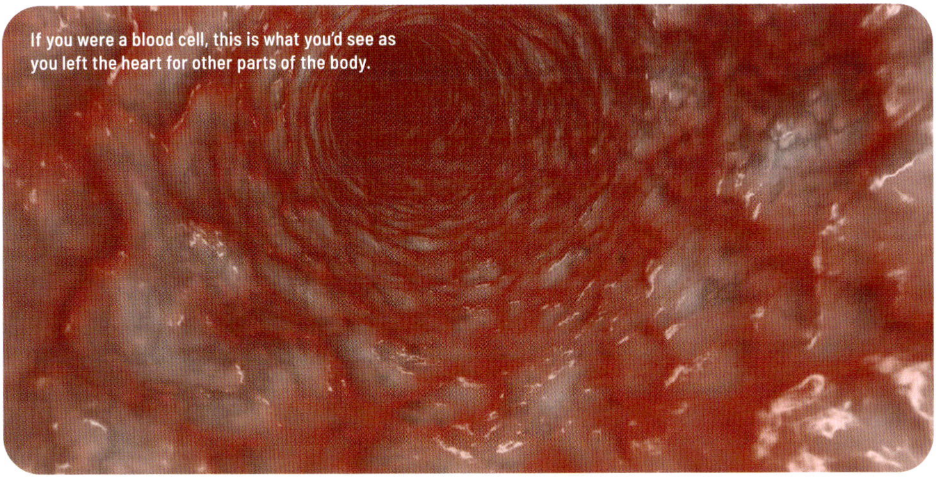

If you were a blood cell, this is what you'd see as you left the heart for other parts of the body.

which carry blood away from your heart. There are the *veins*, which take blood back to your heart. And there are the *capillaries*, which are tiny vessels that supply your entire body with oxygen and other nutrients. The capillaries are the smallest blood vessels. Most of them are so small that blood cells have to line up single file just to pass through them.

EXPLORING THE HUMAN BODY

If you want to learn more about how your body works, you can find mountains of information in your school library and on the internet. A good way to do your study is to investigate the systems in the human body one by one. Here they are: the circulatory system, the dermal system, the digestive system, the endocrine system, the excretory system, the lymphatic/immune system, the muscular system, the nervous system, the reproductive system, the respiratory system, and the skeletal system.

Your Respiratory System

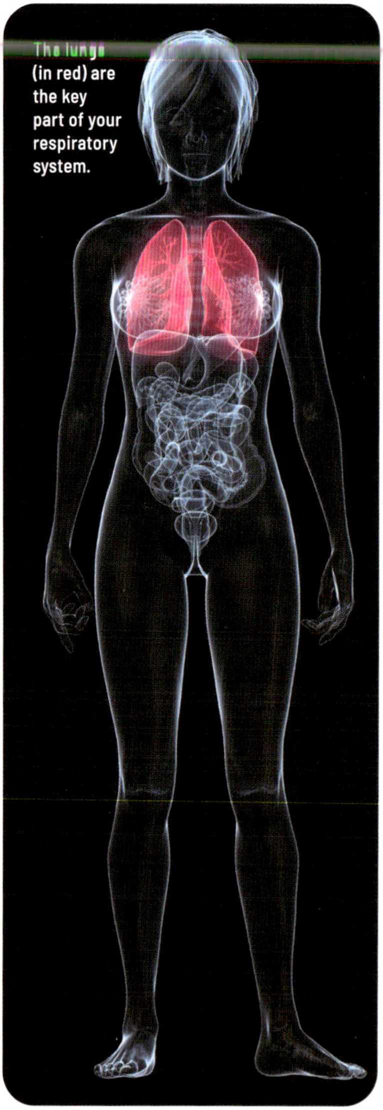

The lungs (in red) are the key part of your respiratory system.

Have you ever had a contest with your friends to see who could hold their breath the longest? If you have, then you know that it's not more than a few seconds after you stop breathing that you really want to take a breath again. That's because it's only a matter of a few seconds before your body realizes you've stopped taking in oxygen and starts screaming at your brain, *I need oxygen!*

Oxygen is one of the elements your body needs to survive. The cells in your body use oxygen to perform every one of the basic functions of life—walking, running, thinking, eating, sitting still. . .even sleeping! When the cells in your body use oxygen, they produce a gas called *carbon dioxide*. Even though there is always carbon dioxide in your body, too much of it can make a person sick or even die.

This is where your *respiratory system* comes in.

Your respiratory system serves one simple purpose: to bring oxygen into your body and to remove carbon dioxide from your body. Your lungs are the biggest and most important part of your respiratory system. They work closely with your circulatory system to bring oxygen to your cells and to remove the poisonous carbon dioxide.

Here's how it works.

When you breathe in, you fill your lungs with fresh, oxygen-filled air. At the same time, your heart pumps blood into the walls of your lungs through your blood vessels. When the blood reaches the walls of your lungs, it releases carbon dioxide into your lungs and absorbs oxygen and takes it to the rest of your body. After the oxygen-rich blood leaves your lungs, it goes back to your heart, which pumps it out through your body. When you breathe out, you release the carbon dioxide into the air around you.

DID YOU KNOW. . . ?

Have you ever wondered why your heart beats faster and you breathe harder when you're exercising—playing basketball with your friends, hiking with your family, or running in gym class? It's because when you exercise, your body uses a lot more oxygen than it does when you're sitting still. Your lungs and heart always work together to take in the oxygen you need and then deliver it to your muscles and other parts of your body to work right, but they have to work harder when your muscles send the signal, *I need more oxygen!* So you end up breathing harder.

What Happens When You Eat—Digestion!

Can you remember the last time you started to feel hungry? Maybe it was almost lunchtime at school, and you began to feel your stomach growl—and maybe hear a few of your classmates' stomachs doing the same thing.

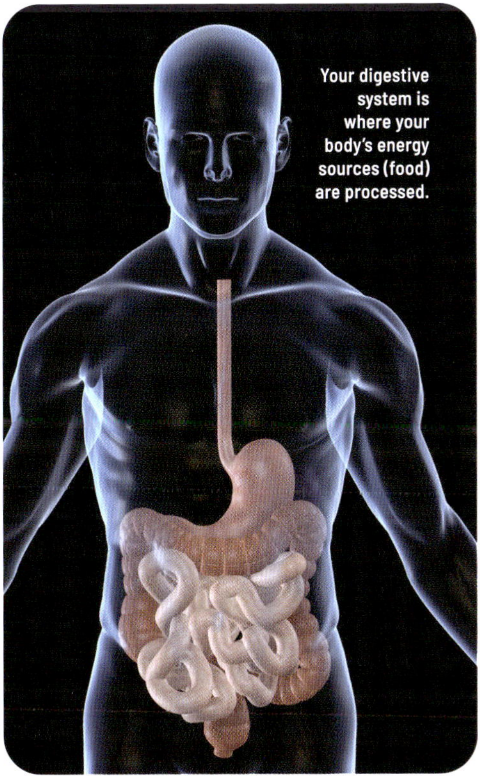

As lunchtime grew closer and you began to think about eating, your mouth might have started to water a little bit. And if you started to smell the food you were about to have for lunch, then your stomach growled louder and your mouth watered even more. It seemed like all you could think about was a delicious slice of pizza or that turkey sandwich you brought to school with you for lunch.

This doesn't happen just because you like food. It's your body telling you it's time to eat!

Like all living things, you need food in order to survive. Food is the source of the energy you need to get through the day, as well as the source of vitamins and other essential nutrients your body needs to grow, develop, heal, and function in every other way.

Your *digestive system* is an amazing system of organs that allows your body to convert food into energy. It includes your mouth, your esophagus, your stomach, and your large and small intestines. That slice of pizza or turkey sandwich wouldn't do your body a bit of good if it wasn't digested, but every part of your digestive system works together to convert the things you eat into energy and nutrients your body can use to keep it running well.

Digestion starts with the part you enjoy the most: eating! When you take a bite of food, your teeth begin crushing it into pieces small enough to swallow—and small enough for your stomach to begin breaking down. At that same time, glands in your mouth and throat produce *saliva* (you might know it better as spit), which moistens your food to make it easier to swallow and which begins breaking down your food.

After you swallow your food, it travels down your *esophagus*. The esophagus is a long, slippery tube that goes from your throat to your stomach. It has muscles inside it that force food down toward the stomach.

Your stomach has muscles it uses to grind and mix the food you have eaten. It also has glands that release the chemicals hydrochloric acid and pepsin, which together break the food down into a goopy mixture called *chyme*. The chyme then moves into your small intestine, where several chemicals break down the food even more. At that same time, your liver adds a liquid substance called *bile*, which helps neutralize the acids from your stomach. That helps move the process of digestion along.

As the chyme slowly moves along in your small intestine—aided by muscles that squeeze and roll it—the process of digestion is almost complete. Inside your small intestine, tiny folds called *villi* absorb all the nutrients from the chyme. What is left is the waste material your body can't use. Those materials enter your large intestine, which helps rid you of the leftover waste.

THAT'S WEIRD!

When you hear the word *bacteria*, you probably think of those little bugs that can make you sick. But there are lots of different kinds of bacteria in your body. Some of them can make you sick, and others are just there not really doing anything. But several kinds of bacteria working in your body help keep you healthy. Believe it or not, your body needs bacteria just to survive! Some of the good bacteria in your body help with digestion of food, with the breaking down of waste products, with cleaning out the bad stuff from your intestines, and with producing vitamins and other nutrients your body needs.

You've Got Muscles!

Remember the last time you saw a super bulked-up bodybuilder? You probably thought to yourself, *Wow! He's really got muscles!* Actually, you have the same number of muscles as even the beefiest-looking bodybuilder in the world. It's just that a bodybuilder spends a lot of time developing his muscles at the gym and making them bigger.

Any time you move, you're using one or more of the muscles your body is designed to have. You use muscles when you run, jump, throw a ball, or pick up a book. You even use your muscles when you smile or blink your eyes.

On average, about 40 percent of a human's body weight is muscle. Your body includes large muscles, like the ones in your legs, to very tiny muscles, like the ones you are using to read this book (yes, your eyes move back and forth because of tiny muscles attached to them). Each muscle in your body is designed to do different kinds of work.

Your body includes three different kinds of muscles: skeletal muscles, smooth muscles, and cardiac muscles.

Most of your *skeletal muscles* are attached to your bones with strong, flexible strands of tissue called *tendons*. These muscles are used in voluntary movements like raising your arms or scratching your leg. The largest muscles in your body are skeletal muscles.

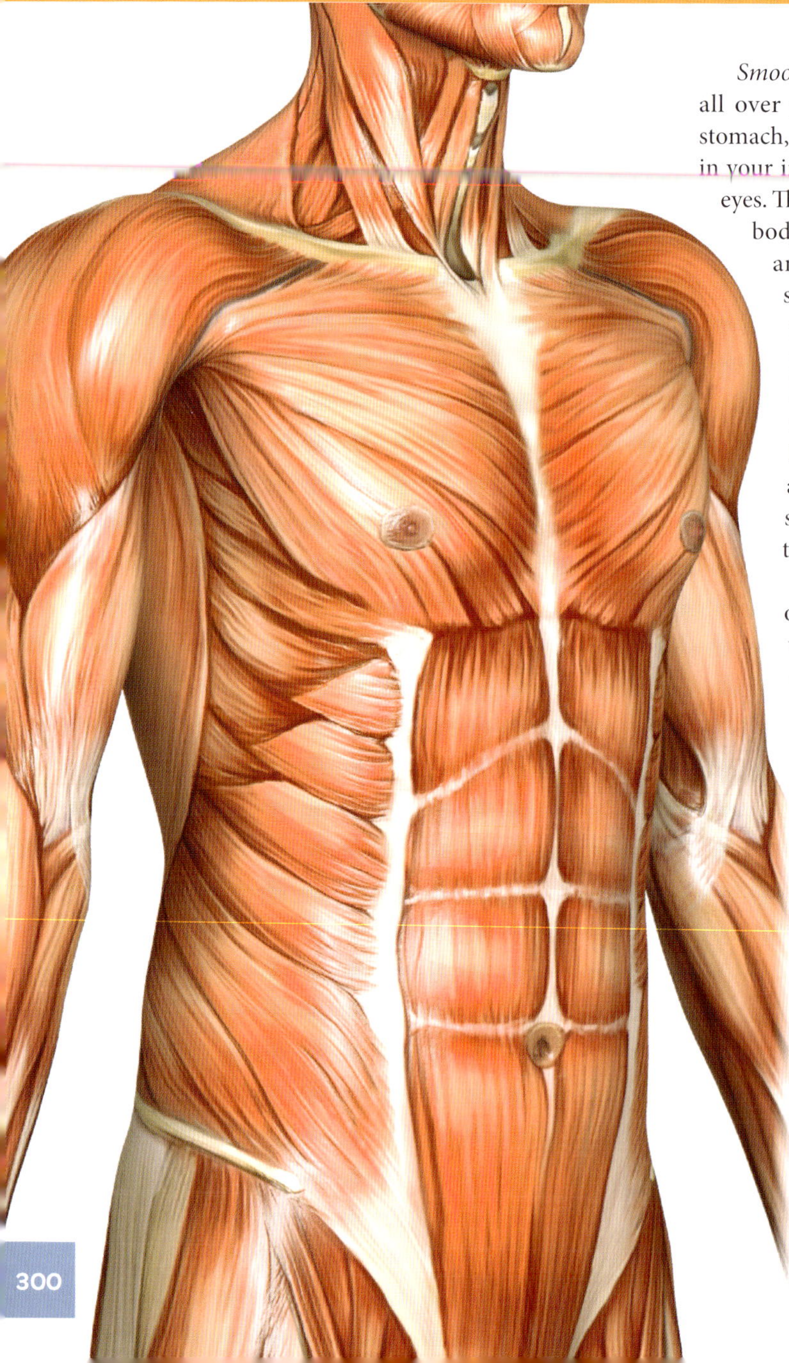

Smooth muscles are found all over your body—in your stomach, in your blood vessels, in your intestines, and in your eyes. These muscles help your body regulate blood flow and digest food. The smooth muscles in your eyes cause your pupils to *dilate* (get larger) when they need to take in more light so you can see, and to *contract* (get smaller) when there is too much light.

There is actually only one place in your whole body that has *cardiac muscles*: your heart! Your heart is a big, strong muscle that beats even when you're not thinking about it.

Your Inner Frame: The Skeletal System

Have you ever gone by a building site and seen how a house is constructed? After the foundation is laid, builders assemble the house's frame—the part that will both support the rest of the house and give the builders something to build on as they work to make the house ready for people to live in.

In a way, your body is constructed very much like a house. But instead of a frame made of wood, you have one made of strong material that forms your skeleton. Without your skeleton, you couldn't run, walk, or stand upright.

Your skeleton is made up of four main types of bones. You have *long bones* in your arms and legs and *short bones* in your hands, feet, and spine. You also have *flat bones* to protect your organs. Finally, you have what are called *irregular bones*, which are bones that don't fit in with the other three types.

Your bones are strong enough to support your weight, hold you upright, and protect your organs, but they are also light enough to allow you to walk, run, and jump. If your bones were any weaker, they would break easily in even the lightest movement, but if they were any heavier, they would make it difficult to move around as freely and quickly as you do.

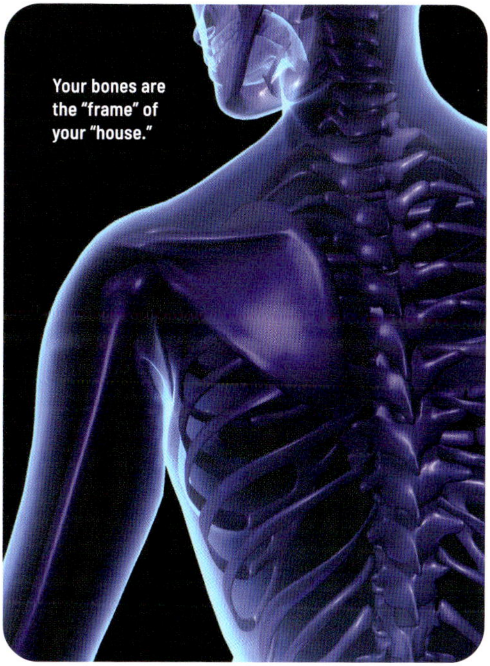

Your bones are the "frame" of your "house."

More than half of the bones in your whole body are found in your hands and feet. These bones, along with the ligaments and tendons in your hands, give your hands the flexibility they need to do things like grasp a pencil or pen or play a musical instrument. And they give your feet the flexibility they need to help you keep your balance when you walk or run.

Your bones also serve one other very important purpose. Not only do they give you strength and support and protect your internal organs, they also produce new blood for your entire body. Your blood is made up of millions and millions of microscopic cells that live for only a few months. That means they have to be regularly replaced. In the center of your bones is a spongy material called *marrow*. The marrow is the part of your bones that creates new blood cells to replace the old ones that die or the ones you lose when you bleed.

RECORD BREAKING

Robert Wadlow was 19 years old—and 8 feet, 7 inches tall—when he was interviewed by the newspaper reporter on the ladder.

The tallest man in medical history was Robert Wadlow, who measured an amazing 8 feet, 11 inches tall at the time of his death in 1940. Wadlow weighed 490 pounds at the end of his life. He was known as the "Alton Giant," after his hometown of Alton, Illinois. The world's all-time tallest woman was Zeng Jinlian, who reached a height of 8 feet, 1¾ inches before she died in 1982 at the age of 17. Zeng Jinlian was the only woman among 12 people in medical history who grew to over 8 feet tall.

THAT'S WEIRD!

Here are some interesting—and really weird—facts about your skin. First, your skin is the largest organ in your whole body, with a surface area of about 21 square feet. Second, humans shed about 600,000 tiny particles of skin every hour, which accounts for about 1.5 pounds of skin a year and about 105 pounds in a lifetime for someone who reaches 70 years of age. Third, humans shed and regrow their outer skin cells about every 27 days. Finally (and this is *really* weird—and gross), most dust particles in your house are made of dead skin.

The color might vary from person to person, but our skin is always working for us!

Other Important Systems

In addition to the ones listed earlier, your body has several other important systems that work to keep your body operating and growing.

Your *integumentary system* includes the heaviest organ you have—your skin. Your skin serves a lot of important purposes. It is designed to protect your body from germs and viruses that can cause you to become sick. It also keeps your body from losing too much water and dehydrating and insulates your body and helps keep it from overheating or from cooling off too much. Finally, your skin actually produces vitamin D when it is exposed to sunlight.

Your *lymphatic/immune system* helps protect you from bad bacteria that could cause you to become ill. This system includes your lymph and lymph nodes as well as your white blood cells. Your lymph nodes produce immune cells that help the body fight infection. Your white blood cells—which are also called *leukocytes*—help defend your body against infections by feasting on bacteria and other dangerous organisms and materials that make their way into your body.

Your *excretory system* serves to rid your body of wastes and toxins that build up as a result of other bodily functions. Your lungs are part of your respiratory system, but they are also part of your excretory system because they help rid your body of the carbon dioxide your blood cells carry back from cells that have processed oxygen. Your large and small intestines are part of your digestive system, but they are also part of your excretory system because they help rid your body of waste that is left over after your body has fully digested the food you eat. And your kidneys work day and night to clean the waste and toxins out of your blood.

Your *endocrine system* is a bunch of glands that serve some very important purposes in your body. *Glands* are organs that release different kinds of chemicals called *hormones* into your body. You have more than 30 different hormones working in your body to cause all kinds of things to happen. Hormones regulate your body temperature, control your growth and physical maturity, and even help you to feel hungry when your body knows it's time to eat. They even help you to handle stressful or frightening situations you may face.

When God created us humans, He made us "male and female" (Genesis 1:27). That is so we could follow His command to "be fruitful and multiply. Fill the earth and govern it. Reign over the fish in the sea, the birds in the sky, and all the animals that scurry along the ground" (Genesis 1:28).

God made all men and women (and boys and girls) in His own image, but He also made them very different in some very important ways. He equipped women with the internal organs they would need in order to give birth to children, and He equipped men with the organs they would need to father children. These organs are all part of humankind's *reproductive system*.

CHAPTER 9

Day 6, Part III:

Creation Complete. . .Now What?

Then God said, "Look! I have given you every seed-bearing plant throughout the earth and all the fruit trees for your food. And I have given every green plant as food for all the wild animals, the birds in the sky, and the small animals that scurry along the ground—everything that has life." And that is what happened.

Then God looked over all he had made, and he saw that it was very good! And evening passed and morning came, marking the sixth day.

Genesis 1:29–31

If you were to go back and read the first chapter of Genesis and take a count of the times God looked at something He had created and said it was "good," you'd find that word used six different times in that part of the Bible. But as the sixth and final day of creation—the day He created us humans—drew to a close, God looked at everything He had created and saw that it was "very good" (Genesis 1:31).

What do you think it means that God saw His own finished work as "very good"? Why not just "good"? One of the reasons creation was "very good" at that point was that it was finished. God had just spent six days creating a home for all living things—as well as a universe to place that home

in—and human beings. When He had finished His work, the heavens and the earth and everything that lived in them were everything He had planned. They were a perfect place for God's most prized creation—you and other humans—to live and multiply.

But what does this mean to you today? Creation happened a long time ago, and some of the things that have happened since then have changed what was once a perfect planet.

Even though creation itself is no longer perfect, it is still a gift directly from God to you today. And one of the first things—if not *the* first thing—you should do when you understand that something is a gift from Him is to give thanks.

Enjoy Creation. . .and Give Thanks

One of the great things about enjoying and studying the wonders of God's creation is that doing these things can remind you of what God is really like in many important ways. For example, when you look up at the stars, planets, and galaxies that are visible from Earth, you can be reminded of just how big and powerful God really is. When you look at the beauty and variety in nature here on Earth, you can be reminded that God likes beauty and variety. And when you look at the amazing detail of your own body, you can be reminded that God made you completely ready to take your place in His carefully constructed plan of creation.

The opportunities to thank and praise God for His works of creation are unlimited. For example, when you go outside and see a beautiful day with lots of sunshine and warmth or a cloudy day with life-sustaining rain, thank God for it! When you see a beautiful woodland area or when you see a desert, a beach, or a valley, give thanks! Or when you see and hear different kinds of birds perching and singing near your home, thank Him for making such a wide array of living things for you to enjoy.

So when you step outside—whether it's light or dark, or whether the sun is shining or it's raining—don't forget to enjoy everything you see around you. And then don't forget to thank the God who made it all happen!

Many towns and cities provide recycling for plastic bottles, metal cans, and newspapers and cardboard. You can help by sorting out your throwaways!

Taking Good Care of What God Has Given You

Do you know what the word *stewardship* means? Basically, it means taking good care of something that doesn't really belong to you. It means treating something that belongs to another person the very same way you would treat it if it belonged to you.

Right after God made the first humans, He blessed them and told them, "Be fruitful and multiply. Fill the earth and govern it. Reign over the fish in the sea, the birds in the sky, and all the animals that scurry along the ground" (Genesis 1:28). So in a very real way, God created the universe and the earth for us humans. His plan from the very beginning was to put people in a higher place than all the animals and other living things. We were meant to multiply and to rule over the whole earth!

At the same time, though, the Bible teaches that even though the earth and the things that live here are for our use, they don't really belong to us. Long after God completed the creation of the earth and universe, King David wrote, "The earth is the LORD's, and everything in it. The world and all its people belong to him" (Psalm 24:1). In other words, everything God created—including your own body—belongs to Him!

How does knowing that the whole universe, the whole earth, and all living things that live here on Earth—including you and all other humans—belong to God change how you see them? Even more important, how does it affect the way you treat them?

Sadly, many Christians in the past have taken the attitude that taking care of the earth wasn't important. But that attitude went against what God specifically told us we should do (take a look at Genesis 1:28 and 2:15). When we damage the earth by neglecting it or overusing it in certain ways, we do harm—sometimes very great harm—to something God created for us and still holds as valuable.

Planting trees is a great way to improve both the beauty and the air quality of your neighborhood.

There are many easy but important ways you can act as a good steward, taking care of what God has given you. For example, when you go out hiking, camping, or fishing, you can make sure you pick up after yourself before you go home. Don't leave anything behind that doesn't belong there. At home, you can encourage your family members to conserve energy by turning off lights when they leave the room, and by not leaving televisions and radios on when someone isn't watching or listening. If you haven't been doing so already, you can also begin recycling the metal, glass, plastic, and paper you use instead of throwing this material in the trash.

Remember, when you do the things that help preserve the world God created for you, you not only demonstrate good stewardship, but you also show God just how much you appreciate all He's done for you—starting with creation itself!

INDEX

Q

R

S

ART CREDITS

High-Z Supernova Search Team/HST/NASA: page 235 (bottom)

iStockphoto: pages 173, 178, 179, 181, 182 (both), 183 (both), 188, 190 (top), 191, 194, 196 (bottom), 197, 198, 200–212 (all), 214–218 (all), 219 (top two), 221 (bottom), 223 (top), 224, 225 (bottom), 226 (bottom), 227 (both), 228, 232, 234, 236, 237, 239 (top and bottom left), 240 (bottom), 242 (bottom), 243, 244–245, 246, 248–257 (all), 258 (top), 259 (both), 260 (bottom), 261 (all), 266 (top), 267 (both), 268 (top), 269–272 (all), 273 (top), 274–275 (all), 276 (top), 277–281 (all), 282 (top), 283 (bottom), 284–287 (all), 288 (top), 289 (top), 290–301 (all), 303–310 (all)

Jan Derk/Wikimedia: page 247 (bottom)

Jeremy Pearson/Flickr: page 221 (top)

Kristian Peters/Wikimedia: page 225 (top)

Lunar and Planetary Institute: page 240 (top)

NASA: pages 195, 230–231, 238

NASA/ESA/G. Bacon (STScI): page 229

NASA/ESA/STScI/J. Hester and P. Scowen (Arizona State University): page 176

NASA/Glenn Research Center Collection: page 177 (top)

NASA/Goddard Space Flight Center/Scientific Visualization Studio: page 258 (bottom)

NASA/John W. Young: page 175

NASA/JPL-Caltech/STCcI: page 242 (top)

NASA/JPL-Caltech: pages 235 (top), 241 (top)

NASA/Raghvendra Sahai and John Trauger (JPL)/WFPC2 Science Team: page 185

NASA/STScI: page 174

Shadowlink1014/Wikimedia: page 199

Shutterstock: pages 163, 165, 171, 180, 189, 190 (bottom), 193, 220, 222 (top), 223 (bottom), 226 (top), 233 (bottom), 241 (bottom), 254 (bottom), 260 (top), 266 (bottom), 273 (bottom), 276 (bottom), 282 (bottom), 283 (top), 288 (bottom), 289 (bottom), 302, 309

SOHO (ESA & NASA): page 233 (top)

Tristan Nitot/Wikimedia: page 247 (top)

US Fish and Wildlife Service/Andy King: page 268 (bottom)

USAsearch.gov: pages 184, 213

Wikimedia: pages 177 (bottom), 196 (top), 219 (bottom), 222 (bottom), 239 (bottom right), 266 (center)

More Great Stuff for Kids!

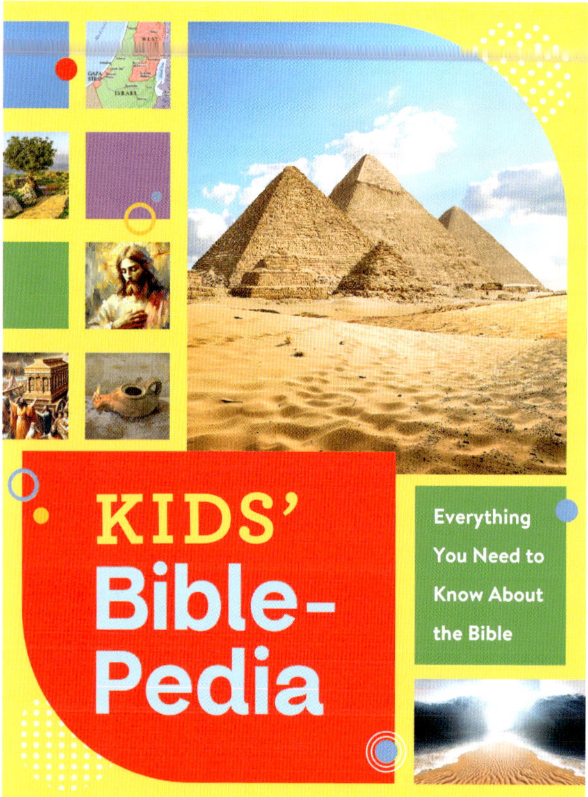

This brightly designed and illustrated reference includes helpful content to give you a better understanding of God's Word: concise, easy-to-follow entries for more than 800 people, places, things, and ideas; a fascinating overview of scripture; and a section of two dozen maps to provide a visual idea of where Bible events occurred.

Paperback / ISBN 979-8-89151-121-7

Find This and More from Barbour Books at Your Favorite Bookstore or www.barbourbooks.com

BARBOUR
PUBLISHING